The War against Marxism

ALSO AVAILABLE FROM BLOOMSBURY

Marx: An Introduction, Michel Henry
How to Be a Marxist in Philosophy, Louis Althusser
Challenging Power: Democracy and Accountability in a Fractured World, Cynthia Kaufman
Georg Lukács's Philosophy of Praxis: From Neo-Kantianism to Marxism, Konstantinos Kavoulakos
The Bloomsbury Companion to Marx, ed. Andrew Pendakis, Imre Szeman and Jeff Diamanti

The War against Marxism

Reification and Revolution

Tony McKenna

BLOOMSBURY ACADEMIC
LONDON • NEW YORK • OXFORD • NEW DELHI • SYDNEY

BLOOMSBURY ACADEMIC
Bloomsbury Publishing Plc
50 Bedford Square, London, WC1B 3DP, UK
1385 Broadway, New York, NY 10018, USA
29 Earlsfort Terrace, Dublin 2, Ireland

BLOOMSBURY, BLOOMSBURY ACADEMIC and the Diana logo
are trademarks of Bloomsbury Publishing Plc

First published in Great Britain 2021

Cover design by Ben Anslow
Cover images: Statue of Karl Marx in St.Petersburg. (© Zoonar GmbH /
Alamy Stock Photo), Black and White Grunge Border (© Panther Media
GmbH / Alamy Stock Photo)

A catalogue record for this book is available from the British Library.

Library of Congress Cataloging-in-Publication Data
Names: McKenna, Tony, 1979- author.
Title: The war against Marxism : reification and revolution / Tony McKenna.
Description: New York, NY : Bloomsbury Academic, 2021. | Includes
bibliographical references and index. |
Identifiers: LCCN 2020055577 (print) | LCCN 2020055578 (ebook) | ISBN
9781350201415 (paperback) | ISBN 9781350201408 (hardback) | ISBN
9781350201422 (ebook) | ISBN 9781350201439 (epub)
Subjects: LCSH: Socialism–History–20th century. | Philosophers–History–20th
century. | Philosophy, Marxist–History–20th century.
Classification: LCC HX40 .M35 2021 (print) | LCC HX40 (ebook) | DDC 320.53/15–dc23
LC record available at https://lccn.loc.gov/2020055577
LC ebook record available at https://lccn.loc.gov/2020055578

ISBN: HB: 978-1-3502-0140-8
        PB: 978-1-3502-0141-5
        ePDF: 978-1-3502-0142-2
        eBook: 978-1-3502-0143-9

Typeset by Integra Software Services Pvt. Ltd.
Printed and bound in Great Britain

To find out more about our authors and books visit www.bloomsbury.com
and sign up for our newsletters.

For my father, Mike McKenna

Contents

Acknowledgements

I am grateful, as always, for my mother Gay's incredible effort in going through the chapters with her fine-toothed comb, thereby making sure they read much more fluidly and legibly; and to both my parents, Gay and Mike McKenna, for the many interesting conversations about the book which have helped pull some of the central themes and ideas into perspective.

I would also like to thank four people whose critical and kind comments on the ideas and themes in this book helped bring it to fruition – Biswadip Dasgupta, Ishay Landa, Sean Ledwith and Katie Terezakis.

Biswadip has philosophical roots in a Hegelian-Marxism similar to my own, but his knowledge of the economics of *Capital* and Value Theory far exceeds mine and I have benefited greatly from the discussions I have had with him on some of the figures I examine in this book.

Ishay's seminal and pathfinding books on fascism and his critique of the 'anti-consumerist' stance which commonly masquerades as Marxism today quite naturally dovetail with my own work and have been exceptionally helpful to informing my critique of some of the Frankfurt School members.

Sean's profound grasp of Marxist philosophy is belied by the light and delicate way he applies it to everything from art to economics, and his criticisms of my work have been acute and penetrating but never less than kind.

But I owe a special debt of gratitude to Katie. She is one of the foremost Lukács scholars in the world today, one of the few to approach that great thinker's work from its roots in the traditions of German Idealism. So I was absolutely thrilled (and rather daunted) to learn she had gone through the whole manuscript. Naturally she uncovered more than a few significant flaws, but these were relayed with great kindness, and her appraisal was nothing short of precious and valuable.

However, the errors, inaccuracies and gaps in the completed book remain the responsibility of the author alone.

In addition, I am grateful to the publishers of the following works for permission to use copyrighted material from them as the basis for the chapters indicated:

'Planes, Trains and Automobiles: A study of Capitalist Reification and the Possibility of Its Overcoming'. *Critique: Journal of Socialist Theory*, November 2018 (Taylor & Francis, Oxon)

'Against Post-Marxism: How Post-Marxism Annuls Class-Based Historicism and the Possibility of Revolutionary Praxis'. *International Critical Thought*, May 2014 (Taylor & Francis, Oxon)

Introduction

In the simplest sense of the word, we describe Karl Marx as a 'communist'; that is how he was known in his own time, and it was also the label by which he identified his own set of politics. Though the word 'communist' can be either positive or pejorative, depending on what exactly you take it to mean – what form of political organization it alludes to, what historical regimes it describes and so on – nevertheless most people today, whether pro- or anti-communist, would probably concur in describing Marx as one.

The word itself doesn't tell us a great deal about the specifics of Marxism it is true, but it gives us a hint as to the thrust of Marx's theory. In their paean to revolution, Marx and Engels use the word 'communist' to describe their famous 'Manifesto' which appeared in 1848, the year of uprisings across Europe. The opening lines are familiar to many; communism is the 'spectre' which is stalking Europe, but the book as a whole laid out a broader historical theory which Engels – Marx's lifetime collaborator and friend – describes in the following terms:

> [E]ver since the dissolution of the primaeval communal ownership of land ... all history has been a history of class struggles, of struggles between exploited and exploiting, between dominated and dominating classes at various stages of social evolution; that this struggle, however, has now reached a stage where the exploited and oppressed class (the proletariat) can no longer emancipate itself from the class which exploits and oppresses it (the bourgeoisie), without at the same time forever freeing the whole of society from

exploitation, oppression, class struggles – this basic thought belongs solely and exclusively to Marx.[1]

So, the proletariat can emancipate itself from bourgeois exploitation, and in so doing emancipates society more broadly from the shackles of class oppression – but how is it to happen? In the same pamphlet Marx answers by saying that the proletariat must 'wrest, by degree, all capital from the bourgeoisie, to centralise all instruments of production in the hands of the State, i.e., of the proletariat organised as the ruling class'.[2]

We have, therefore, something of what the word 'communist' denotes in the context of Marxism. It is a reference to the capacity of the modern proletariat to expropriate capital by placing the 'instruments of production' in its own hands, under the control of 'the proletariat organised as the ruling class' – and by so doing, it relieves the means of production of its character as private property; that is, it now becomes the *communal* property of all the people who work it in their capacity as labourers.

Or to say the same, the means of production become the communal property of the mass of the people whose economic product is now under the political control of those same individuals, and is distributed in accordance with their needs – instead of being alienated by a small elite of investors, owners, managers, shareholders and so on, who use it to undergird their own phenomenal wealth and power. In this way society sheds its class character and becomes something which is organized on a communal or a *communistic* basis.

In Marx's magnum opus, *Capital*, the way in which the capitalist is able to appropriate the economic product of the proletariat – the way in which labour-power in its commodified form generates an excess of value which the capitalist is able to alienate as capital – is elaborated in a much more precise fashion. But Marx's conclusions – which were first laid out in *The Manifesto of the Communist Party* – remain essentially intact.

In *Capital* Marx continues to argue that historical processes of class conflict eventually yield the capitalist epoch in which the prime mode of exploitation is that of wage-labour by capital and, furthermore, that this relation – in organizing proletarians on a collective and concentrated basis in and through the privately owned means of production – also sets the possibility for the appropriation of capital and the means of production on the part of waged-labour itself. Marx describes this historical process and its revolutionary culmination with a pronounced Hegelian inflection when he writes:

> The capitalist mode of appropriation, the result of the capitalist mode of production, produces capitalist private property. This is the first negation of individual private property, as founded on the labour of the proprietor. But capitalist production begets, with the inexorability of a law of Nature, its own negation. It is the negation of negation. This does not re-establish private property for the producer, but gives him individual property based on the acquisition of the capitalist era: i.e., on cooperation and the possession in common of the land and of the means of production.[3]

In addition, when Marx talks about the proletariat's struggle for liberation which opens up against the bourgeoisie in our own epoch, he phrases it in a very particular manner. In the *Manifesto*, the proletariat's ability to gain control of the means of production and its own alienated labour is synonymous with the need 'to destroy all previous securities for, and insurances of, individual property',[4] in the proletariat the bourgeoisie is confronted by 'its own gravediggers',[5] the 'victory of the proletariat' and the 'fall' of the bourgeoisie are 'equally inevitable',[6] the formation of the proletariat as a class will precipitate 'the overthrow of the bourgeois supremacy, conquest of political power by the proletariat'[7] and so on.

This is the tub-thumping, furious invective which speaks of class war and revolution; we are talking about an incredibly radical transformation in which the proletariat 'makes itself the ruling class, and, as such, sweeps away *by force* (my italics TM) the old conditions of production'.[8] In *Capital,* the prognosis is no less fiery and absolute, with Marx writing: 'Centralization of the means of production and socialization of labor at last reach a point where they become incompatible with their capitalist integument. This integument is burst asunder. The knell of capitalist private property sounds. *The expropriators are expropriated.*'[9]

Marx, therefore, was a communist in as much as he postulated communism as a stage in a history which was driven by class struggle, and culminated in the creation of a modern proletariat which had the capacity to take control of the means of production and thereby relieve society of its class character. Furthermore, he envisaged the transition to communism as part of the endeavour of the oppressed proletariat to raise itself to political supremacy and economic domination in and through the furious repression of the class (bourgeoisie) it sought to displace. In other words, class struggle and proletarian revolution are not auxiliaries to Marx's economic theory and his conception of historical unfolding; they are the fundaments which undergird the very possibility of communism and the creation of a classless world. Denuded of these elements, Marxism itself is simply a clock without a spring.

Looking back, of course – after a century and a half – there are innumerable theorists and books which reject Marx's revolutionary prognosis and the possibility of a classless communist society. Many have sought to 'bury' Marx in the outmoded Victoriana of the nineteenth century; for we are no longer dealing with the horny-handed sons of toil labouring away in smoke-clogged factories and blackened mines; now the 'traditional' working class has been dissolved in the world of computer technology, call centres, the great financial hubs of cities – the so-called information economy which has apparently succeeded the industrial world of yore. In addition, the rise of Stalinist states throughout the twentieth century gave many theorists the empirical 'justification' to argue that a so-called dictatorship of the proletariat in the Marxist vein would always and inevitably lead to a dictatorship of the totalitarian variety; that a classless utopia was a dangerous mirage behind which more brutal elite interests were allowed to manifest.

I've written in detail on these criticisms – which I regard as being unjustified on all counts – elsewhere. But the current work is not about any of this. It is not about the criticisms which have been made against Marxism by any of the camps which are hostile to it. I am sure you are as familiar with these as I – they're ubiquitous and unavoidable in today's political climate, after all. This book is about something else. It is about a series of thinkers who describe themselves as being Marxists. And yet, they have, without exception, sought to negate the two elements within Marxism which are fundamental to it: i.e. the history of civilization hitherto as being constituted by class struggle, and furthermore that such class struggle is eventually to yield in the capitalist epoch the prospect of a proletarian revolution and the possibility of the emancipation of humanity therein.

The majority of thinkers I examine in this book are 'Marxist' thinkers who claim to 'modernize' or 'update' or 'develop' Marx but in so doing – whether consciously or unconsciously – they displace the fundaments of Marxism itself; that is, they annul the role of class as the motor force in Marx's theory of history, thereby blunting his revolutionary conclusions. However unlikely or absurd one might find the Marxist prognosis today, Marx nevertheless *did* theorize a proletariat which was compelled to attain a level of development whereby it might emancipate itself through the revolutionary supersession of capitalist society. This was the fundamental conclusion evolved out of Marx's philosophy of history and it was one from which he never departed.

The luminaries of the Frankfurt School, however, or those of the post-Marxist affiliation, or of the other schools of thought which I look at in this book – do not believe this. In fact, they choose to actively argue against it. Of course, whether one elects to go with one position or the other is entirely one's own choice. But the simple and stubborn fact remains that these thinkers are not Marxist if, by that, one refers to the historical trajectory which Marx himself outlined by which a new social system (communism) could emerge from the 'womb of the old order' in and through class struggle.

For this reason, I describe such thinkers as being 'anti-Marxist' – not primarily in terms of a moral category of condemnation – but by way of the simple fact that they disagree with the fundamental conclusions of Marxism itself. To put it baldly, they deny the possibility of Marxist communism and his theory of historical development therein; that is why they are not Marxists. This shouldn't, by the way, be a particularly controversial claim to make. It would be difficult to describe someone as a true follower of Schopenhauer if they rejected the concept of the 'Will' and no good Darwinian could afford to deny the principle of evolution. But why – if their methods and conclusions so clearly contravene the fundaments of Marxism – do these thinkers seek to locate themselves as Marxists? And why, given the fact that they are quite clearly anti-Marxist, have they been so easily assimilated into the revolutionary and philosophical tradition of Marxism itself?

If this book has any originality, it is about figuring out some kind of answer to these questions. And here we must begin with the fact that radical ideas are like dynamite, precisely because they prove so dangerous to the prevailing social order. In the last decade alone we have been witness to the rise of some truly explosive ideas and movements – the Fourth Wave Feminism, for instance, which has been spreading around the world, from the glorious Slut Walks to the MeToo movement. In many countries the depth and scope of the unrest and the power of its protests have forced changes in abortion and employment laws and gender rights, and have led to the incarceration of some supremely powerful men who would have otherwise remained untouchable. Of course, the powers-that-be reply to such movements often with murderous vitriol and the most desperate repression, but naked brutality is not the only response they can muster.

On another level, they seek to co-opt radical ideas, to assimilate them to the status quo in order that the sting be taken out of the tail – and this we can see with so many of the 'progressive' representatives of the ruling elite. One glaring example is that of Harvey Weinstein, who was very vocal about his feminist credentials, even participating in a Woman's March, before the MeToo dam broke. Hillary Clinton is another who has evoked the politics of feminism even though she was involved in a systematic and orchestrated attempt to undermine and slander a series of women who have accused her husband of sexual harassment and worse.[10] And, though figures like the editor of *Vanity Fair* magazine Tina Brown and the high-profile actor and writer Lena Dunham testify to having warned Clinton or her aides about Harvey Weinstein's treatment of women,[11] Clinton continued to pursue media projects with the Hollywood mogul, perhaps because Weinstein had funnelled vast amounts of cash into the Democratic Party, and Hillary Clinton's political campaigning in particular. Clinton's 'feminism', then, provided the type of radical façade which would allow the dirty business of sullied money, big corporate interests and the unadulterated use and abuse of power against women to continue rolling on from behind the scenes.

In a similar fashion, Hillary Clinton also sought to hitch her political brand to the Black Lives Matter campaign, meeting with their representatives and retweeting their slogan at a time when it was felt that the Black and Latino vote in America might be key to providing the political impetus to launch her into the White House in the election that would take place in late 2016. This wasn't the first time that Clinton had brandished her radical anti-racist credentials; in 2007 she described how seeing Martin Luther King speak as a teenager was a life-changing moment, how his 'grace and moral clarity' illuminated the 'social revolution occurring in our country' and reminded her never to stray from 'the cause of justice'.[12]

And yet, stray she did. For the Clintons ascendency to the White House in the early 1990s was predicated on a political campaign of demonization which used a codified racial rhetoric as a dog-whistle to excite hatred and animosity towards the Black populations of the inner cities. Hillary Clinton herself – as part and parcel of this process – infamously alluded to Black youth as 'super predators',[13] feeding into a broader political agenda which would see her husband's administration promote itself as tough on crime, setting the basis for a vast spike in prison numbers, introducing draconian sentencing measures such as 'three strikes' and opening the prison system to an influx of private capital. Needless to say the mass incarceration of poor Black people, and the brutality against them on the part of police, was exponentially exacerbated by the political reforms the Clintons had introduced, and the racist rhetoric in which such reforms were couched.

And lest the reader thinks I am singling out Clinton – I certainly don't wish to; on my side of the pond, I could just as easily refer to the equally noxious Tony Blair, who managed to pursue a series of vicious neoliberal policies which empowered big business and shredded the social-safety net at home while launching a series of imperialist wars abroad causing the loss of hundreds of thousands of lives and destabilizing the Middle East – all of which the prime minister was able to achieve under the rubric of 'socialism' and 'democracy'. There are, of course, countless other examples of elite power adopting the mantle of social movements from below precisely in order to render such movements innocuous and hence preserve the status-quo – examples stretching back into the distant past.

One could, for instance, call to mind the Roman Emperor Constantine who made the move to co-opt the radical vision of egalitarianism which was part and parcel of early Christianity[14] and fuse the practices of the religion with the Roman state, thus relieving it of much of its democratic and incendiary power. Was Constantine conscious of what he was doing? Was it part of a self-aware political strategy? Probably not, but nevertheless the organic power of a movement from below was channelled into the state machine to be better harnessed by a glittering imperial elite. If feeding the Christians to the lions wasn't doing the trick, lionizing the Christians just very well might. In such ways, the revolutionary power of ideas and movements is defused.

In our own time, the revolutionary power of Marxism has been defused by those who have chosen to adopt the mantle of Marxism, and in so doing they have whitewashed the very components in the Marxist description of history which make it one of the most powerful, emancipatory and revolutionary currents to have ever taken shape. They strike at the core of revolutionary Marxism, seeking to obliterate the description of history as one driven by the conflict of particular classes which stand in a specific and objective relationship to the means of production – and so they obviate the possibility of the proletariat taking control of those same means of production and abolishing the capitalist social system and the system of classes in and through its revolutionary act. But the attack on class isn't always posed in a simple and transparent way. Often, instead of actively proclaiming the dissolution of class conflict as their foundational principle, these venerable academics and intellectuals talk instead of something called 'class reductionism'.

What does such a phrase mean? What does it entail? Class reductionism is the idea of reducing all cultural and political forms – all the myriad richness of our social consciousness in its entirety – to the immediate and reflexive categories of an economic base. The notion, for example, that the opinions of an individual judge or shop assistant are constituted simply and directly by the economic interests of the class from which that person comes. Individuals as abstract cyphers which have been reduced to the anonymous representatives of broader class interests. That this is a supreme caricature of Marxism should be obvious to anyone who is immersed in the subject and the writings of its founding thinkers, but even in Marx' and Engels' own time the charge of class reductionism was already being levelled against them. In responding to the charges of class reductionism and economic determinism, Engels wrote:

According to the materialist conception of history, the ultimately determining element in history is the production and reproduction of real life. Other than this neither Marx nor I have ever asserted. Hence if somebody twists this into saying that the economic element is the only determining one, he transforms that proposition into a meaningless, abstract, senseless phrase. The economic situation is the basis, but the various elements of the superstructure ... political, juristic, philosophical theories, religious views ... also exercise their influence upon the course of the historical struggles and in many cases preponderate in determining their form.

There is an interaction of all these elements in which, amid all the endless host of accidents (that is, of things and events whose inner interconnection is so remote or so impossible of proof that we can regard it as non-existent, as negligible), the economic movement finally asserts itself as necessary.[15]

In Marx' and Engels' own time the idea that Marxism involved the crude and mechanistic reduction of the richness of human subjectivity and consciousness to the passive after-effects of economic categories was already a weapon which the intelligentsia of an increasingly anxious bourgeoisie could wield against a revolutionary theory which was more and more gripping the imaginations of the masses.

And yet, it should also be acknowledged that – in the years and decades which followed – certain currents in Marxist thought emerged which did indeed reduce the complex, organic and dialectical relationship which opens up between social being and social consciousness to something in which the latter was merely the reflexive and passive echo of the former.

I have in mind here things like the *Proletkult* tendency which developed in the aftermath of the 1905 revolution in Russia but would achieve cohesion after the proletarian revolution of 1917. *Proletkult* considered the art of a Rembrandt, for example, as irredeemably individualistic and decadent, fatally stamped with the class character of the bourgeoisie from which that great artist had emerged. Indeed members of the *Proletkult* hoped to slough away the whole outer layer of bourgeois art history – the Davids and the Constables – in order to facilitate an inner core of 'proletarian' artists who painted directly and vividly the political interests of the proletariat – from class to canvas, so to speak.

Of course, nothing could have been more damaging and more philistine to the development of art history, as Lenin and Trotsky both realized, when they argued vehemently against *Proletkult* and in favour of all humanity partaking in the universalism and the beauty of the great figures of 'bourgeois' art. Later still, the Stalinist regime in the

USSR promoted extreme forms of class reductionism and economic determinism and, in so doing, claimed it was following an authentic Marxist ideology.

In actual fact, however, the ossified and mechanical 'Marxism' of Stalinist-Soviet ideology was simply the reflection of an ossified and mechanical state which had helped grind into the ground the very same industrial proletariat and impoverished layers of the peasantry which had affected the revolution of 1917.[16] Stalinism was anti-Marxism in the most murderous and grotesque form, and yet part of Stalin's power was premised on the fact that he could employ the rhetoric of a revolutionary Marxism while gutting it of all its meaning and content, thus reducing it to the most mechanical and deterministic of dogmas.

It is my contention that much of this past has come together in order to provide an alibi for murder in the present – the death of an authentic and revolutionary Marxism. Many of the thinkers I examine in this collection who call themselves Marxists begin with these premises; that is to say, they begin with the idea that Marxism has been warped into a form of class essentialism – has been expressed in the form of an economic determinism in the Stalinist fashion – and that they have arrived to release Marxism from these shackles. Many of the thinkers examined in the following pages purport to free Marx from the grip of 'economism', 'economic determinism', 'class essentialism', 'teleology' or some other riff on the same theme, but it is the contention of the author that what they actually do is to decouple the Marxist conception of history from its grounding in class altogether. Despite what they say, it is not the problem of 'class essentialism' they seek to annul; rather they seek to vanquish the realities of class and class conflict itself. And it is in this way that the dynamite is defused. It is in this way that the revolutionary power of an idea is expunged.

And that brings us to the concept of 'reification'. 'Reification' is one of the seminal philosophical concepts in the classical Marxist lexicon. In Marx himself the concept arises in and through what Marx describes as 'commodity fetishism'. In the first chapter of *Capital* he describes how commodities appear on the market as independent things with independent values – and yet, this appearance occludes the reality of the social relationships which set the basis for the production of such 'things'. A bar of chocolate appears as a determinate and independent thing with a given 'value', but in actual fact such 'value' contains in itself as a ghostly echo the social relationships of production, the measure (value) of the labour expended in bringing that particular commodity to market.

The social relationships between different strata are, therefore, in some way materialized in commodities in and through the value they achieve, but in the first instance, these commodities appear as entirely separate and self-contained things which are to be exchanged for one another in a realm wholly independent of the very social relationships which underpin their creation. On the issue of commodity fetishism Marx writes:

> [T]he commodity-form, and the value-relation of the products of labour within which it appears, have absolutely no connection with the physical nature of the commodity and the material relations arising out of this. It is nothing but the definite social relation between men themselves which assumes here, for them, the fantastic form of a relation between things. In order, therefore, to find an analogy we must take flight into the misty realm of religion. There the products of the human brain appear as autonomous figures endowed with a life of their own, which enter into relations both with each other and with the human race. So it is in the world of commodities with the products of men's hands. I call this the fetishism which attaches itself to the products of labour as soon as they are produced as commodities, and is therefore inseparable from the production of commodities.[17]

'Reification' is the term the great Hungarian Marxist Georg Lukács used to describe this process of commodity fetishism in his master work *History and Class Consciousness*.[18] In its most basic sense, the concept of reification denotes the transfiguration of living social relationships into 'things'. And such a concept is integral to the current work – for the central thesis of the author is that the thinkers I examine here – those who seek to denude Marxism of the social relationship of class which underpins it – are able to achieve this in and through a process of reification; that is to say, they transform social, class-rooted categories of exploitation which evolve out of a living history into transhistorical 'things'. The theorist in question will often replace class as the driving force of social development with some ahistorical abstraction – the post-Marxists Mouffe and Laclau talk about a thing called 'the Field of Discursivity' for instance, while Althusser refers to a transhistorical abstraction called 'Ideology'.

This book, then, is an attempt to provide an account of the way in which various thinkers and tendencies throughout the twentieth century and beyond have declared war on Marxism but in the name of Marx himself. How they have systematically transformed that thinker's revolutionary theory of history from one which is driven by living social classes locked into relationships of exploitation and antagonism – into a series of reified 'thing-like' entities which interrelate in a vacuum and are often borrowed from the most fashionable concepts in psychology, semiotics and linguistics. And how, ultimately, this has created a form of 'Marxism' which is particularly prominent in academia, a form of Marxism which is respectable, sanitized and denuded of its revolutionary implications.

And for that same reason, it is a form of Marxism which can be wielded by the left-wing of the bourgeois intelligentsia, which can be featured by the most prominent literary reviews and media outlets of the left-of-centre establishment, a form of Marxism which will not hinder your possibilities of publication, visibility and career advancement – precisely because it is never in danger of challenging the foundations of the class power of the bourgeoisie itself. And yet, it is a form of Marxism which allows you the frisson and moral vitality to believe that you are in some way an outsider, a critical thinker, and a rebel against the status quo.

I am not saying that the thinkers who achieve this 'reification' of Marx are necessarily doing this in a self-conscious and politically aware way. I am sure that Constantine did have a vision where he saw a great cross blazing in the sky, that he genuinely believed he was saving his own individual soul and those of his subjects by legalizing Christianity and eventually making it the official religion of state. Nevertheless, his action also marks a broader moment in which an empire transforms its ideological purview in a radical fashion so as to defuse the revolutionary momentum from below, binding its subjects to itself by raising up a philosophy in which they recognize something of their own struggles and a glimmer, perhaps, of the nature of their own divine power.

Likewise, many of the thinkers who have helped warp Marxism into a shape which is more conducive to the status quo are not conscious of the role history has allocated for them. Nevertheless the role they actually perform – on this count at least – is a remarkably poor one, certainly from the perspective of what Marxism actually is as a political philosophy and the kind of world-historic transformation it advocates.

At this point I should offer up an important qualification. The trends of thought which have been particularly prominent in reifying revolutionary Marxism by extirpating the role of class which I have outlined in this book are the Critical Theory devised by the Frankfurt School, the Literary Theory which emerged as part and parcel of post-modernism and structuralism, and the school of post-Marxism which came a little later, but was touched by some of the same philosophical concerns having been strongly influenced by the thought of Louis Althusser.

But this book does not purport to give anything approaching a comprehensive account of these various schools and intellectual movements. I am not a Frankfurt School specialist; even less, an Adorno scholar. I am not in a position to give you an effective critical account of Adorno's analysis of horoscopes or the work he devoted to understanding the role of teaching and education under late capitalism or his ideas on the philosophy of music. In my chapter on the Frankfurt School I only look at three of their thinkers – Benjamin, Adorno, Horkheimer – and the first of these I reference very briefly.

Nor will I speak to the psychoanalysis which Erich Fromm developed under the Frankfurt School umbrella, or Marcuse's work on aesthetics or Grossman's work on economics. Or to say the same, I am not offering either a positive appreciation or a critical appraisal of the Frankfurt School or that of any other tendency featured here. I am only concerned with their methodology and their conclusions in as much as they relate to the specific problem of the Marxist theory of history and its class-character therein. And that is to target a very small element – and a minority of thinkers – within the wealth and diversity of these tendencies, traditions and schools as a whole.

I aim to demonstrate how the 'reification' of Marxism has been achieved. I aim to reveal that many of the thinkers who have been automatically accepted as part of the Marxist tradition are anything but. And, in one sense, this is something of a grim task; breaking down the convoluted prose of an Althusser or an Adorno when it comes to the subject of the Marxist philosophy of history is a laborious and joyless procedure much of the time. But as Hegel noted in his famous reply to the philosophy of Spinoza, all negation is simultaneously affirmation. Demonstrating how these thinkers misread and misrepresent Marx, at the same time, helps call forth something of the revolutionary power and poetry of the authentic Marxist philosophy itself. A negation of negation, if you will.

It allows me to bring out ideas like 'reification'[19] – which seems like a rather esoteric and obscure concept belonging to the annuls of dusty academic debate – but is, in fact, an incredibly fecund and rich conceptualization of a tendency which is at work in the world all around us, which has a powerful and compelling bearing on our destinies every day of our lives, even if we are not always aware of it. That is why – alongside chapters on how certain thinkers have 'reified' the historical theory of Marx – there are also chapters devoted to the processes of reification in a broader sense; how it structures our working existences, how it affects our love lives, how it shapes our culture, the TV programmes we watch, the novels we read, the impact it has had on the way politics are conceptualized and how art is produced.

And so, while this book is an attempt to document the war on revolutionary Marxism which has unfolded, to show how Marxism has been eroded and undermined 'from within' – at the same time it endeavours to provide a positive affirmation of Marx's thought, to show how his conception of the historical process not only continues to provide a powerful conceptual lens through which we can understand the social world in which we live – but also how its revolutionary and profoundly democratic tenor speaks to the possibility of creating a new one.

Chapter 1

Why the Founding Fathers of the Frankfurt School should be considered anti-Marxist

I want to begin with a brief examination of Walter Benjamin's essay 'The Work of Art in the Age of Mechanical Reproduction'. There is some debate as to whether Benjamin was a 'paid-up' member of the Frankfurt School, or whether he was just a presence on its periphery, but whatever the case, it is fair to say he had a significant influence on the School. Moreover, I think 'The Work of Art in the Age of Mechanical Reproduction', perhaps Benjamin's most celebrated essay, exhibits a certain philosophical logic which would eventually cross over into the political and ideological thrust of the Frankfurt School more broadly in terms of its attitude to the role of class – a direction which is not just non-Marxist but, in my view, is actually profoundly anti-Marxist in its methodology and conclusion.

The thesis which lies at the heart of 'The Work of Art in the Age of Mechanical Reproduction' is a relatively simple one. Following on from the Industrial Revolution, the means of production reach a level of development by which it is possible to reproduce individual works of art on a mass scale: 'Around 1900 technical reproduction had reached a standard that ... permitted it to reproduce all transmitted works of art.'[1] For Benjamin, this fact is an unhappy one. The original work of art is something which has a 'unique existence', specifically 'its presence in time and space ... the place where it happens to be'. This 'unique existence' is the consequence of its production by the artist. The 'unique existence' is what binds the artwork to the history it arose from as a result of the productive activity of the artist. Such a history not only links the artwork to the traditions of the past. It also refers to the changes the work of art endures after it has been created: 'the changes which it may have suffered in physical condition over the years as well as the various changes in its ownership'.[2] In short, its historical framework is a unique and binding condition of the existence of the *original* artwork itself. Benjamin goes even further. Such a framework, bound up with the physical existence of the *original* art object, confers upon it a transcendental aspect, something which Benjamin describes as an 'aura'. Every original work of art exhibits such an aura. However when that work of art is mechanically reproduced 'the technique of reproduction detaches the reproduced object from the domain of tradition' and the aura 'withers', the 'authenticity' of the work of art is lost.

The concept of the aura and its destruction through the processes of mechanical reproduction provide the underlying theoretical premises of the essay. A number of criticisms can be made. The first is the confusion Benjamin rings between the physical and the metaphysical. To be more precise, he reduces the history of the art object to its physical nature at the expense of the metaphysical. So it is the physical mode of the object – i.e. the fact that the original art object exists in a specific place at a specific point in time – which provides the key to its originality. The metaphysical details of the artwork – i.e. the social content which the painting embodies – are not the decisive thing here, for *they can be mechanically reproduced*; what is crucial is that which can't be mechanically reproduced – i.e. the location and physical matter of the original artwork, the specific points in time and space which it, and it alone, occupies for the duration of its existence. This, and this alone, preserves the aura. Or to say the same, the aura of a Picasso painting, its originality and authenticity, is not embodied in the fact that he developed (alongside Braque) a Cubist technique whose form gave life to the shattered, fragmented content of modernity. The Cubist technique and the social content which it reflects can be accurately recreated in and through mechanical reproduction. What cannot be reproduced is the immediate existence of the original physical painting itself.

So, from the outset, Benjamin's analysis of the art object involves what is actually a rather vulgar conflation; that is, he substitutes the immediate material being of the artwork for the social essence when he describes what is key to aesthetic truth and originality.

Why does Benjamin conflate the social aesthetic essence of the art object with the 'uniqueness' of the physical matter in which it is first manifested? I don't think this is any great mystery, and the answer chimes with the spirit of the epoch more generally. Although thinkers such as Benjamin claim to be Marxists, nevertheless the driving spirit of their philosophies often expresses a fundamental disgust to the culture of the masses and, therefore, to the masses themselves. The 'aura' is an aesthetic power which is set against the forces of mass production. The authenticity of the art object is lost when it is reproduced on an industrial scale; the 'aura', therefore, is lost once the artwork in question becomes reproduced on a scale which renders it cheap and ubiquitous – for display in houses; on fridges; in pubs, offices and workplaces, and so on. In other words, the 'aura', the true authenticity of the classical work of art, is displaced and lost once that artwork enters the sphere of mass consumption; once it can be experienced by the majority. Benjamin writes:

The simultaneous contemplation of paintings by a large public, such as developed in the nineteenth century, is an early symptom of the crisis of painting … Painting simply is in no position to present an object for simultaneous collective experience … it does constitute a serious threat as soon as painting, under special conditions and, as it were, against its nature, is confronted directly by the masses. In the churches and monasteries of the Middle Ages and at the princely courts up to the end of the eighteenth century, a collective reception of paintings did not occur simultaneously, but by graduated and hierarchized mediation. The change that has come about is an expression of the particular conflict in which painting was implicated by the mechanical reproducibility of paintings. Although paintings began to be publicly exhibited in galleries and salons, there was no way for the masses to organize and control themselves in their reception.[3]

Benjamin's line of thinking here is quite remarkable if one considers the fact that he purported to be a Marxist. When one steps back from the 'serious', 'high-faluting' tone of the phrases, one encounters what is simply a vulgar form of snobbery. It is 'against the nature' of classical art to be 'confronted directly by the masses' because those same masses are unable to 'control themselves in their reception' of such works. It is fitting and appropriate, however, that such works once entered into a 'hierarchized mediation' with the select elites of the European past, 'the churches and monasteries of the Middle Ages … the princely courts up to the end of the eighteenth century'. In other words, the possibility for aesthetic appreciation of profound and meaningful art on the part of the masses is a negligible one; it is the refined aesthetic sensibilities of a minority elite which truly hold the key to artistic meaning. Crude and aloof, such thinking invariably leaves a bad taste in the mouth, but what is most astonishing is the sheer lack of critical fire the essay has received from Marxists and radicals more broadly; it is almost as though there would be something uncouth, something vulgar, in attacking a 'world-historic' thinker of Benjamin's calibre. It speaks to what kind of elitist assumptions one can smuggle in if one is first prepared to call oneself a Marxist and use a language which has been coated with a veneer of radicalism.

In terms of its theoretical fundaments, the essay is equally crude. The 'aura' expresses a kind of transcendental essence; it is the fetishization of a former form of producing (individual artisan) which is then set in lofty opposition to the epoch of mass production; this, in turn, provides the methodological apparatus for the dismissal of mass culture from the purview of a kind of petty-bourgeois romanticism which is one-sided and retrograde and looks at the 'massification' of culture with a mix of derision and dread. 'The "modern" [is] the time of hell',[4] writes Walter Benjamin. Well, of course he does. Such an element of despair is a necessary excrescence of the logic of this particular theoretical standpoint. Benjamin is arguing that the labour practices of the masses themselves, in and through mass production, are what causes the loss of 'authenticity' or 'aura' in the art object. For this reason it makes sense that the masses themselves are unable to appreciate what true aesthetic authenticity is for their whole mode of being is directly implicated in the process which yields its annihilation. For the same reason, those forms of art which have arisen in the epoch of mass production are by their very nature inauthentic, ripped from any set of organic traditions and history; so, for example, Benjamin says of film that it involves 'the liquidation of the traditional value of the cultural heritage'.[5] Benjamin is prepared to acknowledge some radical elements in such a 'liquidation', it is true. He acknowledges that filmed behaviour can be analysed more easily and thus allows for the 'mutual penetration of art and science'[6] in a highly modern fashion which might otherwise have been stymied by tradition.

Nevertheless, despite these progressive noises, the analysis is unable to shake off its conservative premises: an individual stood before a great work of art in a museum is able to bask in its aura and authenticity *qua* individual, is able to contemplate and reflect and so actively encounter aesthetic truth; but when an individual is sat in a cinema watching a film, then no 'sooner has his eye grasped a scene than it is already changed. It cannot be arrested.'[7] In support of this Benjamin quotes the French author Georges Duhamel who describes the effects of a film on the observer as follows: 'I can no longer think what I want to think. My thoughts have been replaced by moving images.'[8] Benjamin's (and Duhamel's) point is clear; in watching a film, it is much more difficult for thought to be active and critical – instead it is rendered passive, pulled along in the wake of a barrage of frenetic, high-octane 'mass-produced' images; before the film, then, the 'contemplative' individual personality is rendered into something generic and inactive; or to say the same the individual is transformed into a single passive atom of a broader anonymous audience. Individuality, in this way, is dissolved in the mass – 'individual reactions are predetermined by the mass audience response'.[9] This is a consequence of the nature of film itself, a nature which is bound to the epoch of mass production (mechanical reproduction) more generally; '*the technique of reproduction detaches the reproduced object from the domain of tradition. By making many reproductions it substitutes a plurality of copies for a unique existence … Both processes are intimately connected with the contemporary mass movements. Their most powerful agent is the film.*'[10]

So in this brief perusal of the methodological character of Benjamin's essay we are able to note several themes which would become concentrated in the work of the key thinkers of the Frankfurt School, particularly Adorno and Horkheimer. While Benjamin's attitude towards film is much less pessimistic than, say, Adorno's (in as much as Benjamin is prepared to acknowledge some radical and positive elements to film), nevertheless the methodological assumptions of the two thinkers are similar. Benjamin, interpreting film in light of his analysis more generally, reaches the conclusion that it is in some way inherently mindless and inauthentic, because it has come to fruition in the epoch of mass production and the labour practice which facilitates it. This is important because it is not only the case that the film industry tries hard to 'spur the interest of the masses through illusion-promoting spectacles and dubious speculations';[11] more profoundly the technology and aesthetic remit of film itself corresponds to the process by which individuality and authenticity are transformed into the anonymous and thoughtless passivity of the collective; or to say the same, it corresponds to the creation of the modern masses themselves and the way in which their social existence is mediated at the level of culture. The film, in and through its ontological nature, reduces the individual to a member of the masses, i.e. a member of an undifferentiated bloc by virtue of its passivity and dull uniformity. Mass production is simply the productive expression of the social being of the modern labourer in his or her totality; the film and other mechanically reproduced art objects are the cultural expressions of the same.

The importance of this can't be overstated. *If mass production provides the economic basis for the loss of individuality which takes place* – either through the loss of the authenticity of true art in and through the destruction of the 'aura' or the loss of the individuality which occurs in and through the creation of the mass audience – then the masses themselves are bound in the cultural and political fields to a form of consciousness which inevitably works to undermine their capacity for both feeling and thought. In this vision, the social being of the masses *vis-à-vis* industrial production generates of necessity a form of social consciousness which works against their own political and aesthetic awareness, against their own creative individuality. Benjamin described such a phenomenon in terms of a phrase which would become a stock-in-trade favourite of some Frankfurt School theorists – that of 'false consciousness'. The masses themselves are subject to the false consciousness which grows out of mass consumer culture, a culture which is itself a consequence of mass production. This, in outline, is Benjamin's most fundamental thesis in 'The Work of Art in the Age of Mechanical Reproduction'.

Most importantly of all, this helps explain the sheer pessimism which is a natural and inevitable component of these Frankfurt School thinkers. If the masses inevitably generate 'false consciousness' from their economic productions at the level of social existence, then the idea of their revolutionary possibility and potential is inevitably called into question: How can they act in a revolutionary fashion when through their very mode of being they generate the forms of consciousness which leave them passive and unthinking, supine and suggestive? And if one removes at a stroke the emancipatory power of the single social agent (proletariat) which is capable of transforming the structures of capitalist oppression on a society-wide basis, then what are we left with except for the melancholic academic of the Frankfurt School mould? Gloomy and brilliant, able to see past the web of false interests in which the masses are inveigled; able to view, from the highpoint of the sublime intellectual, the reality of capitalist exploitation and the vulgarity of consumer culture – but at the same time compelled to lament the sorrowful fact that the masses themselves will never have the prescience or perception to go beyond the veil of ideology which has so mystified them. And so capitalism gradually morphs from something historically specific – to something which more and more resembles an eternal present; an implacable and unchanging system which has the potential to sustain indefinitely, for it has the capacity to subsume the minds of those who would resist it in and through the hissing, warping power of its industrial monolith.

Adorno's thought contains what is already latent in Benjamin's essay – the idea that the cultural ignorance of the modern masses is in some way responsible for the perpetuation of the capitalist social system and their own continued oppression – but Adorno makes what is implicit … explicit, especially after his relocation to the United States.[12] Adorno would spend over a decade in the United States and it was to be a formative experience. He was living in the belly of the beast, the most concentrated centre of global capitalism, and it provided a cultural and political encounter which would indelibly mark him. Adorno was privy to the birth of a brave new world; the post-war world which saw a massive global boom emanate out from the United States, and on the domestic front, in California itself, a consumer revolution – the epoch of the shopping mall and McDonald's, of the easily accessible wireless and the heyday of the Hollywood film; the time of the first mass-produced microgroove records and the earliest forms of pop music with crooners such as Frank Sinatra becoming the world's original modern-day celebrities. Co-extensively, a florescence of advertising; colourful brands, witty skits and catchy jingles designed to draw the attention of the consumer, and new forms of consumer interaction – every waiter, every petrol pump attendant wearing a radiant smile and exhorting you to 'have a nice day'.

At the same time Adorno also experienced the darker and more sinister underbelly of the reality of 1940s America. In 1941 the United States entered the war, and émigrés such as Adorno and Horkheimer were swiftly classified as 'enemy aliens', preventing from leaving their houses at night, or venturing out further than a five-mile zone. The sense of oppressive and relentless vulgarity of what Adorno and Horkheimer would later term the 'culture industry' was to some extent fused with the darker more totalitarian tendencies of a nation at war – and of course, back in Europe itself, the ongoing persecution of millions by the Nazi regime, a persecution which resulted in the eventual suicide of Benjamin himself.

All of this flowed into a critique of mass culture which built upon Benjamin's premises while at the same time concentrating them to the nth degree. In Adorno and Horkheimer's most famous work, *Dialectic of Enlightenment*, the two authors lay out a similar thesis to that of Benjamin's before them. The period before the mass production and mass culture of the modern age was a period in which art allowed the artist to reach the heights of both aesthetic individuality and a critical awareness towards the social order in which he was located: art 'became rebellious and, in the period from Romanticism to Expressionism, asserted itself as free expression, as a vehicle of protest against the organisation.'[13] It also privileged the authentic individual content over the generic universal form: 'In music the single harmonic effect obliterated the awareness of form as a whole; in painting the individual colour was stressed at the expense of pictorial composition; and in the novel psychology became more important than structure.'[14] Of course, in the epoch of mass production and mass culture this sense of the unique individuality of the art object alongside the critical faculties such an object awakens in the mind of the individual who experiences it is obliterated. While Benjamin had already divulged the thesis of the film stunting the critical faculties of an audience which had been subsumed in a single 'mass' before the flickering images of the cinema screen, Benjamin was, at that time, still prepared to acknowledge some radical possibilities to the medium. Adorno and Horkheimer preserve the underlying conservatism of Benjamin's analysis regarding the film; that is, that it converts the audience into a single mass who are increasingly bereft of the ability to respond critically – '[t]he sound film, far surpassing the theatre of illusion, leaves no room for imagination or reflection on the part of the audience, who is unable to respond within the structure of the film'. At the same time they (Adorno and Horkheimer) eradicate any of the positive though incidental concessions to film Benjamin made. In their vision virtually every film corresponds to the same generic template: 'As soon as the film begins, it is quite clear how it will end, and who will be rewarded, punished, or forgotten.'[15]

Now this is partly because the banks which finance the large Hollywood studios are going to want to invest in films which in theme and tone support the hegemony of the powers-that-be and retain the status quo (certainly a valid point). But it is also much more than this. The medium of film itself – as something which arises in the epoch of mass production and so contains its vapid characteristics – is socially-historically structured to dull the critical faculties of the observer: 'The stunting of the mass-media consumer's powers of imagination and spontaneity ... the loss of those attributes ... [is an expression of] ... the objective nature of the products themselves, especially to the most characteristic of them, the sound film.'[16] Just as with Benjamin, the frenetic pace of the film itself (a characteristic of modern production) is what works to assure 'sustained thought is out of the question if the spectator is not to miss the relentless rush of facts.'[17] And just like Benjamin, though more explicitly, Adorno and Horkheimer note that the development of such mass entertainment conditions a 'mass' in which individuality and imagination are dissolved and each audience member becomes identical with every other. They are reduced to automatons;

> no scope is left for the imagination. Those who are so absorbed by the world of the movie – by its images, gestures, and words – that they are unable to supply what really makes it a world, do not have

to dwell on particular points of its mechanics during a screening. All the other films and products of the entertainment industry which they have seen have taught them what to expect; *they react automatically*.[18]

In other words, the effects of mass culture are not only superficially and immediately political – i.e. the dark, devious capitalists coercing film directors in and through their economic leverage in order to procure capitalist friendly films (though this is part of the 'culture industry' for sure). More profoundly, the masses and mass production enter into a specific relationship; once modern industry produces art and entertainment on a scale such that it can be consumed by the masses easily and ubiquitously, it also produces the masses themselves as an inherently uniform and mindless collective as they go about enjoying the items and artefacts of culture their forms of social organization and economic production have set the basis for. For the Founding Fathers of the Frankfurt School, the real cleavage which separates the beautiful, unique individual artworks of the past from the crass uniformity of art in the modern age is not simply the bald fact of mechanical reproduction – what this technical process overlays is a more profound anxiety and even disgust; for the epoch of mechanical reproduction is at the same time an epoch in which the great unwashed are flooding the museums and the cinemas, are more decisively than ever before exerting an influence on music and art, and are (in many cases) becoming the musicians, artists and actors themselves. What the very 'serious' and 'theoretically profound' language of the Frankfurt School theorists attempts to mask, in the aloof idiom of an objective sociology, is the disgust of the rather sensitive, refined and upper-class aesthete who feels a shudder of repulsion on seeing the lower classes enter the artistic world *en masse* and more and more in the role of protagonists.

There is nothing original, in terms of theoretical acumen, in Benjamin's rather banal essay, nor the riffs on the same theme which follow it in the 1940s, 1950s and 1960s with the 'significant' works of Adorno and Horkheimer. In terms of method it harkens back to Nietzsche. Nietzsche's work took place against a specific historical background; a time, during the nineteenth century, when the urban masses in Western Europe were increasing in number at an exponential rate. Despite the poverty of their living conditions, nevertheless improvements in technology – the ability to identify diseases at the bacterial level, the purification of drinking water, the mass production of food and an increasing variety of diet, use of sewage pipes and so on – meant that the masses were multiplying and living longer than ever before; at the same moment such longevity was also facilitated by the gains won by the masses themselves organizing through trade unions and political movements – gains such as the shortening of the working day, legislation limiting child labour, the creation of health insurance and pension systems. Nietzsche's philosophy was an eloquent and devastating indictment of this process of 'massification', the increasing presence of the masses in the political arena and the public spaces. Such an indictment was framed in a very specific way – a rather bloodthirsty fairy story where once-upon-a-time, 'aesthetic' noble upper-class individuals indulged their individuality in and through the unadulterated exploitation and brutalization of the legions of people below. But at some point the masses were able to infect the 'masters' with a 'slave morality', and managed to reduce what was a strictly hierarchical society – one which promoted creativity and individuality – to a stagnant pool in which the uniqueness of the higher human personality was dissolved in the monotone equality of a vast featureless mass. Quality was replaced by quantity in what was essentially a levelling out process where individuality was subsumed in the undifferentiated and grey expanse of the herd: 'Nobody grows rich or poor anymore … Who still wants to rule? Who obey? Both are too much of a burden.'[19]

When one considers Benjamin's 'The Work of Art in the Age of Mechanical Reproduction' one realizes it is infused with the Neitzchean spirit; its central thrust is how the art object loses its unique aesthetic individuality in the very moment it becomes massified, i.e. mass-produced. The individual loses their creative individuality in the moments they sit before the cinema film and become part of the *mass audience*. More broadly, Adorno talks about 'the enigmatically empty ecstasy of the fans in mass culture'.[20] In going to the cinema and in listening to forms of popular music like … shock, horror … jazz, the mass audience fastens onto 'the culture masks proffered to them … They become a collective through the adaptation to an over-mastering arbitrary power.'[21] This is very much patrician disgust at 'the collective' coming into being before their eyes; the horrified sense of the priggish bourgeois before the awful phenomenon of the masses entering into the field of culture and more and more producing their own creations which – to the refined tastes of the upper-middle-class individual – can only ever appear to be loud and uncouth and mechanical and indistinct. In the very first paragraph in the chapter on the 'culture industry' in *Dialectic of Enlightenment,* Adorno and Horkheimer reveal the fundamentally Nietzschean trappings of their overall thesis, i.e. the shift from quality to quantity which takes place in the human spirit once the masses begin to invade the cultural realm: 'Culture today is infecting everything with sameness.'[22]

To recapitulate, false consciousness is not something the masses are simply tricked into believing by the ruling classes, although this is certainly part of it. More profoundly, false consciousness is part of what it means to be 'the collective' in the modern age; the lack of agency, individuality and creativity are all part and parcel of *the masses essence as mass*, i.e. as the bearers of 'sameness'. For this reason, only those intellectuals who stand outside the masses, who – by the powers of their own intellectual virtuosity – can be the ones to see past the 'false consciousness' of the culture industry, i.e. those truly profound and visionary individuals in the mould of an Adorno or Horkheimer. But although the reduction of quality to quantity in and through the creation of the modern masses has an explicitly Nietzschean overtone, Adorno, Horkheimer and others were at a disadvantage when compared to their older and more rabid right-wing precursor. Nietzsche was able to lament the power of the masses in modern-day society while at the same time *proposing a solution to it in practice*; that is, he was able to postulate a form of proto-fascism which could facilitate practical, political change. It is true that Nietzsche was not a fascist thinker in any typical sense; he was repelled by anti-Semitism (he quarrelled with his sister on this basis) and extreme forms of patriotism and nationalism were abhorrent to him. But the trajectory of his theory of history specifically anticipates the way fascism itself comes into being,[23] the way in which an elite group of masters are able to take the reins of state and subjugate the masses in and through a programme of brutal repression which even touches on extermination: 'That party of life which takes in hand the greatest of all tasks, the higher breeding of humanity, together with the remorseless extermination of all degenerate and parasitic elements, will again make possible on earth that superfluity of life out of which the Dionysian condition must again proceed.'[24]

The problem of 'massifcation' is thereby overcome in practice; quality triumphs over quantity in and through the practical, 'revolutionary' activity of the incorruptible masters and so the creative wellspring of the human essence is once again unleashed in the form of the soaring individuality of the world-historic superman. But because these leading lights of the Frankfurt School are trying to prosecute a left-wing agenda, because (ostensibly) they retain some level of commitment to Marxism and because they were genuinely anti-fascists in spirit who suffered under fascist persecution, the attempt to attack the political power of the masses in and through the creation of a broader, reactionary social movement would never have been an option for them. So while they had, on the one hand, devised a theoretical apparatus which revealed that the masses and their form of social organization were the precondition for the mindlessness and pacifying uniformity of a modern popular culture and the false consciousness which overlays it – at the same time they could not posit a social agency which had the power to transform mass culture by transforming the organization of the masses themselves at the level of social being – not without moving into the camp of explicit fascist reaction. 'Profound' intellectuals like Adorno and Horkheimer could see past the veil of false consciousness and the pacifying oblivion of the culture industry, but there was no social force which their knowledge could mobilize in order to transform the conditions at the level of the social-historical existence which gave rise to them. In other words, social consciousness becomes irrevocably divorced from social agency, theory forever divorced from practice. This is clear when one considers the Frankfurt School's concept of 'Critical Theory'. Critical Theory, according to Adorno and Horkheimer, provides a tonic to the uncritical optimism of establishment thought which seeks (like the culture industry) to inculcate passivity and thoughtlessness by providing a description of reality which is saccharine and sentimental. Critical Theory endeavours to expose the true realities of exploitation and oppression. In the words of Andrew Fagan, in a very comprehensive and positive appreciation of Adorno's thought, Critical Theory aims to 'take a cold, hard look at the sheer scale of human misery and suffering experienced during the 20th century in particular', and to demonstrate how the 'ultimate causes of such suffering are, of course, to be located in the material, political, economic, and social conditions which human beings simultaneously both produce and are exposed to'.[25]

Almost as an afterthought, Fagan acknowledges that 'critical theory refrains from engaging in any direct, political action'.[26] This, again, is more than incidental. Critical Theory is not brought to fruition as the consciousness of a particular social group or agency becoming aware of its own interests. It cannot be the expression of the consciousness of the masses, for as we have already seen, the masses by virtue of their social structure and the way in which it dissolves quality into quantity provide the natural stronghold and historical basis for the culture industry itself. But nor can Critical Theory be used as a means to mobilize the most powerful social groups, the aristocracy, the bourgeoisie, for it experiences itself as 'critical' – i.e. as something which is able to ideologically penetrate and expose the ways in which the power of the establishment works to systemize and maintain exploitation and oppression. So Critical Theory is, on its own terms, detached from any practical and structural interest[27] at the level of social being; it refrains 'from engaging in any direct political action' precisely because there is no social agency whose interests it might reflect, thereby compelling the possibility of action and historical transformation on a society-wide basis. Again, the breach between theory and practice is what lends to the work of Adorno and Horkheimer not only its intellectual aloofness but also an inevitable component of despair. The moment of false consciousness can be 'critically' recognized by the insight of the penetrating intellectual but there is no practical agency which can reform or revolutionize the conditions of social life such that the moment of false consciousness can be overcome.

For this writer, such an approach inevitably invites a contrast with Georg Lukács and the Marxist theory of reification. Adorno and Horkheimer, like Benjamin before them, begin with the fact of mass production and mass consumption – they treat these things in a thoroughly un-Marxist way; that is to say, they treat them as generic phenomena abstracted from the relationship of class exploitation which underwrites them. Lukács' analysis, on the other hand, is based on the commodity form, but specifically a society in which the commodity form as the fundamental economic unit has become generalized such that it encompasses human labour; that is, labour appears in its commensurable and quantifiable aspect as labour power which can be alienated before the market, and so some portion of it can be appropriated by the capitalist therein. In the Marxist scheme, a commodity attains its value from the amount of socially necessarily labour which is required to create it and to bring it to market so that it can realize its exchange value; that is, it can be sold for a specific price. A diamond is worth more than a banana, for instance, because there is more socially necessarily labour embodied within the finished commodity; it has to be mined, hewn, cleaned, transported, shaped and then shined – all of these operations requiring different forms and applications of labour. The banana, on the other hand, is relatively easy to extract from the tree. Labour power, like any other commodity, is also defined by the socially necessary labour embodied within it which is required for its appearance on the market. Its value is determined by the amount of socially necessary labour required to feed, clothe and shelter the worker so that the worker can bring her labour power to the workplace in order to labour for the day/night. But, and this was Marx's great discovery, labour power is unique in its commodity form in as much as it is capable of producing a value over and above its equivalent. If, for example, the amount of socially necessary labour to feed, clothe and shelter the worker for a day is equivalent to four hours of that worker's labour in the work place, the same worker has the ability to work beyond that initial four hour period; that is, they can work for six hours, or eight hours or even ten. In this way, labour power creates a surplus value which is over and above the socially necessary labour which sets it into motion. The capitalist pays, in the form of a wage, a monetary equivalent of the socially necessary labour which allows the worker to feed, clothe and shelter herself, but in working for a longer period of time, the worker creates an excess of value which the capitalist can accrue for 'free'; it is this surplus value which is accumulated by the capitalist without remuneration and henceforth appears in the guise of profit.

What appears as a simple and equal exchange of 'things' – i.e. a 'fair day's work' for a 'fair day's pay' – in actual fact throws a reifying cloak over a social relation of exploitation – i.e. the capitalist's appropriation of a portion of unpaid labour which the worker expends. The true social relationship of exploitation which occurs at the metabolic level appears to immediacy as the mere exchange of equivalents – of things or services which have an equal value. This is the essence of reification; *it is the moment when social relationships appear to consciousness in the guise of things.* For this reason, the reified appearance provides the capitalist social system with tremendous ideological fortitude, because the relationship of class exploitation – which is based on the profound inequality of surplus appropriation – is buried at the metabolic level; whereas, at the level of surface, the act of exchanging one's labour for a wage appears as merely an exchange of equivalent 'things' on the part of free and independent owners – the owner of labour power and the owner of capital. The important thing to note is that the appearance of this in consciousness is not the result of some ideological mystification which is consciously carried out on the part of the ruling classes in order to deceive those they are exploiting; rather the appearance of 'equal exchange' facilitated by 'generic individuals' operating as 'independent economic actors' (as opposed to those who are tied into pre-existing class relationships which have been historically constituted); such an appearance, in the words of Lukács, is a necessary outcrop which is grown from 'the real life-process of capitalism, the extraction of surplus value in the course of production'[28] itself. That is not to say that the appearance does not become 'ideologized'; the basic tenets of bourgeois individualism in philosophy and economics rely on making a fetish in theory of the reified surface; consecrating the isolated individual, making him sacred, at the expense of the network of socio-historical relationships which operate behind the scenes and provide the precondition for the possibility of either his ascendency or destitution.

Lukács' analysis, then, begins with the fundamental unit of capitalism, the commodity. Specifically, however, Lukács is able to show how forms of consciousness are structured by the reified appearance which, in the last analysis, is the product of the relationship of exploitation which opens up between bourgeoisie and proletariat *centred on the commodity in its form as labour power*. It is the essential social relation, the appropriation of surplus labour in and through capital (above all else) which necessarily manifests the reified appearance. For this reason both the proletariat and the bourgeoisie encounter reality in its reified aspect, i.e. as the disparate, perpetual and never-ending exchange of things on a market – a market which assumes a gargantuan and independent existence, an alienated realm with its own ghostly and artificial life, occluding the diversity and richness of all the human relationships and labour operations which set the basis for it. But while the bourgeoisie and proletariat both encounter reality in its reified aspect, Lukács describes how such an encounter is qualitatively different for each by virtue of their social positions.

For the capitalist, the appropriation of surplus value is disguised by what appears to be an exchange of equivalent 'things'; but for this very reason it can appear to him – in and through the way in which he invests money in wages, technology and property – that the real form of productivity and profit creation are the direct results of his own immanent powers mediated by the market. That is to say the creation of profit and, subsequently, capital expansion, all seem to issue out of the process by which the capitalist uses his ingenuity and guile to decide exactly how he will exchange one 'thing' (his money) for another set of 'things' (labour services, machinery, land etc.); the capitalist, then, is confirmed in his existence in and through his encounter with the reified reality, for profit creation 'necessarily appears as an activity ... [whose] ... effects emanate from himself'.[29] For a similar reason, it serves bourgeois economic thought more generally to never breach the reified and ossified surface, for to do so would yield the true nature of profit (surplus value manifested concretely) as something which issues forth from a living social relationship which renders one class parasitical on another: 'the bourgeoisie use the abstract categories of reflection, such as quantity and infinite progression, to conceal the dialectical structure of the historical process in daily life'.[30]

For the proletarian, however, the situation is radically different. When the capitalist 'decides' to pay the worker more or less (i.e. when he 'decides' to consume either a lesser or greater amount of the surplus value the worker generates) this decision has a fundamentally quantitative aspect which issues from the reified prism through which the capitalist perceives the worker; that is, the capitalist decides to expend more or less money on the worker in the same sense he might decide to expend more or less money on a new machine or a new office space. That is to say, he relates to his worker as simply another 'thing', another quantifiable element, another 'mere object of the process of production'[31] his capital sets into motion. But the decision to be taken, which appears to the capitalist in a merely quantitative guise, is experienced by the worker in a fundamentally qualitative form; that is, the same decision *vis-à-vis* wages impacts directly on the quality and innermost nature of the worker's complete existence. It determines whether she is able to send her children to a good school, provide adequate healthcare for her family and so on. As Lukács says, '[t]he quantitative differences in exploitation which appear to the capitalist in the form of quantitative determinants of the objects of his calculation, must appear to the worker as the decisive, qualitative categories of … [her] … whole physical, mental and moral existence.'[32]

Whereas the capitalist is compelled to perceive reality at the level of the quantified, reified appearance by virtue of his social existence, the worker's social existence encourages the transformation of quantity to quality at the level of self-consciousness; she is increasingly compelled to experience her own exploitation not only as a relation between 'things' which happen to coincide on the market but also as a deep and intimate fact which has absolute bearing on her human existence. Her exploitation throws into relief the true nature of surplus appropriation as a social relationship which is created by human beings and impacts human beings, for it has profound qualitative implications for the inner life of the worker who is in thrall to it. In mediating not only the quantitative and reified aspect of the commodity in its form as exchange value, but also containing in herself the hidden basis of this exchange value as a use value – i.e. as an authentically human existence which must first pertain in order to set the basis for her labour to appear in its commodity form and generate added value – for this reason, the worker is capable of recognizing her working existence as a reified one set against her deeper more authentic self; ergo she is capable of perceiving the true nature of the set of social relationships which are submerged beneath a reified world that perpetually posits the exchange of things. The knowledge of the object – of the capitalist social system itself – at the same time manifests as a knowledge of self (of subject) for the worker, for she is a living commodity, and she holds the contradictions between exchange and use, between quantity and quality, between 'thing' and 'social essence' within the confines of her own being. Her consciousness is thus capable of being propelled from the first moment to the second – from the reified appearance to the social reality – by the very nature of her existence within capitalist society and the way in which its relentless determinations more and more work to throw into relief the cleavage between an authentic humanity and its alienated, objectified powers.

Such knowledge – the knowledge of the true 'secret' of capitalist society, i.e. labour power as the value adding commodity – is something which can be only won from the standpoint of the proletariat itself because it is the expression of proletarian social existence in practice; it is, therefore, radical in the most active, practical sense. Lukács writes:

> [W]hen the worker knows himself as a commodity his knowledge is practical. That is to say, this knowledge brings about an objective structural change in the object of knowledge. In this consciousness and through it the special objective character of labour as a commodity, its 'use value' (i.e. its ability to yield surplus produce) which like every use-value is submerged without a trace in the quantitative exchange categories of capitalism, now awakens and becomes a social reality ... The specific nature of this kind of commodity had consisted in the fact that beneath the cloak of the thing lay a relation between men, that beneath the quantifying crust there was a qualitative, living core. Now that this core is revealed it becomes possible to recognise the fetish character of every commodity based on the commodity character of labour power: in every case we find its core, the relation between men, entering into the evolution of society.[33]

In more and more coming to recognize all 'things', i.e. the totality of all the objects of production as the materializations of the alienated value which is extracted from the proletariat by the bourgeoisie in and through a social relationship of exploitation – the proletariat is able to self-consciously raise the possibility of the appropriation of the means of production; or to say the same thing, the proletariat is able to raise the possibility of the appropriation of its own alienated labour (surplus value). Such an appropriation involves taking over the workplaces, expelling the capitalists, creating workers' councils or 'soviets' which would then begin to run the means of production on a fully democratic basis which fuses the economic realm with the political one and allows the class as a whole to organize the rational distribution of its labour product according to its own immanent needs, i.e. according to the rich and multifarious set of needs of the majority in society at any given moment. But leaving to one side the question of whether one believes this is feasible or impossibly utopian, we should note that in Lukács' account the question of self-consciousness, of self-awareness, is ineluctably bound to the question of freedom in the most practical fashion; that is, when the proletariat becomes consciously aware of the true character of its own exploitation in terms of its alienated labour, it simultaneously becomes aware of the necessity of its own freedom – i.e. the possibility of appropriating its own alienated powers. In so doing, in taking control of production under its own auspices – the proletariat abolishes the capital-labour relationship, or to say the same, it abolishes the class relation, the very relation which sets the basis for reification in the first place.

One can detect, I think, a certain pristine beauty in the Marxian/ Lukácsian account of reification and its overcoming, in as much as social being enters into a dialectical harmony with social consciousness, theory enters into a perfect unity with practice, and the moment of necessity yields the moment of freedom. And, of course, the profundity of such a vision throws into relief the paucity of Adorno's approach. The supreme irony of all is that the work of Benjamin, Adorno and so on. provides us with a vivid example of reification; that is, they begin from the 'thing' – the fact of mass production abstracted from the social relationship (appropriation of surplus value by the bourgeoisie) which underpins it. Mass production, in this account, comes into being as a fully formed and 'independent' thing which generates the supine and uncritical 'mass consumer' and 'mass audience'; the social consciousness of the masses is not, therefore, tied into the relationship of exploitation which opens up between bourgeoisie and proletariat, but is simply the passive, inevitable and inescapable reflection of the thing, i.e. of mass production itself.

For this reason, it is impossible that the masses extricate themselves from capitalist exploitation because their social being has not been historically posited; they are simply the appendage of the 'thing', of mass production as a generic ahistorical phenomenon. In this way, the 'Adorno account' cleaves social being from social consciousness, and therefore severs irrevocably theory from practice; mass production isn't posited as a social relationship of exploitation so neither can it be overcome through the revolutionizing of that same social relationship. And so we end up with a 'false consciousness' which is detached from any social-historical conflict at the level of practical existence and which, for the same reason, the masses can never see beyond; we therefore come to understand that the revolutionary supersession of capitalism can only ever be a chimerical proposition; hence the moment of deep abiding despair. Of course, Adorno didn't understand Lukács' theory of reification, any more than he understood the Marxist economics and philosophy which underpinned it. Nevertheless, that didn't stop him from criticizing it with all the disdain of the great world historic figure he no doubt felt himself to be. It is to his criticisms we turn now.

Adorno's criticisms essentially flow from his analysis and critique of the Enlightenment. For Adorno and Horkheimer, Enlightenment thought developed in a very specific fashion, out of a particular way of relating knowledge to nature. Both Adorno and Horkheimer argue that Enlightenment thought claimed to be progressive but in actual fact (like mass culture) had an inherently destructive and totalitarian element to it: 'in the most general sense of progressive thought, the Enlightenment has always aimed at liberating men from fear and establishing their sovereignty. Yet the fully enlightened earth radiates disaster triumphant.'[34] For Adorno and Horkheimer, Enlightenment thought was fundamentally instrumental in character. Which is to say it made of nature only a mere means to an end, only an object to facilitate human will and need. This had the consequence that the human subject becomes ever more patriarchal, ever more inclined to see the natural object as something to be mastered and subordinated to the subject:

> Human beings purchase the increase in their power with estrangement from that over which it is exerted. Enlightenment stands in the same relationship to things as the dictator to human beings. He knows them to the extent that he can manipulate them. The man of science knows things to the extent that he can make them. Their 'in-itself' becomes 'for him'. In their transformation the essence of things is revealed as always the same, a substrate of domination.[35]

For Adorno and Horkheimer the problem with Enlightenment thought deepens further. Firstly there is an element to the object as nature which defies rational cognition, which cannot be known by reason. As Timothy Hall comments, Adorno's materialism does not begin simply with the mediation of man's powers with nature but also with the recognition of 'the irreducible otherness in things, with the acknowledgement of an irreducible distance between subject and object'.[36] Reason, in the context of the Enlightenment, seeks a total dominion over the natural object, but nature, by its very essence, cannot be fully penetrated by reason. As a result, the comprehension of the natural object by the Enlightenment inevitably yields a system of thought which is totalizing yet also abstract, and deficient thereby. It cannot truly reflect the natural object. It creates an accumulation of hard facts, of what Adorno and Horkheimer call 'factuality'. Such a schema subsumes all the richness, diversity and particularity of nature into a single, mechanical and uniform 'mass', a vast and undifferentiated substratum of 'abstract matter' which exists in order to be quantified – classified in an instrumental fashion and in line with the overweening demands of an increasingly totalitarian form of human sovereignty. This is something which goes beyond the analysis of 'mass culture'. It is a broader ontological argument about the human subject and its mediation with nature, and how that creates a certain form of knowledge, i.e. that of instrumental reason which becomes the defining feature of Enlightenment thought more generally.

But although the argument is broader, its logic operates along the same lines: i.e. the richness, the particularity and the individuality which are a component part of the natural world are, by reason, subsumed in a single undifferentiated 'mass'; thus in the same way mass production creates the masses as the bearers of 'sameness', the attempt to rationally cognize and transform nature in accordance with the human subject's own ends, creates a systemic and totalized conception of the natural world in which everything becomes the same: 'Nature, stripped of qualities, becomes the chaotic stuff of mere classification, and the all-powerful self becomes a mere having, an abstract identity.'[37] Adorno coined the term 'identity thinking' to describe this way of conceptualizing the world. The fundamental problem for the human subject lies in the fact that such thought, and the totalizing 'sameness' it generates, does not stop with nature; rather, as Hall says, the means by which nature is mastered are then 'rebounded upon us. The attempt to fully dominate nature culminates in the institution of a social and political order over which we have lost control. If one wishes to survive, either as an individual or even as a nation, one must conform to, and learn to utilize, instrumental reason.'[38]

Adorno' and Horkheimer's critique of Enlightenment is a stale one. The idea of reason as an abstract and totalizing mechanical force which subsumes all the richness and particularity of nature within its remit, before assuming a sinister and spectral power over and against those who have called it into being has a distinguished pedigree in anti-Enlightenment thought going right back to the *Sturm und Drang* philosopher Hamman, 'the Magus of the North', who was writing in the eighteenth century before the French Revolution had even taken place. The idea that the 'object' is impenetrable by reason has a clearly Kantian flavour, although Adorno and Horkheimer do not ground their critique of reason within the context of a broader philosophical system in the way that great thinker did. Instead they simply assert the unknowability of the object (as nature) in a fundamentally dogmatic fashion. The only aspect of originality in Adorno and Horkheimer's critique of Enlightenment is that they rehash certain retrograde components in the history of philosophy in order to merge them together in the context of what purports to be a Marxist school of thought. But how much of any of this could be said to be Marxist from a philosophical point of view?

There is, of course, a genuine critique of Enlightenment thought to be had from a Marxist perspective. Enlightenment thought, in the last analysis, is an expression of the rise of the bourgeoisie and the ascension of a generalized market economy in which more venerable and time honoured relationships – the traditions of communities, the old religious and social bonds between people – are increasingly warped and eroded by the ghostly and interminable gravity of capital expansion; i.e. that which seeks in the individual not the richness and diversity of their individuality – the tribe that they come from, the set of interests they have, the position in their family they hold – rather capital seeks only that which appears in all people as an abstraction, the generic and universal capacity to labour; and it begins to shape and restructure the social world in accordance with this prerogative. That relation between the richness and authenticity of the human personality as a 'use value', and the capital which swallows it up in its aspect as an abstract exchange value in some way becomes the precondition for much of Enlightenment thought; documents like *The Declaration of the Rights of Man and Citizen*, so profoundly shaped by Enlightenment thought, contain this element of abstract universality within themselves. That is to say, they strive to assure a universal political equality,[39] but an equality which in its abstractness absolves the very real socio-historical and economic determinations which open up between people as members of different groups and particular classes. The French writer Anatole France provides a pithy epigram which nicely denotes the limits of such abstract universality. He writes how '[t]he law, in its majestic equality, forbids rich and poor alike to sleep under bridges, to beg in the streets, and to steal their bread'[40] – the point being, of course, that despite its formal equality, it is only ever the poor man who is going to be punished for sleeping under a bridge by the law, because the rich man has enough money to always keep a roof over his head. Enlightenment rights tend to imply the universal form overwhelming a concrete content, exchange value over and against use, quantity against quality and so on. Now clearly this has certain affinities with what Adorno puts forward. Adorno's critique of Enlightenment thought, as we have seen, proceeds from criticizing its abstract universality – i.e. the way in which it dissolves concrete particularity in a more uniform natural substance and how this lends itself to a conception of nature and social reality which has a purely quantitative bent.

Here, once more though, we stumble across the critical difference. The Marxist analysis and subsequent 'critique' of Enlightenment thought are premised on the dominance of exchange value over and against use value – but specifically, it is the exchange value solicited from the individual as she mediates the commodity labour power with the market. In other words, the analysis of the limitations of the abstract universality of Enlightenment thought again flows from the social relation of exploitation which opens up between bourgeoisie and proletariat, as the former consumes the surplus labour of the latter. Because we focus on a social relation, and not a thing, the same social relation contains the possibility of its own overcoming. For the proletariat, 'bourgeois rights' can only ever provide a political form which lacks the necessary economic content; that is to say, such political rights do not touch fundamentally the economic realities of its position as an exploited class. But if the proletariat is to appropriate its own alienated labour through the democratic and self-conscious control of the means of production, then, of necessity, it abolishes the empty formality of 'bourgeois right' for it abolishes the social relation – the exploitation of surplus labour on the part of capital – which sets the basis for bourgeois right as an ideological proscriptive in the first instance.

The theoretical criticism of bourgeois right, therefore, goes hand in hand with its practical criticism in and through the revolutionary unfolding of proletarian class struggle. Again there is a unity between theory and practice, social consciousness and social being. However, the formal universality of Enlightenment thought isn't simply negated by the coming of the proletarian revolution and the eventual emergence of a classless society. Rather, that universality is provided with a concrete content. The political rights which the Enlightenment promises to every human being can never be fully actualized within the context of a society divided and fissured by class, but the proletarian revolution creates a (concrete) universality and an equilibrium at the level of socio-economic existence which can harmonize with the political equality which, in the context of bourgeois society alone, can never shed its formalistic character and make good on all its promises. In one sense, therefore, Marxism can be understood as a critique of Enlightenment thought, but only in as much as it pushes the universality of Enlightenment towards a deeper and more meaningful formulation, only in so much as it provides the Enlightenment with a more concrete socio-historical culmination.

All of this flows inexorably from the methodological understanding of the formalistic character of Enlightenment thought as, in the last analysis, grounded in the social relation of exploitation which opens up between capital and labour power. But Adorno's recognition of the 'abstract universality' of Enlightenment thought does not flow from a specific social relation which is subject to historical development; rather it stems from the postulation of nature as a 'thing' which has a Kantian element of unknowability to it. When human reason is applied to the 'thing' as nature, it inevitably falls short; that is, it forms a concept of nature which is inexorably alienated from the true reality of nature itself, a reality which is, in a fundamental sense, unknowable. The concept of nature which is posited by reason sees nature in purely quantifiable and instrumentalist terms. Such a conception then rebounds back on human society and begins to dictate the way human beings see each other. It creates an increasingly totalitarian social world. In other words, social oppression is no longer a product of a living history in which social and economic conflicts are fought out on the class terrain; instead oppression becomes something which results from the interaction between two given and ahistorical things, i.e. a nature which is inherently unknowable – which becomes a Kantian 'thing in itself' – and a generic humanity whose reason is inherently defective precisely because it cannot come to terms with its natural object.

Both components, therefore, are isolated and eternal 'things' which stand outside historical experience and class struggle. They combine to inform the character of social exploitation in the modern world, this is true. But as the product of the thwarted interaction of a generic reason with an impenetrable nature, such 'social exploitation' itself exists outside the historical process. Why Enlightenment rationality occurs – why reason seeks out nature in such a way and therefore forges the basis for Enlightenment thought – why this happens at this point in time, neither Adorno nor Horkheimer will ever be able to explain because the nature-reason interaction provides a formula in which all genuine social-historical development is dissolved. For the same reason, there can be no transcendence of the 'totalitarianism' of Enlightenment modernity – for there is no socio-historical conflict which called it into being, and so there can be none to overcome it. Again, a sense of profound pessimism abides.

Adorno' and Horkheimer's critique of Enlightenment then is, in essence, irrationalist and ahistorical. Whereas the theory of reification as espoused by Lukács posits the possibility of moving from the reified appearance to the relationships and realities of the social essence precisely because it takes into account the structure of the commodity in its form as labour power and the social relationship of exploitation which undergirds this – Adorno and Horkheimer posit the reified appearance itself as an immutable essence. Their analysis does not take wing from the social relationships which grow out of history and which in their totality constitute the structures and contradictions of capitalist existence but rather they derive the character of 'social exploitation' in the modern world (via the Enlightenment project) from the interaction of a generic, undifferentiated and ahistorical humanity with an implacable and opaque natural object.

In the theory of reification and its overcoming as espoused by Lukács, 'reason' is bound up with 'historicism' – *i.e. it is the historical position of the proletariat as an exploited class which sets the basis for its 'rational' capacity to solve the riddle of the commodity form*, to identify the true value-generating nature of its own labour power; such rational 'self-consciousness' then becomes the necessary predicate for revolutionary action. In Adorno' and Horkheimer's theory all of this is undone; socio-historical struggle is replaced by the interaction between a generic humanity and nature, with the consequence that reason cultivates totalitarian sensibilities in 'society' more broadly precisely because it cannot truly know its natural object; precisely because the object repels reason at the most fundamental level. As a result, in Adorno and Horkheimer we encounter the inverse of what Marxism truly is: i.e. an account which binds reason to historical formation is replaced by an account which uses irrationalism to obliterate the possibilities of historical development, and therefore revolutionary action.

The logic of the irrationalist and ahistorical ontology which Adorno and Horkheimer bring into the light is then used to attack the Marxian/ Lukácsian theory of reification and its overcoming. How so? First and foremost, the character of Adorno's irrationalism stemmed from the fact that the object (as nature) can never be truly known by reason, and that the attempt to do so results in an increasingly quantified and totalitarian warping of the social world. By posing nature as an implacable and ultimately unknowable object, the dialectic between subject and object which is mediated by labour (which Marxism describes) is broken down and the possibility of reading humankind's revolutionary emancipation from the potentials of living history is foregone. The point about Lukács' (and Marx') account is that the object – the objective forms and structures of capitalist social existence – is called into being by the historical process through which the bourgeoisie comes to alienate the labour of the historical subject, i.e. the proletariat.

In recognizing the nature of this social relationship, in becoming conscious of itself, the subject can then appropriate the object by taking control of the means of production in and through the revolutionary supersession of capitalism itself. In appropriating the object, the proletariat thereby facilitates an identity of subject and object (in as much as the object itself is nothing other than the subject's own alienated labour). But for Adorno, subject and object are not mediated by labour. Instead they are drawn together by 'Enlightenment thought'. And such thought is deficient. The object, therefore, is from the outset rationally unknowable and implacable by its very essence. It cannot be comprehended and appropriated by the proletariat as historical subject in and through humanity's mediation with nature as part and parcel of capitalist production and the development of class relations. For this reason, the object will always have an autonomy and an independence which will render it impervious to both human reason and historical development. For Adorno, to suggest otherwise is a form of idealism. Hall describes Adorno's critique of Lukács in the following terms:

The charge of idealism derives from Adorno's belief that Lukács's philosophy of praxis confounds the realization of autonomy with overcoming the dependency on the object, a position most emphatically articulated in Fichte's subjective idealism. What, in Adorno's eyes, the philosophy of praxis shares with subjective idealism is the view that the demonstration of the actuality of the autonomous subject – the absolute ego in Fichte and the identical subject-object in Lukács – turns on showing how the object is ultimately derived from the subject. This in turn leads to a purely 'productivist' account of the subject that in some sense produces its own reality. To this conception of the praxical subject – as producer of its own history – Adorno opposes the priority of the object and the heteronomy of the materialist subject.[41]

In articulating the fundamentally irrational nature of the object (and the way the attempt to know it through Enlightenment reason rebounds on human society *in toto*), Adorno dissolves the dialectic of subject and object which takes place through the mediation of labour activity with nature – a mediation which, over the course of history, eventually leads to the objectification of the proletariat's alienated labour substance as capital and thus also to the possibility of its reclamation on the part of the revolutionary subject, the proletariat, itself.[42] And so Adorno annuls the possibility of the 'praxical subject – as producer of its own history'. Or to say the same, the possibilities of revolution and emancipation from capitalist oppression are by Adorno and his ilk rendered utopian and unrealizable. In his later work, particularly *Negative Dialectics*, this attack on Marxism increasingly crosses into the question of philosophical methodology. The writing in *Negative Dialectics* is simply awful; there is no other word for it. Rambling screeds of consciousness which amble anarchically this way and that before petering away into complete meaninglessness. On the psychological level you have the impression of someone who believes that everything they utter is a world-historic pronouncement, that they are revolutionizing philosophy, reinventing the wheel such is their genius – and yet at the other extreme you also have the sense of a writer who is not quite in control of his own thoughts; a form of verbal incontinence in which every random, half-baked thought is spattered out in the most jargon-heavy, torturous form of prose to have ever been put to page. Of course, that is the very point; the impenetrability of the language – just like so much else in the Adorno project – is designed to differentiate the middle-class academic from the vulgar masses; its esoteric, incomprehensible idiom is meant to demonstrate to the reader that they are dealing with the type of thought which can only be grasped by a glittering and select intellectual elite. In reading Herr Adorno, you confirm yourself as someone in the avant-garde, on the cutting edge, stood on the radical frontiers of thought, dazzled by the sheer import and weight of what you have just read, even if there is some small nagging voice inside which wonders vaguely what any of it actually means!

Nevertheless, if you are able to endure the utter pretentiousness of tone alongside the impenetrability of the boggy language, at the murky heart of *Negative Dialectics*, there are several core principles. Firstly Adorno continues to critique the concept of identity which he sees as the dominating and corrosive abstraction which characterizes modern Enlightenment thought. In *Negative Dialectics*, his criticism is levelled against Hegel in particular. Although Adorno is aware that Hegel often uses the phrase 'identity in difference' to characterize a moment of dialectical synthesis, Adorno doesn't feel this matters in the scheme of things. What happens according to Adorno – inevitably, inexorably – is that the moment of identity comes to overwhelm all else in Hegelian dialectical development and evolution.[43] Specifically, the subject overwhelms the object in its own identity, or more precisely, it overlooks the radical and qualitative difference of the objective from itself: 'Hegel's substantive philosophizing had as its fundament and result the primacy of the subject.'[44] In Hegel, as Adorno sees it, the subject swallows 'everything non-identical and objective in … [its] subjectivity, which is expanded and exalted to the absolute Mind'.[45] Why is this the case? Well, according to Adorno, the Hegelian dialectic, despite its pretentions, is profoundly dogmatic. It assumes in advance that the object can be made identical with the subject. Subject-object identity in Hegel is 'a universal conceptuality … already presupposed at the outset'.[46]

This is, of course, a gross misreading of Hegel. Subject-object identity (in difference) is not presupposed at the outset. Its possibility emerges from the processes of human labour, i.e. self-conscious thought which is embodied in the world (the object) in and through practical activity. Subject-object identity is mediated and deepened through labour; that is, the object – the world – is infused with subjectivity, transformed by the activity of the subject, specifically the means by which human beings produce and reproduce the conditions of their own existence. Marx called that process 'labour'; Hegel called it 'work'. In changing the world, the subject thereby transforms itself; i.e. new forms of social organization and epochs are called forth. Hegelianism and Marxism are both attempts to read this historical process according to its own immanent logic driven by its own internal contradictions. In becoming self-conscious of such an ontology of labour and the necessary moments which comprise it, humanity can become aware of the form and pattern of its own historical development; in so doing, it can consciously harness the powers of production and the most progressive social tendencies which develop around them, culminating them in a form of social organization which is rational and accords to the needs and concrete freedoms of all those who participate in it.

In Hegel, *the most concrete expression of subject-object identity* is postulated in the form of an idealized state; in Marx, it arrives with the development of the proletariat which has the ability to unite in its own subjectivity the objective forms of capitalist production. But what is important here is not the viability of either Hegel or Marx's conclusions; what is fundamental is how Adorno misreads utterly the analysis which yields them. Adorno says of Hegel that his method is dogmatic because he simply assumed the identity of subject and object in as much as the subject simply assimilates the object to itself: 'Hegel's substantive philosophizing had as its fundament and result the primacy of the subject.'[47] Hegelianism is dogmatic, therefore, because it doesn't take into account the moment of absolute difference between subject and object as logical postulates. But the truth is the subject-object dichotomy can only appear in Hegel as a moment which involves the mediation of man with the world in and through labour; it cannot appear as a purely logical postulate and makes no sense to treat it as such. At the most abstract level, at the level of pure thought and its unfolding of its categories in *Hegel's Science of Logic* there is no subject-object dialectic,[48] and nor can there be, because the latter does not appear until the point at which *a subject* can mediate its object through human labour; that is, it does not appear until the third part of Hegel's system which is its most concrete and deals with the question of human history, i.e. *The Phenomenology of Spirit and The Philosophy of Right*.

In criticizing the subject-object formulation in Hegel, Adorno treats it as a purely logical postulate; he therefore tears it from its organic context in the living system of Hegelian thought. When Adorno criticizes Hegel's subject-object formulation, he does not even mention labour – and I don't think this is because he is lazy. It is because, for all his high-faluting phrases, he simply doesn't understand the basics of what Hegel was trying to do. By abstracting the question of subject-object contradiction from the realm of labour and living history, *Adorno himself treats it in a dogmatic manner.* For Adorno, the issue of subject-object identity is not premised on the way in which the subject mediates its object in terms of human practice in the world and the possibilities this throws up. Rather it is postulated that the subject cannot attain identity with the object in advance – because there is some element in the object (the object as a logical, generic postulate) which is unknowable, untouchable, irreducible; some element of the object which is inexorably other to the subject (herein lies the dogmatism). As we have already seen, this Kantian aspect was an integral part of the way Adorno theorizes Enlightenment thought; that is to say, the subject is unable to conceptualize what nature truly is, and so subsumes nature under its own form of abstract identity and in a purely instrumental fashion. But here Adorno moves from a specific point in historical time (the Enlightenment) to a general postulate about the impossibility of thought ever truly apprehending its object as a concept. Thought cannot apprehend the object because the object is always something qualitatively different from thought; it always has within it an unknowable element which refutes the attempt to be conceptualized.[49] As David Held argues, for Adorno thought concepts 'cannot be identical with objects by definition. So this isn't simply a problem of a poorly conceived concept that could be remedied by creating a better concept.'[50] It is rather a problem of the inadequacy and limitation of thought itself. In other words, the irrationalism which is part and parcel of Adorno's description of the forming of Enlightenment thought is now generalized to thought per se.

Of course if Hegelian dialectics has this limitation – if in fact all thought is so limited – then the point of creating a 'Negative Dialectics' in order to 'correct' the Hegelian dialectic and thought more broadly is a moot one. But Adorno is not even aware of the terminal contradiction in his own position, precisely because he is in no way a dialectical thinker.

What does his 'method' of Negative Dialectics actually involve? How does it actually improve on Hegelian dialectics? It is hard to say because so much of the book is simply nonsensical. But this much we can ascertain. By dogmatically asserting that Hegelian dialectics is bound up to 'identity thinking' and in the same dogmatic tone proclaiming the impossibility of a genuine conceptualization of the object by the subject in and through a rational dialectical formulation – Adorno reaches what is perhaps the main conclusion of the book. When the erroneous dialectical method is brought to bear, it inevitably produces a 'false positive'. The idea that a dialectical progression can actually result in a higher and more concrete synthesis is a product of the 'renewed delusion; the projection of consistency-logic, finally that of the principle of subjectivity, on the absolute'.[51] Rather, according to Adorno, '[n]othing positive is to be obtained from philosophy, which would be identical with its construction. In the process of demythologization positivity must be negated all the way into the instrumental reason, which demythologization supplies. The idea of reconciliation rejects its positive positing in the concept.'[52]

It is worth mentioning how fundamentally odd all this is. Dialectics, in the broadest sense, is just the tracing of processes according to their own internal and immanent logic. Sometimes the process can be truncated, aborted, broken, but sometimes it does yield a higher moment. But for Adorno, any positive resolution which emerges from dialectical process is illegitimate. Of course, if one was to assert *that only positive moments* can emerge from this or that process, such an assertion would be dogmatic and grafted onto the process from the outside. But equally, positing an all-encompassing abstract negativity, as Adorno does, is just as dogmatic. But Adorno is very keen to emphasize the power of the negative in the abstract; to show that the possibility of a more concrete and positive result is truncated in advance. In particular he targets Hegel's description of the 'negation of the negation' (loosely speaking the description of how one moment is negated by another, and then both are negated in a higher unity). Adorno says of this: 'The equation of the negation of the negation with positivity is the quintessence of identification, the formal principle reduced to its purest form. With it the anti-dialectical principle wins the upper hand in the innermost core of dialectics.'[53]

Why is this so significant? It is the point at which Adorno's attack on Hegelian dialectics has a fundamental bearing on Adorno's relation to Marx. Marx had described the processes of primitive accumulation which severed the direct producer of old from his means of production on the land and thus created the basis *for the eventual possibility* of labour organized on a vast socialized scale through private property in the means of production. But at some point along the line, the 'socialization of labour' in its industrial form is more and more thrown into irreconcilable collision with capital and the cycle of capital expansion, at which point there is created the potentiality for the worker to re-establish control of his or her means of production – no longer as an isolated individual (a peasant working a plot) but rather in terms of the new collective character of labour which has been bestowed on the direct producers by capitalism itself. The early form of the isolated producer is negated in and through primitive accumulation and the eventual formation of capitalist private property in the means of production; but this form is, in turn, negated in a higher and more complete moment whereby the direct producers take control of the productive process in its socialized capacity. Indeed Marx describes the process in a dialectical and classically Hegelian fashion as a 'negation of negation':[54]

> The capitalist mode of appropriation, the result of the capitalist mode of production, produces capitalist private property. This is the first negation of individual private property, as founded on the labour of the proprietor. But capitalist production begets, with the inexorability of a law of Nature, its own negation. It is the negation of negation. This does not re-establish private property for the producer, but gives him individual property based on the acquisition of the capitalist era: i.e., on cooperation and the possession in common of the land and of the means of production.[55]

The central methodological claim of *Negative Dialectics* runs as follows: 'Negative Dialectics is a phrase that flouts tradition. As early as Plato, dialectics meant to achieve something positive by means of negation; the thought figure of the "negation of the negation" later became the succinct term. This book seeks to free dialectics from such affirmative traits without reducing its determinacy.'[56] The way in which class conflict is played out, the way in which the social contradictions of the epoch yield the basis for revolutionary transformation and the emancipation from capitalist exploitation, has, from a Marxist point of view, a dialectical and Hegelian character which Marx explicitly posits as a 'negation of negation'. For this reason, Adorno's attack on the Hegelian dialectic, seeking to 'free' it from 'affirmative traits' in the sphere of logic, was *also* necessary in order to free human development from any of its 'affirmative traits' in the sphere of history in and through the proletarian emancipation encompassed by the 'negation of negation' which Marx posits. Everything Adorno does is, in the last analysis, driven towards this end, i.e. the dissolution of class conflict and the abrogation of each and every revolutionary possibility (though I don't mean to suggest that he does this in a conscious and politically aware way).

I hope, by this point, has been revealed, albeit in vague and general terms, the true outline of Adorno's philosophy and its methodological thrust. It constitutes a supreme example of reification. It begins by positing the character of mass production as a generic 'thing' outside the crucible of class struggle and the 'thing' then generates a supine 'mass' which lacks agency and intellectuality; such a mass is particularly susceptible to the false consciousness of the culture industry, and thus incapable of resisting the economic exploitation it is in thrall to. Mass production and the modern world more generally are then described in terms of an anti-Enlightenment irrationalism which opposes a fundamentally unknowable nature to a generic humanity. Such a relation severs indelibly the character of exploitation and oppression from living historical development and the conflict of classes. At the ontological level Adorno argues that genuine knowledge of the object by the subject is impossible because the subject must remain inexorably alienated from its object, that there can be no true identity between them either in terms of theory or practice. Last but not least, Adorno mounts an attack on the dialectical method and 'the negation of negation' which is used to describe, in Marxist terms, the possibility of the radical unfolding of working-class power which culminates in the 'affirmative' control of the means of production by the proletariat itself (and thus the basis for a new classless society). Adorno does all this from within the context of the Marxist tradition. His attack on Marxism is styled as the attempt to update and improve Marxism, to free it from the baggage of 'economism' by demonstrating the relative autonomy of culture. His attack on dialectics is likewise couched as an attempt to improve and develop dialectics, which is why he terms his own thoroughly undialectical method to be 'negative dialectics'. His 'originality', alongside that of his intellectual partner Horkheimer and their comrade Benjamin, lies in the fact that they are able to smuggle in the most stringent and potent form of anti-Marxism whilst proclaiming themselves to be arbiters of the Marxist tradition. They claimed to be thinkers who wished to resist capitalist forms of exploitation and yet they generated on every level – ontology, epistemology and politics – the eternalization of those forms through the vision of the world they called into being.

Why? The deflation of the revolutionary moment in Germany which occurred with the defeat of the German revolutions in 1918 and 1923 was always going to introduce an element of pessimism into the Marxist radical scene which would eventually find its echo in theory. But the popularity of these thinkers, even today, is about more than that. There is a section of the Marxist intelligentsia, and the left more broadly, which have attached themselves to the kind of vision that Adorno *et al.* helped put forward. Thinkers like Stuart Jefferies – whose recent book *Grand Hotel Abyss: The Lives of the Frankfurt School* provides an appreciation of the Frankfurt School – have mobilized their approach, again seemingly in the service of anti-capitalist sensibilities, but in reality as a way of attacking the stupidity of the masses evinced in and through the dull and pacifying patterns of mass consumerism, whereby the majority continue to yearn for the 'worthless, the trashy, the things that seemed to promise utopia' or the 'disposable tat'[57] to be found on the shelves of Primark. Citing Herbert Marcuse, Jefferies draws attention to the classical Frankfurt School stance of how the masses have become fully corrupted by false consciousness in and through mass consumption: 'if they all read the same newspaper, then this assimilation indicates not the disappearance of classes, but the extent to which the needs and satisfactions that serve the preservation of the Establishment are shared by the underlying population'.[58] Jefferies himself, just like his mentor Adorno, has the ability to resist 'assimilation',[59] to avoid being transformed into one of the mindless automatons of the mass who seek their 'utopia' in 'the worthless' and 'the trashy'. Like so many members of the middle-class radical intelligentsia, Jefferies experiences himself as having a level of aesthetic sensibility and intelligence which raises him up out of the sordid quagmire of mass consumption, but one can't avoid the suspicion that Jefferies and his ilk will always have access to a level of funds which means that they won't have to shop at the more downmarket places and that they themselves will always have the phones, the computers, the cars and the modern conveniences which will more effectively facilitate their own existences.

Jefferies' article was written apropos of Black Friday, an event which was developed in the 1950s at the outset of the consumerist boom, where stores allowed a few customers bargain basement prices on the latest consumer goods, provided they were the first through the doors. Over the decades following, the Black Friday event grew in scale, the prices were slashed even further and the desperation of those trying to be first into the shop grew ever more intense. Eventually, inevitably, some fatalities were clocked up as a consequence of large crowds stampeding into buildings. Such deaths occurred in countries across the world, for now corporations on a global scale had factored in just what a lucrative marketing strategy the Black Friday phenomenon represented. But, and this was the curious thing, the reportage provided by much of the media in the aftermath seemed less about criticizing the companies that had instituted the practice of Black Friday (and continued to operate it even as news of injuries and deaths came flooding in); rather the tone became about berating the masses of people who were desperate to buy the items. The vast majority of these journalists had probably never heard of Adorno or Horkheimer. And yet, the tone of their puff pieces – somewhere between repulsion and fascination – was indelibly faithful to the spirit of the Frankfurt School in as much as it located the true evil in capitalist society not in the social relationships of exploitation which opened up between the powerful and the disempowered, but rather in the way in which vast numbers of people, congregating together as a mass, become mindless and acquisitive, thoroughly hypnotized before the alter of consumerism. In *The Odyssey*, Kaylin Johnson wrote about Black Friday and how it makes 'me sad to see the greed that comes along with this form of mindless consumerism'.[60] In the same vein an article in *Salon* bemoaned how Black Friday marked the point at which 'consumerism loses its last mooring to civilization'[61] while a protest which developed against the Black Friday phenomenon urged you to boycott the event and thus avoid becoming the type of person 'who will trample and fight ... to get their hands on next year's landfill'.[62] A slew of articles appeared all carrying the same refrain, the same ideological thrust; taking part in Black Friday as a consumer would render you 'uncivilized', would make you 'trample and fight' as you were reduced to yet another 'mindless' automaton in the flowing, stampeding mob desperate to get its hands on vapid consumerist tat. These articles were written in a spirit of radical-anti-capitalism, but they were written by predominantly moneyed, middle-class journalists who found it easy to look down on the 'vulgarity' of the masses and 'consumer culture' from the perspective of those who'd had all their own material needs taken care of from day one. At the same time, these same writers in some way tended to define themselves as critical, edgy, and they were often desperate not to be seen as members of the establishment they were so clearly a part of. Thus their complacency, snobbery and outright disgust towards the lower orders had to be syphoned into a critique which, on the surface, could seem to be about challenging the power and hegemony of capitalism. But of all the responses to Black Friday which have appeared over the last few years, the one which most stayed in my mind was offered up by the activist and filmmaker Michael Moore. Moore is one of the few leading figures on the left today who actually comes from a working-class background. And perhaps because of his early life in the then highly industrial town of Flint, Michigan, where his father worked as an automotive assembly-line worker, Moore had a very different take on the whole Black Friday phenomenon. He wrote:

So who do u think those people are? Rich people? Ivy Leaguers? Parents with nannies in tow? No. They're poor people. Working people. People living from paycheck to paycheck. You think they want to spend half of Thanksgiving Day in the cold wrapped in a blanket in the parking lot of some soulless big box store? They have families. They might like to be home. But they know this is the one day of the year they get the chance to risk frostbite or a punch in the nose to get their kid a laptop that they otherwise couldn't afford. They're willing to get pushed and shoved and ridiculed on TV to get that one thing they hope might give their child a slightly better chance to have the life the hipsters at home laughing at them may have.

Of course by the time they stumble into the electronics aisle, the 20 piece-of-crap laptops discounted to $50 are gone and all has been for naught. They then look around and see the cacophony of signs announcing '50% OFF!' and, to cheer themselves up, they buy a few things they don't need and leave.

Tsk, tsk, the rest of us go – 'consumerism out of control!'[63]

Moore's description here contains pathos and a profound sense of understanding. He understands that the companies may well end up having the last laugh, as a result of the desperation which drives a parent to struggle so desperately to 'get their kid a laptop', but he also understands how, more often than not, such need is about something more than the vapid yearning for transitory material satisfactions which emanates from an underclass blinded by bling. It is true, of course, that some people will buy products – the most fashionable brands, the latest phone – merely as a way of emphasizing their material and social standing, simply as a way to mark themselves out from the crowd, to manifest a sense of individual superiority. It is also true that a lot of stuff is cheap and disposable and often doesn't serve any kind of profound human need. But acknowledging this does not exhaust the question of consumerism, nor does it give us any real sense of just how important it is for us all to have access to the products of mass production. What a difference this can make and how it can revolutionize the lives of ordinary people. Raymond Williams, another writer from a poor working-class background, wrote about this with some poignancy.

At home we were glad of the Industrial Revolution, and of its consequent social and political changes. True, we lived in a very beautiful farming valley, and the valleys beyond the limestone we could all see were ugly. But there was one gift that was overriding, one gift which at any price we would take, the gift of power that is everything to men who have worked with their hands. It was slow in coming to us, in all its effects, but steam power, the petrol engine, electricity, these and their host of products in commodities and services, we took as quickly as we could get them, and we were glad. I have seen all these things being used, and I have seen the things they replaced. I will not listen with any patience to any acid listing of them – you know the sneer you can get into plumbing, baby Austins, aspirin, contraceptives, canned food. But I say to these Pharisees: dirty water, an earth bucket, a four-mile walk each way to work, headaches, broken women, hunger and monotony of diet. The working people, in town and country alike, will not listen (and I support them) to any account of our society which supposes that these things are not progress: not just mechanical, external progress either, but a real service of life.[64]

Of course, just as with Benjamin, Adorno and Horkheimer themselves, the anti-consumerist critique of capitalism is often styled as a Marxist one, which makes it worth looking at what Marx actually had to say about mass consumption. In the chapter on Alienation in the *Grundrisse,* Marx talks about how the capitalist relates to 'the world of workers'[65] who 'stand toward him as consumers' by seeking to 'spur them on to consumption, to give his wares new charms, to inspire them with new needs by constant chatter etc'.[66] So far, this is not out of sync with the Frankfurt critique. But as the Marxist philosopher Ishay Landa points out, Marx then goes further. Marx argues that it 'is precisely this side of the relation of capital and labour which is an essential civilizing moment'.[67] What does Marx mean by describing 'consumerism' as representing a 'civilizing moment'? I think it interlocks with his theory of humankind more broadly. Specifically, in producing and reproducing the means of his own existence in and through the forms of social organization his labour activity throws up – man produces himself in the same moment. The more sophisticated his forms of social organization become, the higher the level by which his productive technique is raised – the more the individual is produced as someone who develops an ever-increasing complex of rich social needs and potentialities which transcend the needs of his immediate biological existence, i.e. the basic requirements for food, drink and shelter. In other words a whole host of 'artificial needs' are created which are in time with the higher development of the human individual as a richly social and cultural creation, a human creation, over and above the moorings the physical body has to its purely natural existence. Marx writes how such artificial needs 'arise out of the social existence of the individual' and are 'those which do not flow from his naked existence as a natural object'.[68] For those bourgeois economists who criticize such needs as somehow 'false' or 'spurious' in comparison with the 'genuine' needs of his physical existence, Marx has only contempt, suggesting that such thinking reveals 'the inner, desperate poverty which forms the basis of bourgeois wealth and of its science'.[69] For Marx, therefore, communist society would not involve the narrowing down of consumption in order to concentrate on a pre-determined set of 'authentic' and 'natural' needs, but would rather encompass the generation of a whole set of new, 'artificial' needs on the part of the consumer in line with the development of a richer and more comprehensive social world. Consumerism, then, would be expanded rather than contracted: 'after the abolition of the capitalist mode of production the part regularly consumed by the direct producers would not remain confined to its present minimum level'.[70]

When one considers today some of the truly remarkable gains of consumption, it is difficult not to be awestruck. For instance, you can now buy a phone which works as a camera, which allows you to watch films, which can act as a method of payment in a shop, which – at the touch of a button – can access an online encyclopaedia drawing upon millions of millions of pages of collective information that encompass the vast spiritual and scientific estate of humanity. It can provide you with video footage of your home, it can be used to open a door for a delivery even if you are miles away, it can monitor your heart rate and alert the paramedics should you have a medical emergency, you can play games on it, you can talk to it – relaying commands as it is also voice activated – and it can give you advice on the best restaurant in the area where you are, along with directions on how to get there and recommendations for which film to watch in the cinema afterwards, before it then buys your ticket. You can write stories on your phone, send emails, you can make music, you can conduct a love affair, or create algorithms, donate to a charity of your choice or coordinate a mass protest. That such multifarious examples of human creativity and possibility can be totalized and condensed into a sleek, thin streamlined piece of technology which fits in your hand is nothing short of miraculous especially when one considers how, only a few decades before, this would have been almost unimaginable.

And yet, there are a couple of dystopic and discordant notes to be struck in the context of such an otherwise idealized vision. The first is that the vast majority of human beings in the world will never have access to such technology because they will never have the funds required to procure it, even though it is their intensive labour operations which set the basis for the extraction of the raw materials and then the manufacture of the finished product in the first place. The question of labour is particularly significant and darkly ominous. Many of the batteries which power such phones are formed in part from a material called cobalt, and much of this material is mined in the 'copper belt' of the Democratic Republic of Congo. Such mines, nearly always run by vast corporations, produce super profits from the backbreaking labour exacted from men, women and children at the most piteous levels of financial compensation. Suffering, ill-health, exhaustion and fatalities run amok with the hot craterous landscape providing a backdrop to scenes which might well have come from a modern-day Dante's *Inferno*.

But it would be wrong to argue that this is a problem inherent to consumerism per se. Rather it is an issue which is inherent to class. The way in which corrupt authorities are bought off in order to not enforce the already inadequate labour laws, the way in which the governments of powerful states such as China and the United States facilitate rather than rein in the rapacious tendencies of their capitalist business interests operating in Third World counties with particularly vulnerable populations. These are issues of the political wing in the ruling class facilitating capital creation and expansion in its economic wing more generally. In addition, even though consumers benefit from the technology they access through consumption, it is not the case that they are engaged in the exploitation of the labour of those who create it. Instead surplus product flows upward; that is, it is the owners and investors of the corporations which mediate the consumer with the product who are the ones to absorb the vast quantities of surplus labour generated by the class of impoverished labourers. That's not to say that the consumers don't have some role in the process; certainly, when the working practices of a particular company are revealed to be barbaric, the consumer can be integral in boycotting such a company and helping to affect more progressive changes in labour law. But again, the key thing to remember is that the exploitation which takes place is not the product of a generic something called 'mass consumption' which stands in a necessary connection to 'global poverty'; rather global poverty is the product a particular set of class relationships which underpin both production and consumption on a national and international basis. To eradicate poverty two things are required: firstly, labour conditions must be relieved of their viciously exploitative character; that is, the capital to labour relationship must be revolutionized and abolished thereby. Secondly, the vast number of people who labour to create the products of mass consumption must be the same people who enjoy those products in their entirety. The first condition – the revolutionizing of the capital – labour-power relationship sets the basis for the second; once the masses appropriate their own labour power at the point of production, they are then able to control and 'consume' the products that their labour creates entirely in accordance with their own needs. In other words, a classless, communist society implies not the reduction of consumption but the extension of it, to all those people whose labour sets the basis for it. This is revolutionary Marxism, but the thought of the Frankfurt School and their ilk stands in precise opposition to this; for them, it is precisely the extension of consumption which leads to the masses being more vulgar, more mindless, more acquisitive and more incapable of radical action. When you cleave away the radical paraphernalia of the appearance – the high-faluting language, the virulent denunciations of the misery of humankind under capitalism – you come to realize that on the levels of both culture and economics the conclusions these thinkers draw have a certain sense of parity. On the cultural level, they lament the fact that the masses have increased influence, and at the level of the economic the same is true, they rue the level of purchasing power the masses have achieved as consumers.

Given the thought of the figures considered here in its outlines does not only *fail to add* to the body of significant Marxist thought more generally, but rather has an explicitly reactionary and often rather vulgar thrust which works against it; given their thought is convoluted and profoundly anti-Marxist, why has it amassed such a following and why has it attained such critical respect? The answer to this is related to what one might nowadays term 'academic Marxism'. It is important to define such a concept as carefully as possible, and to note in advance that I am not advocating some type of anti-intellectualism. There are a good few Marxist teachers and professors, students and lecturers, who maintain a great moral and intellectual fidelity to Marxism and are integral to the expansion and concretization of our tradition. I know this because I have benefited from the work and the teaching of a number of them and indeed several of them have helped improve this book with their insights.

'Academic Marxism', however, is something which refers to a particular and predominate tendency of thought within academia; in its loosest outlines it seeks to 'appropriate' Marxism for the professional intellectual; it seeks to do this by displacing class struggle as the critical ontological category which underpins revolutionary Marxism and instead make the head of the privileged, super intelligent intellectual the crucible in which real human progress (or the lack of) is achieved. This is often wrought through a combination of pessimism and privilege.

When the class struggle is in the downturn, the faith more radically inclined academics have in the popular movements from below is, quite naturally, diminished, and we have experienced several decades of struggle and defeat, amid the backdrop of the domination of neoliberalism in countries across the globe. In such circumstances, it is always easy to question the efficacy of working-class struggle, to be acutely aware of its failures and limits, and if one is able to view these things through a lens of privilege and relative prosperity – these failures can sometimes be quickly and easily linked with a more general and essentialist description of the masses, their lack of intellectual capacity, lack of culture and so on. Adorno *et al.* give such a vision a theoretical and systematic expression. The culture of the masses, mediated by mass production, is vulgar and false and only the refined sensibilities of the middle-class intellectual are able to see past the veil. In Marxist scholarship more generally many of the same sensibilities pervade because it is more and more dominated by a middle-class elite at a time when working-class struggle more broadly is in abeyance. There is often, in Marxist academic circles, a certain disdain for the products of mass culture. *Harry Potter*, for instance, is the single biggest literary phenomenon of all time; and not only a great work of art, but also one which has as its core motif the development of fascism[71] and the way in which the left rises to fight it. And yet, remarkably, the attention which Marxists (especially those in the academy) have paid to this has been almost completely non-existent. And when Harry Potter has been written about it is often with a great deal of contempt.[72]

More broadly, great examples of popular culture have been neglected, from films like *Planes, Trains and Automobiles* which address specifically the question of reification and its overcoming to great series like *Frasier* which puts the question of class difference at its centre. Programmes like *Breaking Bad*, *The Sopranos*, *Oz*, the whole HBO 'revolution', all these things have a pitiful representation in Marxist scholarship proportionate to the millions upon millions of people who enjoy them. When it comes to Shakespeare there is an ocean of material and books, and rightly so. My point is not that Shakespeare is unworthy, but simply that there are a good few Shakespeares who are developing writing and music and art in our own epoch, and they are equally worthy of our attention. But instead we come to understand that Shakespeare is part of high classical culture and Harry Potter, while amusing, is about witches and wizards and is really just a form of 'light entertainment'. Not as if Shakespeare would ever write about witches. But apart from all the hubble, bubble, the toil and the trouble, it is worth remembering that in Shakespeare's time he was *an immensely popular and commercially successful author*. He was attacked by an elite with more 'refined' sensibilities precisely because he was popular, precisely because – in mixing bawdy comedy with earthly tragedy – he violated the principles of the classicists, he created a more 'vulgar' form of art which was designed to appeal to the lower classes as well as the royal court. His audiences were, in the majority, composed of 'groundlings', that is to say seamen, servants, shopkeepers, ironworkers and so on. It was only retroactively that Shakespeare was appropriated as an example of 'high culture'.

Perhaps more paradoxically, there is a certain attraction to the pessimism of the Frankfurt School on the part of the middle-class intellectual or academic. Immersing yourself in this sort of stuff allows for a very esoteric experience; the ridiculously convoluted and often nonsensical language of a Horkheimer or an Adorno allows you to imagine that you are dealing with the most sublime and profound work of genius which only the thinking power of a tiny elite can hope to penetrate, while at the same time its Marxist lexicon allows you to believe that you are part of a radical set of politics which lets you enjoy the rebellious frisson of someone who defines themselves as anti-establishment and profoundly critical of the oppression and exploitation of the status quo. But the pessimism which lies at the theory's core – the means by which it is able to divorce theory from practice by removing the motor of class struggle at the heart of history – also gives you the sense that any real convulsions and social transformations are now beyond reach; that, regrettably, capitalism can never be fundamentally superseded, and that your own place and privileges within the context of what you know and experience will always be a given. It allows you to masquerade as a sceptic – as someone who is against the crass commerciality of an industrially produced culture which seeks to pacify and demean – and for the same reason, it allows you to separate yourself out from the common herd by the awareness of the radical and highly developed nature of your own artistic and political sensibilities; in the last analysis, it secures and eternalizes the very structures and apparatus of class this 'left-wing' variety of elitism grows out of; above all it makes clear that your own material privilege, your own sense of social superiority, will remain forever undisturbed by the formless and protean forces broiling underneath. Lukács understood the political psychology of the Frankfurt School to a tee, when he wrote that a 'considerable part of the leading German intelligentsia, including Adorno, have taken up residence in the '"Grand Hotel Abyss" … a beautiful hotel, equipped with every comfort, on the edge of an abyss, of nothingness, of absurdity. And the daily contemplation of the abyss between excellent meals or artistic entertainments can only heighten the enjoyment of the subtle comforts offered."'[73]

Chapter 2

Planes, Trains and Automobiles: A study of capitalist reification and the possibility of its overcoming

Planes, Trains and Automobiles is the 1987 film that tells of the travails of two strangers who are thrown together as they attempt to navigate their way home one snowy Thanksgiving weekend. Because of blizzards, the transport infrastructure is heaving under the weight of thousands of stranded travellers, the hotels are overflowing, and the icy conditions ensure every type of delay and diversion. And so what should be, for Neal Page, a brief, painless trip of less than two hours by plane from New York to Chicago is warped into several days of relentless trudging from airport to train station, from hotel to hotel, from car hire firms to dodgy locals with beaten down trucks. Throughout, he is accompanied by the ebullient, generous, overbearing Del Griffith who provides Neal with both companionship and irritation, as the two men battle the obstacles which their epic journey entails.

The word 'epic' might seem a little out-of-sync here. After all, a journey which takes place in and through the mundane environs of airports, and stations and the kind of generic motels which are frequented by travelling salesmen the world over hardly provides the fodder for the type of heroic pilgrimage in the classic Lawrence of Arabia type vein. But one of the most abiding elements of the film is how the journey Neal and Del undertake really is quite momentous – for it forms an almost David and Goliath type opposition between the two men themselves and the sheer anonymous power of the system they are trying to navigate. *Planes, Trains and Automobiles* brings out one of the most disempowering elements of the individual faced with the sheer bureaucracy of modernity; that is, much of the time you have so little control over anything, and when something doesn't go your way there is little you can do. When a great flashing screen informs you that your flight has been delayed or cancelled, it matters not how passionately you remonstrate with the person behind the counter, for there are already objective forces which have been set in motion, and which cannot be reversed. The details of your life, your own individual set of needs, your whims and aspirations – through precious to you – matter very little in the scheme by which those higher objectivities are unfolded, and one of the great strengths about *Planes, Trains and Automobiles* is that it lays bare this truth in all its comic absurdity.

It is exemplified, for example, in a scene where Neil, rundown, natty and exhausted, finally arrives to a rental car company, only to find the car he has booked is missing. The sheer frustration at once again having his plans undermined is translated into an infamous four-letter tirade against the rental clerk behind the desk. He unleashes a rant in which every sentence lashes the underserving worker with the f-word, before she calmly enquires if he has a copy of the car-hire agreement he has signed (he has not). When he tells her this, she looks back, without missing a beat, turning the tables on him – 'oh boy …. *you're fucked'*.[1] The scene works on several levels. Firstly it emphasizes what we already know about the character of Neil Page. He is an advertising executive who has bought into the ethos of seeing those he meets in the wider world, not in terms of the quality and content of their personhood, but rather as bearers of the particular service they can provide him with. Page is able to be so rude to the worker behind the desk at the car rental shop because, in his eyes, she appears as nothing more than a facet or extension of a company which has failed to honour its contractual obligations. In the same moment, Page's rant also illustrates the absurdity inherent in the endeavour to reduce another person to a particular commercial function, for in the moment you do so – you too are endanger of having your own personhood undermined. Of being converted from a living individual to a paragraph or phrase in a contract – a cipher for a given sum of money which is indifferent to the richness and complexity of human personality and ends – 'May I see your rental agreement? ... Oh boy ... you're fucked'.[2] In Marxist terms, the scene represents the way in which human contact is transfigured from the prerogatives of use to those of exchange. When Page first comes across the rental worker in order to make his complaint, she is on the phone talking with a sibling about the Thanksgiving meal she is planning for their parents. She is giggling, but when Page reaches the desk – his expression stormy and furious – her hilarity at once evaporates, and she puts on a terse smile – 'Welcome to Marathon – may I help you?'[3] To say the same, she is transformed from her aspect of authentic personhood in and through her exchange with Page; the scene demonstrating, more broadly, the absurdity of a realm in which the relations between people are, of necessity, transformed into a transaction and interaction of things or services.

All of which brings us to Del Griffith. Del Griffith is a shower curtain ring salesman so ostensibly he too is very much embroiled in the prerogatives of exchange. We see him, for example, using the gift of the gab in order to hawk his wares, spinning some colourful yarns regarding the exotic lineage of each of the shower curtains he wishes to sell, and thus relieving some of his more credulous clients of their money. Del certainly has a roguish and even manipulative side to his personality, but this is necessary for it speaks to the authenticity of the character. Del's existence as a travelling salesman is precarious and hard; living hand-to-mouth, he has picked up certain survival skills which are undoubtedly unsavoury but also to be expected. But, while Neil is unable to see the strangers who enter his orbit as anything other than living commodities – i.e. the bearers of a particular good or service which might help facilitate his overall 'end' (the endeavour to make it home) – Del from the outset treats Neil as a person he reposes a real interest in. Del wants to know about Neil's thoughts and feelings, and history and background, because he, Del, is actually, genuinely interested. In the same way, Del gives everything of himself; he is a font of rambling anecdotes, spontaneous thoughts, cheeky asides and helpless laughter. When Neil and Del find themselves sitting in the same row on the plane near to the start of the film, Del takes off his shoes, groaning luxuriously before turning to the horrified Neil and remarking with a grin – 'My dogs are barking!'[4]

On one level the scene has a devilish comical value because the gesture of Del taking off his shoes verges on the obnoxious, and the audience is invited to enjoy the comic contrast between Del's obliviousness and Neil's palpable discomfort. But at the same time, the scene is far more than just a cheap body-odour gag, because it gives us a glimpse into something more fundamental about Del's character. He is easy in the company of strangers, he trusts their empathy, relies on their sympathy; in a word, he imagines them to be as genuine and kind as himself. But such a sensibility is fundamentally problematic. Under capitalist social relations the majority of people one encounters in the external world – outside the remit of family and friends – are those drawn into your orbit as a result of the fact that they are the bearers of a particular commodity. When you buy something at McDonald's, when you jump into a taxi, when you get a haircut – all these things[5] are underpinned by the processes of commodity exchange, and thus both yourself and the people who are interacting with you appear not in the guise of persons paramountly but in the reified aspect as the bearers of particular services or things. Even when there is no direct exchange of commodities, even when, for example, you are on the tube in the middle of the rush hour, you are surrounded by other commuters, the majority of whom are taking the journey in order to get to work; or to say the same thing, to realize the sale of their labour power in its commoditized form.

The manner in which individuals encounter one another in the broader capitalist reality, then, is thoroughly permeated by a process of reification in which they appear foremostly in the guise of things – as bearers of particular commodities. Inevitably, therefore, the rich life of the personality is exiled to an increasingly private and solipsistic realm – one which is, of necessity, invisible, impenetrable and undisclosed. When you are sitting on the tube on the Underground, for instance, and you open a book, it is into this realm which you fall, and it is thoroughly liberating for the same reason. In the moments when you open up your book or your magazine, you are no longer in thrall to the awareness of yourself as a bearer of labour power who is compelled to realize that commodity by getting to work and deploying it for a given number of hours. In the moment when you begin to read, you are (providing the reading is not work related) most likely indulging the idiosyncratic set of interests which corresponds to your authentic, private individuality. And if, in that situation, one finds oneself being observed, if, for example, someone is reading the book over your shoulder – and if they go further still; if they remark positively on what you are reading, expressing how they too have read it, and sharing with you just how inspired they were by it – the typical reaction to all of this would not be to enthusiastically agree with the person who is relaying this information, but rather – perhaps – to express a certain wary acquiescence, to feel an inner sense of discomfort, to mollify them and hope they get back to whatever it was they were doing before ASAP.

On the surface we experience such anxiety because it is unusual to be approached by a stranger in this way – perhaps we question the anonymous person's intents – do they want to rob us, are they possibly even a little bit unhinged? But beyond all of these imaginings there is something more fundamental which has taken place, and which undermines us at a more profound level. When a stranger opens up a dialogue in that way, he or she is also breaching the threshold of a specific ontological parameter. As strangers, commuting to and from work, the various passengers on the train necessarily appear to each other as bearers of exchange value – as multifarious but mutually discrete processes by which exchange value seeks its realization in a set of given workplaces; all of this calls forth a mode of behaviour, of ritual, of formality – which acts as a buffer between one's private essence, one's rich inner world and authentic consciousness, and the role one is compelled to assume as an economic actor exchanging one's labour for a wage or partaking in some similar economic relation. When that person, that stranger on the train, leans over and comments on your book, he or she is in effect crossing a metaphysical Rubicon – the threshold between one's objectified essence as a bearer of the commodity form and one's authentic essence as a unique human being rich in interest and particularity. This marks nothing less than a metaphysical breach, a social trauma, an ontological rupture which suddenly sees use value in the form of the authentic human personality erupting and bursting forth into the realm of exchange – the same realm which provides the modes and forms of its antithesis.

Again this brings us back to Del. Del *is* that person on the train who leans over and comments on your book, for Del is an aberration, in as much as his personality manifests as a pure authenticity which is set against the prerogatives of exchange and the reifying consequences they exert in the region of social behaviour. If the scene where Neil confronts the clerk at the car rental agency represents, in microcosm, the way in which human relations become capitalized according to the prerogatives of exchange, the way in which one is in some way alienated from one's inner personality and sensibilities by the demand for an etiquette and mode of behaviour which, in the last analysis, corresponds to the structure of the commodity form as the fundamental economic unit of the capitalist social system; if Neil's interactions with those he encounters in the broader world navigate the trajectory from use value to exchange value, then Del's way of being encourages the very opposite movement; that is, it endeavours to 'dereify' the set of relations between people which are first and foremost posited as a set of relations between things.

And it is this conflict which provides the rationale for one of the most poignant scenes in the film. When the two men are compelled to share a room (there are no others available because of the business of the holiday season), Del's presence finally becomes too much for Neil. Now the way in which Neil's frustration and anger build is handled with expert and hilarious comic effect – Del occupies the bathroom for ages, and when Neil finally gets a turn the hot water runs cold. When he goes to mop his face with a flannel, what he in fact presses to his nose, mouth and eyes, are the huge set of underpants which Del has left soaking in the basin. The camera zooms in on Neil's face as the realization of what he is using to massage his face sinks in. Again a lot of this stuff is slapstick, almost silly, and yet it sets the basis for what is to come. As they climb into bed together (there is only the one double bed), as Neil closes his eyes against the world, his whole body locked into a clench of irritation – even the blessed escape of sleep is not permitted to him, for it is then when Del begins to make bizarre snorting noises, an attempt to clear his sinuses.

Finally Neil explodes. And it is here where the tone of casual playfulness vanishes in the face of a genuine pathos. We watch as Neil lays into Del, eviscerating his personality with a vicious and prolonged diatribe:

Didn't you notice on the plane when you started talking, I started reading the vomit bag? Didn't that give you some clue that this guy's not enjoying it? Everything's not an anecdote. You have to discriminate. You choose things that are funny or mildly amusing or interesting. You're a miracle. Your stories have none of that. They're not even amusing accidentally. Honey, meet Del Griffith. He's got some amusing anecdotes. Here's a gun so you can blow your brains out. I could tolerate any insurance seminar. For days, I could listen to them go on and on. They'd say, 'How can you stand it?' And I'd say, 'Cause I've been with Del Griffith. I can take anything.' You know what they'd say? 'I know what you mean. The shower curtain ring guy.'[6]

We watch as Del's face crumples, his eyes well with tears, but he doesn't break down. For the first time the large, kind man's face assumes a real solemnity, he straightens himself up, as though he wants to fully expose himself to the anger of the other man. And then in a soft, halting voice Del says:

You want to hurt me? Go ahead if it makes you feel better. I'm an easy target. Yeah, you're right. I talk too much. I also listen too much. I could be a cold-hearted cynic like you, but I don't like to hurt people's feelings. Well, you think what you want about me. I'm not changing. I like – I like me. My wife likes me. My customers like me. 'Cause I'm the real article. What you see is what you get.[7]

The scene, able as it is to transition so seamlessly from light comedy to genuine pathos, is one of the finest, most delicately crafted set pieces in which deft writing merges harmoniously with some of the most pitch-perfect acting ever seen. It is truly affecting. But the basis for its emotive power is provided by the way in which it harnesses the contradiction between use and exchange. Superficially, it is true, Neil becomes enraged because of the set of incidents he endures sharing a room with Del – the underpants, the cold water and so on. But what is happening is more fundamental than that. Neil is unable to tolerate Del's personality because it constantly threatens to breach the ontological boundary between the ossified, dispassionate, external and 'thing-like' persona the etiquette of exchange demands from us in our dealings with others – and the interiority and private consciousness of the genuine individuality which we all bear and which is exiled to a private realm. Neil's anger towards Del is more than simple irritation; it is the rage of someone who feels fundamentally threatened, for he is so rooted in the prerogatives of exchange, that the pure authenticity which Del represents undermines his way of being.

The difference between the ontological realms which each character represents is also described in terms of class. Again one must avoid too literal a reading here. As we have already observed, Del is a travelling salesman, and so by most economic designations a member of the petit bourgeoisie. This is a necessary device – being a salesman allows the Del character to be mobile, always on the move, and provides the premise of his contact with Neil in the first place. But beyond this the contrast is quite clear. When the two men make it onto a bus full of other wayward travellers, everyone's spirits are high for they are all finally making progress. In the atmosphere of bawdy enthusiasm the travellers all join in for a sing along. Del is enjoying himself so much that he wants to bring his friend into it – he announces to the bus that Neil is going to lead them all in a song. Again, Neil looks mortified, but not wanting to deflate the obvious mood of enjoyment, he gamely tries to press ahead, singing 'Three Coins in a Fountain' – a song which is greeted with utter silence because nobody has ever heard of it. Del, wincing at Neil's discomfort, manages to rescue his travelling companion by launching into a boisterous rendition of 'Meet the Flintstones' – at which point, inevitably, the whole coach begins to sing in enthusiastic unison once more.

Now the scene is making a quite obvious point in a rather amusing way; that is, Del is able to connect with ordinary people whereas Neil, who is from a higher social stratum, finds it difficult and awkward. In the rough and ready context, Neil's song sounds absurdly effete and precious, and the scene is made all the more painful, by the look of abject failure and discomfort on Neil's face once Del is able to instantaneously rouse the others in the rendition of his own song. Although it is a comedic moment, we nevertheless experience a glimpse of Neil as an extremely lonely man. Through this, the scene is speaking to the question of capitalist reification more generally. The people on the coach are clearly less well-off and more working class, like Del himself. The fact that they are all strangers, and yet can bond so easily, represents – in microcosm – the burgeoning possibilities of working-class solidarity. The ability that those at the bottom have to transcend reified relations is one which is a product of the class structure, process and dynamic; one in which the reification of workers as 'living commodities' which bear value can only be overcome by the collective revolutionary activity which the working class is able to assert in order to take control of the means of production, to universalize them, and to abolish the capital – wage-labour relation thereby. It is the capital – wage-labour relation which most profoundly generates the reified appearance; it is the means by which the social relation of capital as it extracts surplus value (profit in its elementary form) from living labour appears primarily as an exchange of 'things' on the market – i.e. of commodities which have an equal value. Its abolition by the revolutionary class,[8] therefore, also implies the dissolution of a given appearance; the reified appearance of an almost infinite network of exchangeable 'things' can now be peeled away to reveal the content which underpins it – i.e. the social relationships between human beings.

In other words, the ability of the working class to overcome reification cannot be viewed from the perspective of an isolated moralism which has a certain Dickensian or Christian flavour and suggests that those on the bottom – in and through suffering and want – are able to evince the type of humbleness and worthiness which smack of a somewhat saintly sensibility. The ability to transcend the given socio-historical conditions of oppression and their reified forms is one which, of necessity, flows from a basis in the historical structure and sweep of the class itself; proletarian solidarity is a necessary adjunct of revolutionary action and a concomitant ability to sweep away the basis for capitalist reification at the level of practical existence. And this has a key bearing on *Planes, Trains and Automobiles* – firstly because the film does, in the scene on the coach (and throughout) show that the reification which Neil is in thrall to can only be truly overcome by those who are connected to the life and development of the masses more broadly – something which is epitomized in the figure of Del. And secondly, that such an identification is in no way saintly or moralistic, but emerges from the organic conditions of the characters' struggle in an alienated world. Del is a beautiful man; sensitive and kind, but he is also profoundly damaged, and can be highly manipulative and at times dishonest. His profound goodness is not unblemished by the world he lives in; he is also devious and wily when circumstances demand.

One of the more gut-wrenchingly funny scenes involves Del driving them the wrong way down a freeway, and when the duo narrowly escape death, and their battered car grinds to a halt, their luggage is spilled out into the road. They go to collect it; exhausted and in shock, they take a few moments to rest, sitting on Del's huge suitcase. Unbeknownst to either, the car behind them has caught fire (the result of a cigarette Del has failed to extinguish). The flames begin to dance, and when they register what has actually happened, Neil's reaction is wholly untypical. Surreally he begins to chuckle, and then to laugh. Uproariously. Del is perturbed by such hysteria but Neil endeavours to explain. Through the snorts of choked laugher he is eventually able to articulate:

> You finally did it to yourself … I mean, good luck turning the car in. They'll be happy as pigs in shit to see you. How could you rent the thing anyway without a credit card? You couldn't. How could you do it? … You can't rent a car with shower curtain rings.[9]

Gradually the laughter dies, and a look of dawning comprehension spreads across Neil's face whereupon Del is compelled to admit – 'Well, uh … somehow your, uh … diner's club card wound up in my wallet, and I, uh, just … '[10] Neil is naturally quite furious and lashes out, but not only is the scene uproariously funny – again that dead-pan look of helpless realization which Steve Martin plays to perfection – but it also speaks to Del's craftiness, and his ability to rationalize his own more questionable decisions, and this gives to us a character whose sometimes skewed moral impulses provide the basis for a searing authenticity.

In summary then, we might note several central themes which underwrite the film. Firstly the two men are faced with the vast anonymity of a modern and impersonal bureaucracy which is constantly undermining and repelling their endeavours. Perhaps more profoundly, it is under the shadow of such a system, where people most often appear to one another in alienated terms; as economic actors who are in the first instance set against one another – each appearing to the other in an objectified form as a service which might be utilized or an obstacle which has to be overcome. Neil's initial experience of Del occurs when the latter happens to snatch the taxi Neil has been waiting for from right under his nose. Their first encounter, therefore, sees them brought into contact with one another as isolated economic actors whose conflicting interests mean they are thrown into competition. Of course, it is later revealed that Del didn't even realize he has filched Neil's cab, but again the literal aspect of the piece here shouldn't be allowed to overwhelm; what is more significant is that the form of capitalist alienation in which people encounter each other as wholly atomized entities subservient to the pull of market competition is from the outset the fundamental premise of the film and forms the basis of the initial contact between the two main characters.

Neil and Del encounter each other as discrete economic actors who are expected to conform to the etiquette of exchange and the impersonal formality of its demands, but the situation that sees them having to share the same hotel room, the same bed even, is a situation which is typically premised on the people in question relating to one another in terms of their authentic personhoods – as lovers, spouses, friends and so on. Or to say the same, relating to one another as use values as opposed to exchange values. The scene is so funny because the cold, hard, rigid borders of behaviour which are in effect are forcibly undermined by the context and situation the two men are embroiled in; thus, despite themselves, they begin to adopt forms of behaviour which accord to use and authentic personhood. So, when they wake up in the morning, for example, they are both wearing dreamy smiles on their faces, Del is cuddling Neil and in his semi-conscious state kisses his ear. Through the fug of his slumber, Neil begins to ascertain that something is not right.

Del.
Hmm? Yeah.
Why did you kiss my ear?
Why are you holding my hand?
Where's your other hand?
Between two pillows.
Those aren't pillows!

The scream which ensues caps off perhaps one of the briefest and devastatingly funny exchanges in the history of film. By this point it should be clear that the whole film is premised on the relationship of these two men – and the way in which it is constantly being forced to transcend the clinical cold parameters of exchange and enter into the organic realm of personhood and friendship. More generally, Del is trying to push for the second set of relations – he is constantly treating Neil warmly and affectionately in the manner of a friend. Neil – as a result of an inhibited character, and as a representative of business (a marketing executive) – is constantly trying to resist this form of behaviour; his tragedy is that he has internalized the world of exchange and capital accumulation; his loneliness and his alienation are a condition which is so normal to him it is as though he truly feels at home within it. The true journey which the film outlines is not simply Neil's struggle to get home – it is his struggle to pass beyond the boundaries of exchange value, and to be able to relate to someone in his broader world in terms of their genuine personhood.

And what is so profound about the film is the way in which this transition takes place. Right up to the very conclusion, Neil still continues to regard Del, on a conscious level, as a burden. In one of the final scenes the two men are ready to go their separate ways. As the men say goodbye to one another, before Neil is due to board the train which will take him the final leg of his journey, they embrace tentatively. Del apologizes for any trouble he has caused Neil but Neil waves his concerns away, after all – 'You got me home, and, uh … a little late. A couple days. But, uh … I'm a little wiser, too.'[11] Neil gets onto the train and watches Del's waving figure grow smaller. The train rounds a bend. At this point Neil heaves a sigh of relief. He is finally free of Del and all his complications. He pictures his wife and his children at home, and imagines seeing them again, and he shrills with pleasure and love at the prospect. And then he thinks about the horrendous journey he has just endured. And Del. He thinks about the absurd situations the two men have found themselves in – the image of them curled up in bed together comes to Neil's mind, and he finds himself chuckling involuntarily. Then a frown passes across his face. He remembers his cruelty to Del, and the character assassination he delivered to the other man that first night in the hotel. After which he remembers a conversation when they were drunk on tequila, and they talked about their respective wives.

At this moment Neil's expression becomes puzzled. Del has talked about his wife 'Marie' regularly, but Neil has recalled a snippet of conversation where Del said, without really thinking – 'I haven't been home for years'.[12] Slowly a realization dawns. At this point we see Neil step off the train, only he has returned to the platform where we last saw Del. He looks for Del, before dashing into the station waiting room. At once he sees Del slumped up against the wall, his luggage gathered around him. Neil asks him in the type of voice which is frightened to receive an answer why he, Del, hasn't gone home. Del looks at him with a slight flinch in his aspect – 'I, uh ... I don't have a home. Marie's been dead for eight years.'[13] The scene is incredibly moving. John Candy plays pitch perfect the aspect of kindness and wounded vulnerability which makes Del such a soulful character. But Neil's intervention is decisively important here. When the character is sat on the train, and Del is waving him goodbye – even at that moment Neil continues to regard Del as an irritation and breathes a sigh of relief at being free of him. But what has also happened by this point is that Del and Neil have formed a genuine friendship which is based on the content and quality of their immanent personalities – no longer orchestrated according to the formal prerogatives of exchange. When Neil starts to think about Del, he can no longer see him in his reified aspect – he is compelled to see him in terms of his authentic personhood, and because of this, he experiences a revelatory moment. He realizes that the other man is in trouble and has in some way been set adrift. And because he no longer sees Del the person as merely one more object in a reified world, because he experiences Del as a living personality – as a friend – he is compelled to go back; *he has to go back*, because he fears for him, and perhaps in that moment Neil already senses the truth; that Marie, Del's beloved wife, has been dead for years.

The last scene sees Neil and Del lugging Del's suitcase down the road, and then Neil introducing Del to his family. The movie closes with the image of Del smiling warmly. Criticisms of the 'trite' and 'saccharine' nature of the ending have been levelled against the film, but what these miss is that it is not simply the case that Neil has decided to act in a kind and charitable way to his fellow man, and thus save Del in his time of need. On a more profound level it is not Del who has been rescued by Neil but Neil who has been redeemed by Del. When we first meet Neil, the director and writer John Hughes is at pains to depict just how unpleasant his protagonist actually is. Neil is snide, aloof and dismissive towards those he comes into contact with, but this also means that he is a fundamentally lonely individual, and part of the brilliance of Steve Martin's performance is that it is able to show how much Neil is missing out on. In and through his relationship with Del, Neil is forced to pass beyond the set of reified relations which had hitherto constituted the landscape of his broader world, and for the first time he is able to encounter another person in terms of their raw humanity and authentic personhood; in the same instant, he is rendered more human himself.

So the conclusion, indeed the whole culmination of the film, is not 'moralistic' or 'trite' in as much as it does not proceed from any abstract sense of morality – rather the central dilemma – Neil's inability to recognize the true form of the human personality from within the furore of the social world – is one which is necessarily posited by the forms and structures of capitalist social-historical existence itself. Del's appearance in Neil's life – at first a bluff annoyance – in actual fact marks the possibility of transcendence; the ability to see beyond the reified veil. For this reason, the conclusion isn't 'moralistic' in the traditional sense; it does not provide the resolution of an isolated 'moral' conflict, but rather a conflict which has grown out of the forms and structures of the world in which the protagonists are enmeshed. The ending appears superficially trite – for it seems like Neil has simply chosen to accord to a nicer, kinder nature and do something charitable for his fellow man, but in actual fact it is Neil who has been rescued by Del, from the loneliness and the anomie that an existence which can only conceptualize others in terms of their reified aspect automatically presupposes.

Not to say, however, that the writer/director was in anyway conscious of these more fundamental underpinnings. Hughes wanted to write a film in which the travel plans of an uptight guy were repeatedly bamboozled by the relentless and bumbling influence of an overbearing slob; he wanted to do this via a series of set pieces and comic gags which were designed to make his audience laugh their asses off. But at some point along the line the film becomes so much more than this. For we, the audience, find ourselves crying too, as we live with these characters and inhabit their contradictions, and the struggle they have to go through in order to truly find one another. It is a struggle which, in an individualized and fantastical manner, gives expression to the way in which the logic of exchange and capital accumulation is able to warp and reify the human personality according to its own imperatives. But the film also gives life to the way in which alienation can be overcome;

the way the distorting prerogatives of exchange can be transcended by the power of the inward content, the authentic personality, rich in possibility and need. At the heart of the film is manifested this truly radical, revolutionary power, for the friendship which develops between the two men, exhibits the true content of the social power that – in and through its activity – is able to divest the world of its reified form – to tear away the veil at last.

Chapter 3

Against post-Marxism: How post-Marxism annuls class-based historicism and the possibility of revolutionary praxis

This chapter provides a brief examination of the theory of Althusser, Mouffe, Laclau and Žižek. Specifically the writer endeavours to provide an account of the methodological categories which underpin the thought of these thinkers at the most fundamental level; an X-ray like snapshot which reveals the bare bones of the theoretical apparatus each thinker deploys.

When stripped of all its external paraphernalia and specific idiosyncrasies, the thought of each of the thinkers considered here attains a fundamental identity; that is, one discovers at the methodological level, a reconfiguring of Marxism according to a post-Kantian paradigm. I will demonstrate how a reversion to a pre-Hegelian form of methodology results inevitably in the annihilation of the living core of Marxism – its class-driven historicism; consequently, I consider some of the grievous political implications which flow from this.

Althusser, Mouffe and Laclau were all heavily influenced by the great Italian revolutionary Antonio Gramsci. The manner in which they misrepresent his thought is integral to understanding the development of their own, so this chapter will also consider Gramsci in brief – specifically his approach to the base-superstructure problem which has bedevilled Marxist scholarship, on and off, since its inception.

✳✳✳

Louis Althusser always considered himself to be a Marxist. However, he thought that one of the ways in which Marxism had been hampered was the manner in which its founders had utilized a base-superstructure model in a one-sided and narrowly deterministic fashion. The criticism is not without any type of foundation, I think. It is probably fair to say that Marx and Engels were occasionally guilty of adducing the relationship between base and superstructure in a somewhat off the cuff and mechanical manner at this or that point.

Peter D. Thomas, among others, has argued that the problem with the formulation, as Marx has elaborated it, is that the metaphor is a 'spatial' one; that its 'simplistic two-dimensional sense'[1] allows for an implicit 'mutual exclusion' between the two terms which is easily conscripted to the service of a more mechanical reading, the type purveyed by the theorists of the Second International, and later the representatives of the Stalinist bureaucracy.

For Thomas, part of Gramsci's importance lies in the fact that he went someway to redress this. Gramsci endeavoured to flesh out the Marxist relationship between base and superstructure by providing a more fluid and organic interpretation. He began with Marx's famous axiom that:

> The sum total of [the] relations of production constitutes the economic structure of society, the real foundation, on which rises a legal and political superstructure.[2]

Thomas argues that Gramsci then combined the original metaphor laid out in the *Economic Manuscripts* by relating it to 'Marx's later characterisation of the "ideological forms" that make up the superstructure, which he [Gramsci] took as licence to speak of "superstructures," in the plural'.[3] These 'superstructures' or 'ideologies' were then conceived 'less in spatial terms than as forms of practice, or forms in which men know their conflicts based in the economic structure of society and fight them out'.[4]

Gramsci's approach helps emphasize and bring out what was already implicit in Marx's original work. The Gramscian articulation of 'ideologies' permits – as Thomas points out – a more fluid exposition of the base-superstructure metaphor 'by taking it literally: if the superstructures arise upon the economic structure, the former is then in fact coextensive with the latter, in a three dimensional perspective, overlaying it'.[5] This, in turn, allows for a model in which:

> The superstructures are agonistic forms that compete to become the essential form of appearance of a content that is itself contradictory ... they [superstructures] seek to resolve the contradictions in the economic structure of society of which they are the (more or less adequate) comprehension, either by pacifying and effacing them, or by emphasising their unstable nature and driving them to a moment of crisis.[6]

Building upon this perspective Gramsci introduces the concepts of hegemony and the collective will. As is well known, he adopted the former from his reading of Lenin. For Gramsci, hegemony involves the notion that in and through the battle of conflicting super structural forms (which are many and various) one group or social agency will manifest imposing hegemony on society thereby – both through the application of force via public and private means, and, perhaps more importantly, through the appropriation of culture; that is, the particularity of its world-view becomes generalized in and through its intellectual activity and its dominance of the cultural network. Its perspective is thus naturalized and its ethical life experienced as the gold standard. As a result its modes and forms of social organization appear immutable and eternal. The maintenance of hegemony by simple physical means is most often exacted through the 'superstructure' of the state, while its cultural power is articulated in and through the organs of civil society, a relation which provides us with the Gramscian distinction between 'domination' and 'intellectual and moral leadership'.

But, in tracing the process by which hegemony is achieved, Gramsci is faced with the mechanical paradigm once more. By introducing competing 'superstructures' or 'ideologies' through which the contradictions at the level of social existence are cultivated, Gramsci has succeeded – to put it as a good Hegelian might – in 'sublating' the vulgar and mechanical opposition between base and superstructure, but the buck does not stop there, for when we examine any of the competing superstructures these too are in danger of being isolated and reduced to a multiplicity of individual units – each one to be understood as the causal reflex of a prior event. The original base-superstructure metaphor is at risk of being replaced with an equally mechanical bases-superstructures relation.

So at the micro-level too, one is required to 'sublate' mechanicalism, and this is one of the advantages which the concept of the collective will provides. The collective will allows for the 'superstructures' or 'ideologies' to crystallize in and through their mutual reciprocity; the class which becomes hegemonic does so because its ideology is filtered through the nexus of superstructure more broadly, pulling other superstructural strands from different social agencies into the process of its own development and ultimate realization. From Gramsci one receives an infinitely richer and more fluid account; ideologies are not simply multifarious but fully formed reflections of objective economic categories but rather they are understood as the mutually determined processes of their own becoming.

Of course, this is his position in its most abstract, thread-bare outline – the logical categories bereft of any historical or specific class content. But it is precisely from such abstraction that structuralist philosopher Louis Althusser proceeds.

Like Gramsci, Althusser draws upon the 1859 preface, where Marx describes ideology as the terrain in which people become conscious of socio-historical contradictions and fight them out. Althusser claims to draw upon the way in which Gramsci attempted to go beyond a mechanical base-superstructure formulation. Althusser describes Ideology[7] as a system of representations by which people 'live' their relationship to the world. 'Ideology', he argues, 'is a system (with its own logic and rigour) of representations (images, myths, ideas or concepts, depending on the case) endowed with a historical existence and role within a given society'.[8]

Now the 'system' Althusser describes – with its 'representations (images, myths, ideas or concepts)' might be broadly encompassed by the notion of 'social consciousness' – and if we then add the caveat – 'endowed with a historical existence and role within a given society', we understand that 'social consciousness' has its role determined ('endowed') by a 'given society' at a particular point of historical development – 'historical existence'. Far from freeing us from a model in which consciousness is determined reflexively by social existence, Althusser has returned us to it.

So how can Althusser purport to transcend the mechanicalism of base-superstructure? Part of the answer lies in what he does next. Chantal Mouffe argues that for both Althusser and Gramsci, transcending the base-superstructure metaphor meant that 'subjects are not originally given but are always produced by ideology … subjectivity is always the product of social practise'.[9]

Mouffe's account is important because it elucidates the critical theoretical move Althusser was to perform in order to 'transcend' base-superstructure. Althusser understood subjects to be 'produced by Ideology', she emphasizes. But, if Ideology 'is … a system of representations (images, myths, ideas or concepts)', and if one acknowledges that 'social consciousness' provides a conceptual umbrella under which 'images, myths, ideas and concepts' shelter – if we then go further, and add the Althusserean clause that Ideology is what creates subjects, we find, camouflaged in Althusser's philosophy the rather more simple concession – 'consciousness (Ideology) determines subjects'. Althusser has responded to the crude 'Marxist' formulation of consciousness presenting as the simple reflection of social being, not by sublating it as Gramsci does, but rather by inverting it. Althusser has simply made 'consciousness' the absolutely determinate term in the pairing albeit that its reality as 'consciousness' is disguised, wrapped as it is in the Althusserean veil of 'Ideology'.

So now we have a situation where social consciousness masquerading as Althusserean 'Ideology' is the means by which social existence is articulated in terms of 'subjects'. What we can see very clearly here is that the Althusserean claim that – 'Ideology produces subjects' – when stripped of the verbal paraphernalia of the tortured Structuralist idiom – is nothing more than a vulgar idealism in which consciousness one-sidedly determines being.

Althusser, of course, would, and did deny he was making any such claim. How is such a denial even feasible? We must look towards his next theory-driven sleight of hand in order to ascertain.

What Althusser now proceeds to do is to convert what he has already (but implicitly) disclosed as consciousness more broadly – 'Ideology' – into something else again. He now describes 'Ideology' in terms of 'structures'. These 'structures', he argues, 'act functionally on men via a process that escapes them'.[10] The move from 'Ideology' to 'structure' is illegitimate in as much as it is merely asserted and, in as much as it has survived critical scrutiny at all, has done so because of the overall incomprehensibility of the Althusserean syntax which simultaneously provides a highly 'technical' and 'scientific' gloss.

But the conversion of 'Ideology' to 'structure' is at the same time an entirely necessary one. We had arrived at the premise – 'Ideology produces subjects' – which actually represents an inversion of the base-superstructure model whereby social consciousness appears under the banner of 'Ideology', and 'Ideology' is then said to create 'subjects'. Now Althusser, having realized an abstract idealism, simply reverses the poles; he proceeds to undergird his concept of Ideology (which harbours consciousness in its midst) – with what appears to be a series of higher, external objectivities – i.e. structures. Structures impose themselves *in and through Ideology* producing the subject but are themselves fundamentally distinct from consciousness – 'In truth, ideology has very little to do with "consciousness", even supposing this term to have an unambiguous meaning. It is profoundly unconscious.'[11]

Structures, therefore, are simultaneously the forms of Ideological consciousness while involving a process which somehow stands outside consciousness and whose external manifestation is experienced unconsciously by the subject in and through her creation as 'subject'. Structures are artificial constructs, fleshed out in a complex and technical idiom – but we are now in a position to see, having traced the process by which Althusser develops his notion of them – exactly what purpose in his philosophy 'structures' serve.

To recapitulate, the original problem was one of the mechanical dichotomy between social existence as the base and social consciousness as the (loosely considered) superstructure. Althusser's structures are neither base nor superstructure, nor social consciousness nor social existence, and at the same time they provide an unholy mix of all. On the one hand, Althusser argues that Structures (of Ideology) 'are perceived-accepted-suffered cultural objects'[12] and are somehow external to consciousness – they give to subjects their subjectivity, while at the same time he also argues they are identical with consciousness, identical with the 'images, myths, ideas or concepts' which characterize consciousness's inner world. In other words the structures of Ideology allow the opposition between base and superstructure, social existence and social consciousness, to be dissolved because both moments are rendered abstractly identical and annulled therein.

This, then, is Althusser's solution to the base-superstructure dichotomy; he first makes consciousness the determinate term as Ideology, and then renders Ideology in terms of the structural forms of a broader existence, thereby fusing 'base' and 'superstructure', and it seems as though he has done something subtle and profound, yet in reality the solution is utterly fantastical and artificial. Althusser simply provides the (unstated) conjecture that base and superstructure, consciousness and existence are abstractly the same. The only complexity lies in the difficulty required to unravel his vulgar methodology through the vortex of claim and counter-claim, all of which are underpinned by an esoteric vernacular which teeters on the incomprehensible.

Nevertheless Mouffe was right when she saw a similarity in the approach of Althusser and Gramsci when it comes to the vexed issue of base-superstructure – but she was right for all the wrong reasons. The similarity lies in the fact the Gramscian approach to the dichotomy also fuses social being with consciousness; but with Gramsci base and superstructure represent not so much a false opposition, but rather a necessary one, albeit an abstract one, which is then 'sublated' in a Hegelian-style progression by which a more concrete unity is yielded.

Social agency, particularly class agency, isn't something fully formed requiring an approximation or reflection in consciousness; rather agency is actualized in and through the process of its comprehension. With Gramsci a class achieves hegemony, and becomes what it is *therein*; it is not the case that it exists fully constituted beforehand – except, of course, in the immediate and empirical sense – as a group of individuals stood in a certain social relation to the means of production.

So while Gramsci allows social existence and social consciousness to supplement one another dialectically and thereby crystallize in a concrete unity, what Althusser does is to simply assert their unity artificially, vanquishing them with the power of an undifferentiated abstraction. As a result 'Ideology' becomes an implacable force which looms over us with the indifference of an impenetrable and alien power.

But because the base-superstructure opposition has not been mediated historically, but rather annulled artificially, it returns with a vengeance. We cannot avoid the question – if Ideology produces subjects by imposing its structures, what is it which determines the forms, shapes and pattern of those structures? Here Althusser has managed to entangle himself in a truly Hegelian contradiction, a 'spurious infinite' in which the initial abstraction – 'Ideology' – is employed to resolve the base-superstructure contradiction, but in resolving it, it simultaneously reproduces it anew. For – we are forced to ask – wherein lies the basis or base for Ideology and its structures? It cannot be with social existence, because we already understand that Ideology itself produces subjects. It is a truly Hegelian contradiction though one which Althusser would fail to see the irony of – for, though he wrote not a little on Hegel, at the same time he understood not a lot.

The 'spurious infinite' which the Althusserean methodology yields has two central consequences for the overall theory, both of which are vital. Firstly, if one cannot identify some agency or element which lies behind Ideology and helps determine and shape its structures, then Ideology becomes de-historicized, converted into a purely ontological proposition, for there is at work within it no fundamental principle of change; it creates subjects, to be sure, but subjects do not create it; nor does anything else – precisely because its *raison d'être* consists in the nullification of the dialectic between being and consciousness.

Consequently it becomes an immutable substance impervious to alteration – a lifeless, transhistorical thing. And so while Althusser begins the discussion by arguing that Ideology is a system 'endowed with a historical existence and role within a given society', one can see quite clearly how the logic of his theoretical development now driven to the point of irreconcilable contradiction inexorably yields one of his more notorious and noxious propositions – 'Ideology has no history', we are told.

The second consequence is related to this first. Althusser claimed to be a Marxist, albeit one of an unusual shade. Ostensibly, therefore, he retained a certain ideological commitment to the proposition that thinkers had previously only interpreted the world but the point was to change it. He had a commitment to a level of historicity. But such a commitment was at odds with the underlying methodological implications of his system. How can one filter political and revolutionary activity into the lifeless, dehistoricized schema of Althusserean structuralism? How is political activity (and change) possible, when the structures of Ideology which inform the very possibility of thought are themselves the product of an ahistorical and transcendental field which entangles and determines us? We do not know what determines it; we cannot look at the structures of Ideology from the outside, as it were, for the very mechanisms by which we seek an objective perspective are nothing other than the same structures and forms through which Ideology constitutes us.

Now we can see what the second consequence fully entails. Having annulled, at the methodological level, the historicity which provides the living core of Hegel and Marx, the Althusserean philosophy quite naturally regresses to a Kantian model – only a Kantian model of a particularly crude and convoluted type. What subjects are before they are constituted by Ideology becomes a question of the noumenal. We cannot hope to penetrate Ideology as an object in itself before we are constituted by it; we unable to determine, therefore, the more profound reality on which our phenomenal existence as subjects is premised. Ideology forms the intermediary, the permanent barrier between ourselves and a prior condition which nevertheless generates us from the mysterious substrates of its noumenal dark matter.

In order to purvey the illusion that the Althusserean philosophy is Marxism rather than anti-Marxism (perhaps even to himself), Althusser tried to maintain the component of revolutionary praxis within the boundaries of the very schema which was designed to strangle it. Because Ideology has no history, because, according to Althusserean methodology, we human beings have no access to the genuine precondition of our existence as subjects, Althusser was forced to invoke yet another artificial clause in order to guarantee the possibility of political practice. It might be impossible to genuinely apprehend the 'real' conditions of being in and through lived 'Ideology' but nevertheless we can 'imagine' them. The astonishing concept of the 'imaginary relation' – startling in terms of both its mendacity and its naivety – is what Althusser now superimposes on his schema in order to escape Kantian dualism. He defines the imaginary relation as follows:

What is represented in ideology is therefore not the system of the real relations which govern the existence of individuals, but the imaginary relation of those individuals to the real relations which they live[13]

'The imaginary relation' allows us to have some mode by which to interpret, and therefore change, Ideology – even though the logic of Althussereanism has already precluded any such possibility – hence the evocation of the 'imaginary' over and against the Althusserean 'Real'. Alas, like every other theoretical manoeuvre Althusser has thus far performed, the current one entangles him in yet another irreconcilable contradiction and one from which escape is possible only by yet another artificial assertion. How – we are compelled to enquire – might one distinguish between differences in the imagined relations? How can one judge Marxism, for instance, to contain a level of truth, to have an objective value superior to that of liberalism, or even fascist thought for that matter? According to the underlying logic of Althussereanism, that can be no way of extrapolating reality from unreality, truth from the imaginary relation. And so Althusser introduces another artificial distinction; what liberates some forms of knowledge from the Kantian-like web of Ideology in which the subject is enmeshed is the fact that some forms of knowledge are 'scientific' (Althusser includes Marxism in this category). Of his concept of 'scientificity', Althusser provides the following definition in *Reading Capital*:

The validity of a scientific proposition as a knowledge was ensured in a determinate scientific practise by the action of particular forms which ensure the presence of scientificity in the production of knowledge, in other words, by specific forms that confer on knowledge its character as a (true) knowledge.[14]

The polish philosopher Leszek Kolakowski managed to extract what little meaning there is to be found in this mangled sentence. 'In other words', Kolakowski argued, Althusser has stipulated that 'science is science when it has the form of scientificity. This grotesque statement contains everything we can find in Althusser about how to distinguish scientific work from other kinds of work.'[15]

Who has access to scientificity? Althusser's answer seems to be top flight intellectuals like himself. But this isn't merely the result of some superficial arrogance. Having cultivated a methodological system which ultimately results in the abnegation of living history; having discovered that subjects are transfigured by Ideology and locked into an ahistorical guise therein, it was never possible that Althusser would be able to place any real emphasis on genuine collective, socio-historical agency. The masses are denuded of the possibility of entering the historic arena as protagonists for the simple fact that there is no such thing as history but only a supra-historical field of Ideology which 'interpellates' (a genuinely imaginary word) them as subjects.

The question of some type of revolutionary supersession therefore becomes, of necessity, an ahistorical one; the attainment of 'scientificity' an ahistorical possibility which is inevitably projected onto a series of abstract qualities in the head of the gifted intellectual; a figure who must proceed – *a la* Althusser – to relieve the masses of their Ideological delusions. It is clear why such a 'philosophy' has developed such a following within Marxist academia and why it remains so attractive today for academics who flirt with a superficial sense of radicalism but actually find terms like 'class' or 'trade-union' to contain a certain vulgar, grossly 'economist' flavour.

And so, Althusser's philosophy, despite its glaring inconsistencies and obscurantist mode of presentation, resonated not only with the Stalinists who found the notion of an 'Ideological' power shaping the political life of subjects with an overarching inevitability compelling for all the obvious reasons, but also with a rash of academics who would have naturally opposed the Stalinist system precisely because of the straight jacketing effects its totalitarianism imposed on intellectual life within the university *milieu*. Such academics were in favour of the Althusserean project for an altogether different reason.

Especially in periods of declining political militancy and working-class stagnation, when any call for collective struggle resonated for many as either utopian or vulgarly demagogic, the Althusserean account provided the impetus for a turn away from any resolution of political problems in and through the modes and forms of social life more broadly, and instead rearticulated them as a series of convoluted transcendental constructs over which the intellectual alone has a privileged dominion. The collapse of Stalinism in many ways dealt Althussereanism a bitter blow and yet it was not sufficient to kill it off for Althusserean structuralism did manage to sustain – resuscitated as it was in the pages of many an academic journal unable to come to grips with the spectacle of an Emperor bereft of garments.

***

Althusser's most visible and influential adherents today are Chantal Mouffe and the late Ernesto Laclau. Their general position, loosely stated, is that Gramsci was correct in his attempt (as understood by them) to move Marxism away from a mechanical base-superstructure model – though his efforts were embryonic and insufficient, at which point Althusser takes up the mantle improving on Gramsci, but even Althusser doesn't sufficiently escape the dread grip of 'economism'.

In her essay *Hegemony and Ideology in Gramsci*, Mouffe outlines some fundamental points of the Mouffe/Laclau prospectus. What is important about this essay is not only its clarity and lucidity, especially by the standards of its author, but also how it reveals the underlying consequences of the Mouffe/Laclau project – i.e. a dehistoricization of Marx as thoroughgoing and as comprehensive as anything Althusser was able to manage, while utilizing a similar array of methodological categories and techniques. Like Althusser, Mouffe attempts to move beyond a 'reductionist model' in which superstructure is simply reduced to the automatic reflex of base. In particular, she appeals to Gramsci to fortify her position by emphasizing his model of hegemony as crystallized in and through a collective will. She quotes Gramsci describing the manner in which a class becomes hegemonic:

> The dominant group is coordinated concretely with the general interests of the subordinate groups, and the life of the state is conceived of as a continuous process of formation and superseding of unstable equilibria (on the judicial plane) between the interests of the fundamental group and those of the subordinate groups – equilibria in which the interests of the dominant group prevail, but only up to a certain point, i.e. stopping short of narrowly corporate economic interest.[16]

For Mouffe, Gramsci's emphasis on 'narrowly corporate economic interest' is what is important here. She argues that a class can only achieve hegemony when it 'renounces a strictly corporatist conception, since in order to exercise leadership it must genuinely concern itself with the interests of those social groups over which it wishes to exercise hegemony'.[17] But this is then supplanted with an interpretation of the collective will which has less in common with Gramsci but more to do with Althusser. Mouffe writes:

> According to him [Gramsci] hegemony involves the creation of a higher synthesis, so that all its elements fuse in a 'collective will' which becomes the new protagonist of political action which will function as the protagonist of political action during hegemony's entire duration[18]

We experience here a transmutation of the Gramscian position. In Gramsci the collective will ultimately allows the 'interests of the dominant group to prevail, but only up to a certain point, i.e. stopping short of narrowly corporate economic interest'. It is part and parcel of the means by which the class becomes; that is to say through its activity it traverses three moments – those of the primitive economic, the political economic and finally the hegemonic, in and through its relationship to the ruling class and other subordinate classes.

But what Mouffe has done is to create 'a new protagonist of collective action' – a collective will which isn't merely the means to an end – i.e. class hegemony, but rather an end in itself; by detaching the collective will from its class basis, Mouffe moves closer towards the creation of a transcendental subject decoupled from any historical premise. The Gramscian collective will is, for Mouffe, a 'protagonist' that 'consists in the production of subjects'[19] though she acknowledges Gramsci himself 'did not quite manage to formulate this theoretically'[20] – however, she concedes rather graciously – he was at least able to 'intuit' it.

We can see quite clearly that the 'anti-reductionist' position Mouffe advocates avoids base-superstructure mechanicalism by curtailing the role of class and replacing it with a transcendental notion of collective will; this, she claims, was already implicit in Gramsci, though he never managed to make it clear because he expressed it in 'an ambiguous form which is now outdated'.[21] The method of Gramsci, according to

Mouffe, is not the method of classical Marxist which has outdated class struggle as its theoretical and practical lynchpin. For Mouffe's Gramsci, 'political subjects are not social classes but collective wills'.[22]

It is true that Mouffe does permit some tenuous connection to survive between the concept of the collective will and a determinate class – 'an ensemble of social groups fused around a fundamental class'[23] but this is little more than lip service, in as much as the methodology itself, through a series of logical progressions, moves further and further away from anything which resembles genuine class agency. For Mouffe argues that classes have the ability to become hegemonic precisely by forgoing the interests which flow from their structural positions; class hegemony arises when a class articulates other class interests to itself, rather than expressing the fundamental economic interests which mediate it through a particular and subordinate role in a set of production relations; relations which have themselves grown out of a specific socio-historic context – 'It is, therefore, by their articulation to a hegemonic principle that the ideological elements acquire their class character which is not intrinsic to them.'[24]

Above all, the necessity between the proletariat as a class and political action is precluded because there is nothing in the historical genesis of the proletariat and the objective position it occupies in capitalist society which would make of it, in Marxian terminology, 'a universal class', or to take the Lukácsian riff on the same theme – 'the identical subject-object of history'. It is true that, here and there, Mouffe still talks about the proletariat as the 'leading class' but again, just as with Althusser, the point here is not about what the theorist says they are doing, or even what he or she thinks they are doing; rather we must concern ourselves with the logical and necessary implications and consequences of the theory itself. In making the collective will a virtually independent protagonist of political action, class assumes an essentially passive and redundant role; it becomes instrumentalized, a mere technical device through which an external, surpra-historical entity manages to constitute its subjects – 'these elements do not in themselves express class interests, but their class character is conferred upon them by the discourse to which they are articulated and by the type of subject thus created'.[25]

In Althusser the transhistorical subject was provided by Ideology – an ontological proposition about which it is possible to say very little with any degree of consistency. Ideology is eternal; it produces subjects, and creates an imaginary relation which, for some unknown reason, and at some unknown point, simply bifurcates yielding the difference between itself and 'scientificity'. At the level of philosophical methodology these tenuous claims are underpinned by the assumption that social consciousness and social being are abstractly the same – fused in a static, non-dialectical identity – 'his ideas are his material actions inserted into material practices governed by material rituals which are themselves defined by the material ideological apparatus from which derive the ideas of that subject'.[26]

The erosion of the dialectic between being and consciousness at the philosophical level naturally finds its counterpart in the abolition of class struggle on the historical plane. The political implications of this are inevitable – 'the object of ideological struggle is not to reject the system and all its elements but to rearticulate it'.[27] Mouffe and Laclau, having converted Gramsci's collective will into a transcendental subject within which the definitive historical forms of different social classes are abrogated, have, in effect, hitched the great Italian revolutionary to the Althusserean wagon – with the end result that a revolutionary politique is eschewed in favour of a process of a 're-articulation of existing ideological elements'.[28]

Mouffe and Laclau 'rearticulate' their notion of the Gramscian collective will through the prism of Althusserean Ideology – the end result of which are 'discourses'. Discourses are similar to the 'structures' of Althusserean Ideology only instead of Ideology, discourses operate in and through the 'field of discursivity'. It becomes clear that we are dealing with a Kantian model once more; like Ideology, the conditions for the 'field of discursivity' cannot be apprehended and attain a noumenal-like invisibility. Mouffe and Laclau write:

> The discursive [or, the field of discursivity – as distinct from discourse] is not … an object among other objects (although, of course, concrete discourses are) but rather a theoretical horizon. Certain questions concerning the notion of discourse are, therefore, meaningless because they can be made only about objects within a horizon, not about the horizon itself … If the discursive is coterminous with the being of objects – the horizon, therefore, of the constitution of the being of every object – the question about the conditions of

possibility of the being of discourse is meaningless. It is equivalent to asking a materialist for the conditions of possibility of matter, or a theist for the conditions of possibility of God.[29]

Like Ideology, the horizon itself, the field of discursivity 'is not an object among other objects' but rather becomes the pre-condition for 'concrete objects'; the thing in itself which cannot be penetrated by thought in as much as thought's natural range operates 'within a horizon' while unable to apprehend the conditions of the horizon itself. In reconfiguring Marx and Gramsci according to a post-Kantian paradigm, Mouffe and Laclau display a profound ignorance of the history of philosophy, and a fatal lack of awareness with regards to Marxism specifically.

For Marxism was born out of the tradition of classical German Idealism. The *raison d'être* of this fabulous, fecund period of thought lay in the critique of Kantian dualism; the attempt to overcome the noumenal-phenomenal divide – an attempt which would produce the absolute ego of Fichte and Schelling's objective absolute principle (owing a great debt to Spinoza) as Nature or *Naturphilosophie*. Their projects were vast unifying philosophical edifices which sought to raise the totality in a conscious and systematic unfolding.

Part of Hegel's great contribution was to show that the Kantian antinomies were not the inevitable aberrations that result from the misapplication of rational thought to the noumenal realm; rather they were contradictions which inhere in the fabric of reality itself, and were therefore susceptible to the processes of historical mediation. The ultimate reality ceased to be indecipherable and was now subject to the genuine political-historical interventions of the majority. Hegel did not simply reject Kantianism, he historicized it by ultimately framing the dialectic which had opened up in Kant between subject and object, and which was further mediated by the opposition of Fichte and Schelling[30] – in terms of a living logical development which was itself eventually concretized in the form of a historical ontology of labour – one which permitted a unity of subject and object. For, in labouring on the object, the world, we disclose its fundamental rationality, developing and realizing our own nature thereby.

But in Hegel the dualism which had fissured across the Kantian project was not fully overcome, in as much as it was reproduced once more in the separation between the highest stage of consciousness

(Philosophy) and the highest embodiment of social existence as the concretely universalized State. There was no necessary reason why the philosopher should also be a statesman – Hegel simply wished for this to be the case, and argued that it should be the case.[31] Ironically enough this was a very example of the type of logic which Hegel had so effectively criticized elsewhere in as much as it allowed the 'is' to be permanently divorced from the 'ought'.

The Kantian dualism which provided the dilemma which classical German Idealism had responded to would eventually be resolved by the historical materialist Marx. Lukács, in his masterful essay – *Reification and the Class Consciousness of the Proletariat* – locates Marx's conception of the proletariat as the means by which the ongoing problem of dualism bequeathed by Kant (at least in its modern form) is reconciled. Lukács argues that the proletariat, by virtue of its structural-historical position within capitalism, is able to realize a genuinely concrete identity of subject-object because it holds the possibility of overcoming dualism not only in theory but also at the level of practical existence. For the proletariat consciousness of the object, of the social world, of the capitalist system, is at the same time a question of self-consciousness; the proletarian is a bearer of the commodity form, a living commodity so to speak; for her – knowledge of the object is simultaneously a knowledge of self.

Though Marxism here follows a dialectical logic of the Hegelian type, it expounded upon the Hegelian solution which was unsatisfactory and had polarized the subject and object once more in the division between the consciousness of the philosopher (stage of philosophy) and the existence of the state conceived as concrete universal. Subject and object remained forever held apart. For the proletariat such a polarization is overcome; its consciousness and its practical existence were inexorably bound in a genuine unity realized in and through its historical activity.

For Marxism, therefore, Kantian dualism is resolved in a concrete historical unity at the level of social existence. For Marx, the culmination of the history of philosophy and the development of the proletariat as a social power are not to be understood as discrete and exclusive events. This is what the unity of theory and practice really signifies; it must be comprehended according to both the German philosophical tradition and the historical creation of a modern working class which provides its living exegesis. In this way alone, the unity of theory and practice can be understood as something more than a vulgar empiricism, a crude experimentalism which appears easily falsifiable in practice – 'ah well the Russian revolution was defeated which proves the failure of the so called philosophy of praxis'. The other prevalent, but equally flawed view, is to associate, as Lucien Goldman did, Marx's attitude to the modern proletariat with a wager along the lines of the Pascalian type – a wager which, if rewarded, would yield a better world. Such a position undermines the true power of Marxism for it reduces it to little more than an act of faith.

It is only in light of all this that the truly destructive consequences of Mouffe and Laclau's Kantian 'post-Marxism' can be fully appreciated. By following Althusser, by fusing existence and consciousness in an abstract identity in and through the forms of 'discourse', Mouffe and Laclau create a noumenal, supra-historical object – 'the field of discursivity' – and in so doing they reassert the very dualism which Marxism evolved as a response to. The brilliant solution which Marx envisaged – and which was simultaneously posed at the level of social existence with the historical development of the modern proletariat – is thus negated. It is not the case, therefore, that Mouffe and Laclau simply offer us a Kantian interpretation of Marxism; rather the negation of Marxism is built into the very theoretical apparatus which they deploy.

Inevitably Mouffe and Laclau are unable to imbue the contents of 'discourse' by consciously and comprehensively drawing upon the forms and mediations of the social whole. And, in as much as they abandon any genuine form of practice, concomitantly they circumvent any painstaking engagement with theory – with the philosophical tradition which produces Marxism – instead choosing to step outside it, using their own unadulterated brilliance to tear away the veil, and reveal the discourses which have, until the arrival of Mouffe and Laclau, held humanity hostage. It is perhaps worth examining their account in a little more detail.

Mouffe and Laclau argue that discourses attempt to 'fix' meaning around a 'centre' but in their attempts to do so these discourses necessarily fail because 'no discursive formation is a sutured totality and the transformation of the elements into moments is never complete'.[32] In addition, discourses emerge through a process of 'articulation'. Articulation is 'a discursive practice which does not have a plane of constitution prior to, or outside of, the dispersion of the articulated elements'.[33] Discourses are not closed systems but are 'penetrated' by the field of discursivity. The field of discursivity is characterized by a limitless play of meaning which is both the condition of possibility and impossibility of discourse. The impossibility of discourse is represented by Mouffe and Laclau by the concept of 'antagonism'. Discourse attempts to transcend this and 'fix that which antagonism subverts'.[34]

Jacob Torfing wrote a short glossary in an attempt to make these concepts clearer to the general reader. Torfing defines a discourse as 'a differential ensemble of signifying sequences in which meaning is constantly renegotiated'[35] while the 'the field of discursivity' appears as an 'irreducible surplus of meaning'. In what would consist a surplus of meaning? We are not told. The concept is clearly too profound to be broken down into something which actually resembles sense. Torfing goes on to talk about hegemony; for Mouffe and Laclau, he says, this involves 'the expansion of a discourse, or set of discourses, into a dominant horizon of social orientation and action by means of articulating unfixed elements into partially fixed moments in a context crisscrossed by antagonistic forces'.[36]

It should be clear that Torfing, in his quixotic attempt at clarification, has laboured in vain. There is very little of any genuine meaning in these overburdened, esoteric sentences. It is no coincidence that the language of Mouffe and Laclau remains, for the main part, nebulous and opaque. Historical materialism is the theory of the proletarian revolution as the unity of theory and practice but the 'post-Marxism' of Mouffe and Laclau is geared towards the splitting of them (theory and practice) once more. As a result, Mouffe and Laclau's concepts, emptied of historical content and genuine human agency, necessarily become vague and solipsistic and we enter into a rarefied academic landscape in which the concepts themselves seem to develop an entirely artificial agency and life; reality becomes 'decentred', society becomes 'dislocated' and meaning is understood in terms of signifiers which, rather surreally, tend to 'float'.[37]

The need to understand concepts which are intended to describe and elucidate subtle social realities without having recourse to the genuine social relationships embodied in living history means that Mouffe and Laclau and others have to find some other way of allowing their concepts to interrelate. The absence of a genuinely social interrelation is amended by a physical one – for instance the fundamental problem of society is no longer constituted as one of class contradiction but instead becomes a question of 'fullness'. Society, you see, rather wistfully wishes it were 'full' however this is a condition it simply cannot attain – 'the social only exists ... as an effort to construct that impossible object'.[38] The 'fullness' is an 'impossible object' because it will be 'incomplete and pierced by contingency'.[39] Again it is difficult to say what any of this really means; perhaps the only thing we can glean from it is that the 'object' is rendered 'impossible' which once more hints at the Kantian character which underpins the bizarre, rambling screeds these thinkers generate. Society never truly realizes its 'fullness', unfortunately. Mouffe and Laclau, on the other hand, are certainly full of something.

∗∗∗

The final thinker I wish to turn to is Slavoj Žižek. Žižek appropriates some of the worst traits of the post-Marxists. Like Althusser, Mouffe and Laclau, Žižek refashions his philosophical apparatus in a neo-Kantian form which necessarily implies the dissolution of historicity. This is doubly paradoxical, because Žižek himself is a Hegelian scholar of sorts, and unlike any of those others, is well versed in what Hegel actually wrote. How, then, does Žižek manage to de-Hegel, Hegel, by ultimately returning that great thinker to an ahistorical Kantianism? I think this is achieved first and foremost by the re-articulation of Hegel through the prism of Žižek's beloved Lacan.

Jacques Lacan, like Althusser (who clearly leaned on Lacan quite heavily), was another French obscurantist philosopher who managed to fashion an ad-hoc form of Kantianism from the wreckage of a ruined theoretical edifice. Lacan, in his mature period, came to postulate an initial, fundamental (noumenal) condition – 'the real' – from which the subject emerges but simultaneously remains inexorably alienated from – as a result of its entry into the language-mediated culture which Lacan described as 'the symbolic order'.

Žižek's task then is to attempt to reconcile the Lacanian concept of the real – with a dialectical movement of the Hegelian type. Žižek approaches the problem in an innovative fashion:

> [T]here is a Real – this real, however, is not the inaccessible Thing but the gap which prevents our access to it, the 'rock' of the antagonisms

which distorts our view of the perceived object through a partial perspective. The 'truth' is not the 'real' state of things, accessed by a 'direct' view of the object without any perspectival distortion, but the very Real of the antagonism which causes the perspectival distortion itself. Again, the site of truth is not the way 'things really are in themselves', beyond perspectival distortion, but the very gap or passage which separates one perspective from another, the gap (in this case, social antagonism) which makes the two perspectives radically incommensurable.[40]

This provides a creative attempt to understand Lacan as a comprehensive dialectical thinker (not simply one who thinks in terms of paradoxes and contradictions) in his own right, and to rescue him from the Kantian dualism which underpins the impossible gap between the real and the symbolic order. Žižek is privileging the movement from one position to the next as the true; in other words he is comprehending the world as a complex of processes rather than a static, pre-given thing (even if it be a thing in itself). The Lacanian real does not persist (exist is the wrong word here) simply as some noumenal pre-condition; rather it is called into being retroactively as the very antagonism which frustrates any attempt to perceive it.

I would like to say a few words on 'retroactivity' in philosophy as a necessary aside. Žižek's insights on the role of retroactivity in philosophy are often intriguing, drawn from elements which are present in Marx and Hegel and, to my mind, Lukács also. Žižek provides a useful, anecdotal illustration of just what is meant by 'retroactivity'. When we listen to an old record, he reminds us, the static which fizzes and crackles in the background – far from acting as a distraction – in fact provides us with a deepened sense of authenticity, as in a Billie Holiday number, for example. The 'crackling' works to give us a sense of the record's age, and thus it carries with it the historical aroma of an older time and this becomes part and parcel of the satisfaction of the aesthetic experience.

But those who heard the background noise at the time Billie Holiday was actually singing would have experienced it as nothing more than an irritant which served to subvert the overall quality of the singer's voice. It is only in retrospect that this 'irritant' becomes something else entirely. And the critical point here is not simply that the listener from the purview of the twenty-first century appreciates the 'sound' of old records with an aural sensibility cultivated over time – one which those in the past happened not to possess. Rather we are dealing with the far more radical and provocative proposition – i.e. in the very act of listening to the music in the twenty-first century, we thereby transform the content of the original music; the future, on some level, is able to retroactively determine the past.

Why is this important from the standpoint of Marxism? In his book on the relationship between Marx' *Grundrisse* and Hegel's *Logic*, Hiroshi Uchida notes that, on the chapter on money in the *Grundrisse*, Marx describes the now-familiar process whereby the identity of a product is differentiated into a dual form (use and exchange), and how, when this product is brought into an exchange relation, it becomes a commodity. When exchange value is further realized as money, 'the immanent difference between use-value and exchange-value becomes an external opposition between commodity and money. As we shall see later, this opposition will develop into a contradiction within money, and from money arises capital.'[41]

At the same time, though, in a capitalist economy, Uchida also notes – 'the product is explicitly defined as a commodity when it is the product of capital, or when capital posits or produces a product'.[42] In other words: 'This means that the product is posited as a commodity through the capital-relation, into which the value-relation has transformed itself. If we inquire why the product exists as such, we must trace it back to capital.'[43] Uchida has drawn attention to an example of 'retroactivity' here – in as much as capital is required to posit the very thing (value-relation) which provides its own 'ground', to put it in Hegelian terms.

Žižek too sees the Hegelian dialectic at work in Marx' concept of capital when he describes how 'the "truth" of its relating its otherness is its self-relating, in its self-movement, capital retroactively "sublates" its own material conditions, changing them into subordinate moments of its own "spontaneous expansion" – in pure Hegelese, it posits its own presuppositions'.[44]

Both Uchida and Žižek are drawing attention to the same phenomenon, and it is interesting that both reference the same section of Hegel's *Logic* as a means of elucidating Marx' dialectical method in the *Grundrisse* and *Capital* respectively – i.e. the transition from Being to Essence. Žižek comments on this section of the *Logic* in order to explicate the movement of the Notion more generally:

Therein, in such a retroactive 'positing of presuppositions', consists the fundamental matrix of the Hegelian 'self-relating of the Notion': in the course of the dialectical 'progress', the initial category 'develops' into a 'higher' category in such a manner that it is 'trans-coded', posited as its subordinate-mediated moment; in the passage of 'being' into 'essence', the entire domain of 'being' is retroactively determined as that of the 'appearance', as the medium in which 'essence' becomes manifest, appears to itself.[45]

And so we receive some inkling of the way in which Žižek seeks to rescue Lacan from the abyss of Kantian dualism; the Lacanian real is no longer to be understood as a noumenal entity but rather as the process of thinking which creates retroactively a distortion or gap in its own fabric – 'The Real is not the In-itself but the very obstacle which distorts our access to the In-itself.'[46]

In so doing Žižek believes he has reconciled Lacan with Hegel. Because *'dialectical process retroactively posits ... [its] presupposed Background'*, the previous moment is of necessity *'incomplete'* and so *'in Hegel, the beginning has the status of the Lacanian Real, which is always already lost, left behind, mediated and so on, and yet simultaneously something we can never get rid of, something which forever insists, continues to haunt us'.*[47]

In other words the Lacanian real is merely the reified expression of the contradiction which drives the dialectical process – at any given moment a thing is not fully equal to its Notion. Žižek says of the Hegelian Idea – 'the universal Idea is nothing but the distortion or displacement, the self-inadequacy of the particular with regard to itself'.[48]

Despite its shrewdness, Žižek's attempt to reconcile Hegel with Lacan fails on two levels. Firstly, his elaboration of 'the real' as considered here has transformed it beyond all recognition with regards to the Lacanian original. (I have not considered Žižek's three-fold classification of the Lacanian real as real-real, symbolic-real and imaginary-real for it is not germane to the overall thrust of the current chapter.) But even if we accept the definition of the real here as 'retroactive gap', it still falls short of a dialectical progression of the Hegelian variety. If Althusser, Mouffe and Laclau all emphasized the static, interminable power of the thing (Ideology, structure, field of discursivity, discourse) over and above process, Žižek has swung to the opposite pole; that is, he now absolutizes the autonomy of process over and against the thing. For instance, he says that in Hegel 'the beginning has the status of the Lacanian real, which is already lost, left behind, mediated and so on', but he does not examine the thing – i.e. that which is 'lost, left behind, mediated' – in terms of its specificity. In Hegelian terms he here makes the mistake of concentrating solely on the 'relation to other' rather than 'relation to self'.

For when Žižek equates the Lacanian real with the Hegelian beginning – 'in Hegel, the beginning has the status of the Lacanian Real' – the comparison holds water only in as much as both 'the real' and 'abstract being' are 'lost, left behind, mediated and so on' in terms of a dialectical progression. But this allows Žižek to overlook the difference of the retrospective contents ('the real' and 'pure being'). In actual fact Hegel begins with pure being for a very specific reason; it is the concept bereft of content such that all that can be said about it is that it merely 'is'. Beginning with 'being' is a response to one of the most fundamental problems of philosophy; the problem of dogmatism – of making a beginning without bringing to bear all sorts of assumptions from the outside in advance. (Lacan's 'real' is thoroughly permeated with dogmatic pre-conceptions – the assertion that there is some natural unity which is experienced before the subject is constituted is entirely dogmatic, for example.)

Being, shorn of all quality and quantity, striped down to only its 'is-ness' is the category which best avoids presupposition, thus yielding the first triad in the system, and underpinning the whole Hegelian edifice. For that which merely 'is' denuded of all quality and characteristics is, at the same time, a 'nothing'. Respectively 'nothing' is also a 'something'. Being collapses into nothing and vice versa; the two terms vanish only to reappear in one another once more; at which point the concept of 'becoming' is generated – for it provides the (temporary) means by which both terms are to be held together in a stable unity. All of this is, of course, Hegelian Logic 101 but it is worth returning to what the maestro writes in relation to that first triad nonetheless:

> Becoming is the unseparatedness of being and nothing ... as the unity of being and nothing it is this determinate unity in which there is both being and nothing. But in so far as being and nothing, each unseparateded from its other, is, each is not ... they sink from their

initially imagined self-subsistence to the status of moments, which are still distinct but at the same time sublated.[49]

In the first Hegelian triad, therefore, becoming involves the 'sublation' of being and nothing; it both preserves and annuls them in a higher unity. But in making the 'real' a pseudo-name for Hegelian contradiction and limitation 'of the particular with regard to itself', Žižek empties it of any content. There ceases to be a first moment – 'the real' – which is then sublated in a more concrete moment (as with being, nothing and becoming); rather 'the real' becomes a synonym for the movement of dialectic itself – only a movement which has been abstracted from the categories in which it moves – 'the very gap which separates one thing from another'.[50]

In trying to transform 'the real' from its original Lacanian aspect as a noumenal entity which cannot be rationally apprehended, to something which can be understood in terms of a rational dialectical development – Žižek abstracts the contradictions in the dialectical movement from the very categories which produce those contradictions; processes, then, are able to overwhelm things. The dialectic of 'the real' *a la* Žižek is a ghostly dialectic, one whose motion is as empty and forlorn as the wind for it remains, in effect, nothing more than movement for movement's sake.

What are the consequences of employing a dialectic thus voided of content? Most critically the gains of 'sublation' – the means by which an early *content* is both preserved and annulled in a later one – are lost. The dialectic which underpins classical German philosophy is important in connection to this. Hegel describes Fichte's philosophy as 'the Kantian philosophy in its completion',[51] in as much as he (Fichte) attempted to overcome the noumenal-phenomenal divide and create a systematic and rational totality by absolutizing the individual transcendental ego – the ego he took over from Kant.

Fichte, therefore, can be said to 'sublate' Kant, in as much as what comes before is simultaneously preserved and annulled in a higher unity. The same must be said of Schelling's relationship to Fichte; Schelling allows to a degree the truth of Fichte's absolute ego – but maintains that it itself is the inverted product of a greater objectivity (Nature); the movement by which subject passes into object and vice versa is, in turn, assimilated into the Hegelian dialectic which endeavours to locate a concrete unity of subject and object – itself the culmination of the re-tracing of the history of thought (and, ultimately, being).

Now, for reasons which have been touched upon in this chapter, the Hegelian solution was inadequate, but in a very real way Marx, and then Lukács, sought to 'sublate' the Hegelian notion of the 'concrete universal' or 'Individual' as state (concrete unity of subject and object) in their conception of the modern proletariat. A profound understanding of what the working class is, therefore, requires – as absurd as it might sound to common sense – an understanding of 'sublation' in the context of the ongoing dialectic between subject and object in classical German philosophy.

All of which brings us back to Žižek – the point about the Lacan influenced pseudo-dialectic he brings to bear, a dialectic in which process overwhelms content – is precisely that the gains of 'sublation' are lost. To illustrate this one need only reference his account of German Idealism where he writes:

> [T]here is no unilateral progress in German Idealism: each of its four great names (Kant, Fichte, Schelling, Hegel) struggled with a fundamental problem and ultimately failed to resolve it, but this does not mean that each linear successor resolved his predecessor's problem in a move of Aufhebung – rather, the successor radically changed the field, so that the problem itself disappeared. Fichte 'missed the point' of Kant's though; Schelling and Hegel 'missed the point' of Fichte's (and each other's)[52]

By removing the activity of 'sublation' or '*Aufhebung*' as the key constitutive in the dialectical process, in tearing the individual moments asunder and holding them in implacable opposition – Žižek achieves in the arena of classical German philosophy, what Althusser, Mouffe and Laclau had achieved in ontological terms more broadly, i.e. the loss of the living historical development. The fact that the dialectic of German Idealism (and Marxism) is now no longer understood in terms of an ongoing process of 'sublation' in which the subject and object contradiction is progressively synthesized in a more concrete unity (one which eventually manifests at the level of socio-historical existence) has consequences for theory more broadly. For it was the awareness of this subject-object dialectic and the 'sublation' of its moments which lead Lukács to perceive in the proletariat the identical subject-object of history. Because Žižek has ceased to comprehend it thus, his understanding of Lukács' (and vicariously Marx') conception is left wanting. He comments on Lukács' formulation thus:

> However, Lukács remains all too idealist when he proposes simply replacing the Hegelian Spirit with the proletariat as the Subject-Object of History; Lukács is here not really Hegelian, but a pre-Hegelian idealist.[53]

It should be clear that Lukács has not simply replaced 'the Hegelian Spirit with the proletariat as the Subject-Object of History'. But Žižek is not the first commentator to suggest the Lukács conception is idealistic. Most famously Lukács himself renounced it in his 1967 preface to *History and Class Consciousness*,[54] but the same formulation has been widely criticized elsewhere as irrevocably idealist. It seems to be a purely metaphysical category which takes the form of an almost mystical 'teleology' purporting to resolve historical contradictions almost independently of real, active people – but it seems that way only if it is understood outside the dialectical contradictions implicit in the history of philosophy, and the historical ontology of labour more broadly.

What Žižek achieves on the philosophical terrain with regards to the German classical period – the annihilation of historicism – is inevitably carried through to the explicitly political realm. Marx posed the question of proletarian revolution as a living historical development in which a series of moments are 'sublated' – a process of primitive accumulation which culminates in the separation of the individual proprietors from control of the means of production by the emergent capitalist class – is subsequently superseded when control of the means of production is re-asserted but in a fuller more concrete form (sublation); particularized, individualized property is re-established in and through a universal form by the social agent which has the capacity to do so as a result of its historical formation and collective power.

Marx even goes as far as to phrase this in explicitly Hegelian terms – as a negation of negation. What we have here, what Marxism is, in fact, is the means by which philosophy locates in the culmination of historical existence the concrete answer to its own most profound riddle, while simultaneously historical existence encounters philosophy as the medium in which it achieves its most complete self-expression. Because Žižek abandons a genuinely historical dialectic at the level of philosophy, it is far easier for him to abandon the philosophically driven 'negation of negation' description of the proletariat at the level of history – and to therefore abandon the standpoint of revolutionary Marxism which sees the proletariat re-appropriate its own alienated labour by taking over the means of production in and through the revolutionary development of workers' councils. For Žižek, the idea of a modern proletariat which 're-appropriates its own content is deeply misleading ... communism should no longer be conceived as the subjective (re)appropriation of the alienated substantial content'.[55]

As a consequence, and like most post Marxists, Žižek entertains the commonplace notion that the orthodox Marxist analysis of the proletariat is antiquated and dogmatic – that Marx simply asserted it as a response to the immediate economic realities he encountered at the time; subsequently, it has been refuted by events, and has little or no place in a 'post-industrial' capitalism (making of Marxism, incidentally, little more than a crude empiricism).

But in abandoning the concept of the proletarian class as the culmination of a historical development orientated around the centrality of the productive process and the modes and forms which facilitate it; in eschewing such analysis, these post Marxists (including Žižek) – in as much as they wish to maintain (superficially) a revolutionary edge – must locate some other social agent which can offer the possibility of some (vague) manner of revolutionary resistance. Inevitably this takes the form of alighting on this or that heterogeneous grouping connected only by the geographical space it occupies, its sheer wealth of numbers, or the sheer level of immiseration it endures. Žižek, for instance, looks towards the inhabitants of Third World slums.

For Žižek, these slum dwellers have a revolutionary potential[56] not because they are enmeshed and unified by the productive processes and an objective mode of economic exploitation in which a portion of the value-added surplus product of their labour power in its commodity form is annexed by an exploiting class; no, rather their revolutionary power stems from the fact that they are in some wise 'free' from such outmoded determinations; they are understood as standing outside society rather than being immanent to it – '"freed" from all substantial ties, dwelling in a free space, outside the police regulations of the state'.[57]

This emphasis on the freedom from determination is an expression of the abandonment of historicism at the level of theory. And because the *possibility* of revolutionary unity is not understood as the culmination of an objective historical process, the political consciousness of the slum dwellers (in Žižek's account) inevitably assumes vague, isolated and profoundly idealistic dimensions – unmoored as it is from the concrete modes of existence in which it takes shape: 'they have to invent some mode of being-together … simultaneously deprived of any support in traditional ways of life, in inherited religious or ethnic life-forms'.[58] Ironically this ('they have to invent … ') is not a million miles away from Althusser's 'imaginary relation' (and of course Lacan's own concept of the imaginary); both of which emanate from a conceptual schema in which historicism is annulled.

Žižek's 'magnum opus' on Hegel and dialectical materialism accomplishes a shift from the realm of historicity to a form of psychoanalytical, linguistic-based ontology in and through the adoption of a Lacanian pseudo dialectic which annuls at the methodological level the possibility of a concrete historical unfolding by disregarding the fundamental categories of social existence. In terms of theory and political analysis the consequences of the loss of historicism are visible and grave. To take only a couple of examples. Categories of gender cease to be understood by Žižek as social historical constructs grown out of particular forms of class oppression in a given epoch but rather – 'Woman is man's prosopopoeia: she is man's symptom, she has no substance of her own, she is a mask through which man speaks.'[59] How on earth does one bring this type of analysis to bear on 'mundane' struggles against oppression at the level of day-to-day reality – like sexism in the workplace for instance? In a similar vein the phenomenon of Stalinism is not understood according to the decimation of the social basis of the revolution – the Russian proletariat – by civil war and foreign invasion, and the subsequent rise of a bureaucratic caste; it was instead a consequence of those Marxists who would 'neglect' theoretical conflicts between freedom as 'institutionalism' and socialism as 'spontaneity'.[60]

In abandoning a concrete historical analysis, the political struggle against capitalism is inevitably weakened for the comprehension of the link between theory and action, politics and philosophy, social existence and social consciousness is evaporated. As a result, when one tries to contemplate the possibilities of political action – one is most often left with an ill-defined but profoundly felt humanitarianism which, in the last analysis, is grounded on little more than hope or faith. When Žižek talks about the Third World slum dwellers as representing the 'germs of the future', he remains remarkably vague about the organizational forms which their resistance will take and the transformative possibilities which it might contain. In fact, even though – like many post-Marxists – he claims to have elaborated a far richer and less dogmatic conception, one can't help but sense that his assurances are simultaneously overshadowed by despair.

In the concluding pages of *Less than Nothing* Žižek asks – 'How are we to break out of the deadlock of post-political dehistoricization?' In the event he endeavours to clarify – 'we' cannot translate the 'energy of the protest into a set of "concrete" pragmatic demands'.[61] What is the answer then? At this point Žižek concludes enigmatically in true Lacanian fashion – 'People have the answers' – he informs us – 'they just do not know the questions'.[62]

For all Žižek's so-called Marxist credentials, it would be difficult to imagine the great German revolutionist ever giving such an answer.

Chapter 4

Reification and its consequences for modern life

Much of what is written thus far has been about expounding the notion of reification, i.e. the means by which underlying social relationships and social qualities are experienced as 'thing-like' in and through the exchanges of products and services which take place all the time at the surface of economic life. This chapter not only examines reification but also explores how it helps determine and shape forms of social behaviour and etiquette which structure both our working lives and our social lives. Sometimes these forms and modes of behaviour are so commonplace as to seem unremarkable or invisible even. And yet, they would have proved quite baffling to people living in pre-capitalist societies.

In selling our labour power in its commodity form, we present ourselves before the market and to the employer as a 'service' or a 'thing', a motive power which can be integrated into the processes of production and distribution in the same way as electricity, machinery and natural resources. In stepping into the workplace, your existence is manifested in its commodified form as a reified 'thing', and because you are reduced to just another abstract force in the processes of production, the experience of work under capitalism for the majority of people is an alienating one; they try to switch off while they are working on the tills or on the factory line – because the fragmented, partial and monotonous character of their labour has nothing in common with the set of interests and aspirations they have outside work. For the same reason, they watch the clock; their working life is something to be wound down and phased out, so that they might put it behind them and return home to pursue the set of interests and concerns which correspond to their authentic lives. Of course, this is not the case for every job or every worker, but it is true for the vast majority, because capitalist forms of labour often tend to reduce the worker to a repetitive and menial set of actions like sliding products across a till or answering phones and delivering the same set of sales options.

In splitting the labour operation in this way capital better develops labour efficiency; if the human beings who mediate industrial labour are each concerned with a particular labour operation in isolation, the overall output is increased because the product is developed more rapidly as all those individual operations are combined seamlessly on the factory line. A feudal cobbler making a pair of shoes is the overseer of the whole labour process from start to finish, fashioning the raw materials, putting them together, shaping the final product. But in a shoe-making factory each stratum of workers is responsible for an individual and abstract operation; some workers will operate the hydraulic presses which cut the initial materials, the next group of workers will stack the shoe parts for stitching, then the shoes will be moved onto a conveyer belt so that another group can facilitate the process by which the material is fused and glued in devices known as 'heat tunnels'. Very few of these workers would have the intellectual skill possessed by a medieval cobbler of old; that is to say, while they are capable and precise in reproducing their own specialized labour operation, it exists as a feat which is repeated in isolation. These industrial labourers are unable to command the technical skill responsible for the creation of a pair of shoes in its entirety, for that possibility has been lost amid the fragmentation of industrial labour more generally in and through the deployment of a variegated and discrete set of machines.

The increased fragmentation of the division of labour is a necessary condition of industrial efficiency under capitalist conditions of production. Adam Smith famously noted it when he described how ten workers could produce 48,000 pins a day if each of eighteen specialized tasks were assigned to each of the specific workers, whereas one worker would struggle to complete twenty pins from start to finish in one day –

if he or she were working on the task in its entirety. There are a couple of things to note here in regard to reification. The way in which the division of labour is expanded within the context of the single workplace, the way in which the labour operation ceases to stem from the intellectual ability of the worker themselves, becomes a profound instance of reification, because the worker is transformed from someone who is the premise of the productive process, who uses his physical skills and intellectual abilities to shape the product from start to finish in the manner of a human being consciously and creatively shaping the material world – into a 'thing-like' entity, that is to say an abstract physical force which is merely part of a series of anonymous inanimate forces which form an aspect of the productive process like electricity, steam, fire or water. Georg Lukács writes:

> This fragmentation of the object of production necessarily entails the fragmentation of its subject ... Neither objectively nor in his relation to his work does man appear as the authentic master of the process; on the contrary, he is a mechanical part incorporated into a mechanical system. He finds it already pre-existing and self-sufficient, it functions independently of him and he has to conform to its laws whether he likes it or not. As labour is progressively rationalised and mechanised his lack of will is reinforced by the way in which his activity becomes less and less active and more and more contemplative. The contemplative stance adopted towards a process mechanically conforming to fixed laws and enacted independently of man's consciousness and impervious to human intervention ... [transforming] ... the basic categories of man's immediate attitude to the world: it reduces space and time to a common denominator and degrades time to the dimension of space.[1]

The fragmentation of the labour process under the conditions of industrial capitalism, therefore, reifies the being of the worker, converting it into an abstract, partial and one-sided force which is subordinate to the objective and overriding process of production itself – a process which appears to the worker as a relentless and alien power which looms over and diminishes him. But what does Lukács mean when he says the productive process 'degrades time to the dimension of space'? If the labour activity of the individual labourer is converted into something resembling an ever more abstract force, a 'thing-like' power of production alongside a series of others – then it also follows that it can be measured and enumerated in the same sense that one might measure the amount of water which flows through a turbine every hour. Under capitalist specialization, therefore, the qualitative dimension of labour is increasingly phased out so that what remains is something which is almost purely quantitative in character, i.e. that which can be quantified and measured to increasingly exact calculations as just another element in the productive capacity of industrial machinery. It would have made almost no sense for an aristocrat of old to commission a painting from a Velázquez or an El Greco and to pay the prestigious artist by the hour for a precisely delineated number of hours determined by a written contract. It would have made no sense because of the nature of the artistic labour itself; each painting would portray a different subject in a unique setting, conditioned by the unconscious moods and feelings of the artist – an artist who would eventually pull all those random elements together as he brought the creative process in its totality to fruition in and through the completed work. It would be virtually impossible to say with any precision in advance just how long the painting might take. A group of men or women working on the factory conveyer belt producing those pins, on the other hand; here the manager of the factory would be able to develop an accurate estimation of how many pins were produced every hour, because he or she would be able to resort to tried and tested experience, to witness the results of the abstract labour of various groups of workers performing the same monotonous repetitions on the factory line, and because such labour is uniform – i.e. because it will involve roughly the same set of operations no matter what group of labourers are performing it or what time of the day it takes place – the overall results will also be roughly uniform. In the majority of cases of production the manager will be able to come up with an estimate of how much can be produced equivalent to a quantified gobbet of time. In this way 'space and time' are reduced to 'a common denominator' and that denominator is human labour in the abstract, the type of labour which develops its most concentrated form in and through the fragmentation of the labour process which takes place under conditions of industrial capitalism.

Abstract labour is the 'common denominator' by which 'time' is degraded to 'space', because the unmediated uniformity of the labour operation – which now presents as a mere 'abstract force', an inhuman 'thing' without qualitative dimensions – is something which can be rationalized, organized and measured in purely quantitative terms. The abstract labour of the human being can be applied to the productive process in much the same way one might apply a given amount of petrol to power a car for a given amount of time at a given cost. The reified character of the individual's labour activity comes to overwhelm their personhood almost entirely in terms of their entry into the productive process. The person now becomes the 'thing', the thing whose capacity to act as a cog in the machine is expressed according to a series of objective and measurable characteristics.

In our period the conversion of the authentic personality of the worker into a mere abstract force of production reaches increasingly horrifying dimensions. In the case of the super-corporation Amazon the process is almost absolute; the productivity targets of the firm have rationalized and measured the potential labour capacity of any given worker to such levels of efficiency that in some factories the labourers themselves are aware how, in order to meet production targets, they do not have time to take bathroom breaks and have instead resorted to urinating into bottles.[2] Naturally, when the processes of reification take such an acute form; when the human being is quite literally treated as a piece of machinery which is to be rationalized, refined and set into motion such that it reaches its very optimum capacity – the degrading effects on the body and the mind of the worker are inevitably manifested. In the same set of warehouses where the survey found that 74 per cent of workers were reluctant to use the toilet for fear of missing production targets – there were also reported hundreds of ambulance call outs to the buildings, including women miscarrying on the warehouse floor. In 2018 the tendency toward reification was given perhaps its starkest expression yet, when Amazon patented designs for an electronic wristband[3] which can precisely track where employees are putting their hands and, if necessary, use vibrations to direct their movements in a more productive fashion. It sounds like something out of a sci-fi movie, but it represents the very real prospect of reification being driven to its necessary and logical conclusion; that is, here the conversion of the human being into a 'mechanized thing' becomes a literal reality, in as much as electronics are to be strapped to human flesh creating what might be described as an 'automated labourer', a piece of humanized machinery. It is also noteworthy that the protests which were mounted against Amazon and the working conditions which we have referenced here were very much articulated as a response to increased reification. The GMB Union's national officer, for instance, couched his complaint to company founder and world's richest man Jeff Bezos by saying that Amazon workers wanted their boss to know that they 'were people, not robots'.[4]

But reification isn't simply a process which takes place in the warehouse or office or factory floor in isolation. In fact, it is in effect before the worker ever steps into the workplace. Consider the act of writing a CV, for example. It seems like the most natural thing in the world, especially if – like me – you were first taught how to do it at school. And yet, there is something artificial, something 'unnatural' ... something reified about the whole process. You are taught to list a set of objective qualities which will better advertise you to any potential employer: 'I am a good timekeeper', 'I work well in a team', 'I am dynamic and motivated'. One lists these qualities in the same way one might list the qualities of a used car you are trying to sell: 'Only a few thousand miles on the clock', '0–60 in seven seconds', 'power-steering' and so on. The point of the CV is an advert which advertises your ability to labour as commodity; to give the employer a sense of how efficiently and effectively your labour can be harnessed to the processes of production. Consequently, the writing of it provides a 'reifying' experience in as much as you reduce yourself to a series of stock-in-trade phrases – 'I am able to multi-task' – but such stock-in-trade phrases have nothing in common with who you really are, they rarely ever touch on the genuine and unique set of interests you yourself hold as an individual and idiosyncratic personality.

And that is why the experience of writing a CV proves dull and wearying, whereas the experience of writing something which is not reified – which does not reduce you to your capacity to labour in its abstraction but which actually references the set of organic interests and aspirations you have in terms of your genuine individuality – can prove satisfying and rewarding. Compare the experience of writing a CV to that of writing say, a diary. In Marxist terms the former mobilizes the aspect of your being which presents as an exchange value, a partial, one-sided and abstract force of labour which can be called forth and sold on the market as a commodity. The latter represents your authentic personhood; it represents your thoughts, dreams and hopes; i.e. it represents the 'use value' which corresponds to your being in terms of its authentic, organic existence.

Of course, I am not saying that every CV works according to the model of 'exchange value'. If you are fortunate enough to have a job which corresponds to your interests, it is not the case that the 'exchange-value', 'reified' aspect of your existence will inevitably be brought to the fore. For example, if you have spent a lifetime studying William Blake, whose poetry first inspired you as a child, and you apply to become a Professor of 'William Blake Studies' then the CV you hand in at a job interview will correspond much more closely to your own authentic personhood and the interests which underlie it. But most jobs under modern-day capitalism which involve unskilled labour often in combination with manual work do not allow for this type of possibility. And even when one discovers a job which better facilitates the type of 'use-value' which corresponds to the genuine personality of the worker, one often finds that the conditions which set the basis for that 'use value' are being progressively warped by the prerogatives of exchange. So our 'Blake Professor', for instance, will often find herself having to spend more of her time working on administrative duties, or she might have to teach a class which concentrates on the 'art' of applying for jobs in and through CV writing, i.e. things which are more profoundly related to the 'quantified' element in labour productivity rather than the joy and interest which flows from the Professor's organic personality and the years of studying Blake she has accrued.

And when the most pronounced form of exchange value is in operation on a society-wide basis – i.e. society is run according to a neoliberal economic model – often one of the first things to be achieved is the progressive decimation of the 'humanities' in the universities, precisely because they are not seen as having any 'practical value'; that is, they do not explicitly conform with the dictates of productivity, exchange value and capital expansion. The socially structured reified existence inevitably calls into being a sense of contempt for the curiosity which seeks to explore what it is to be human in terms of history, art and philosophy – for these are issues which pertain (most fundamentally) to humanity in its aspect as a 'use value' – as something qualitatively unique and authentic, and they are not issues which readily convert themselves into the dull dogmas of an entirely quantifiable and mechanically rationalized economy whose sole measure of the human soul is carried out in terms of dollars and cents. Such an economy generates a particularly dull form of pragmatism which pervades everyday life, which imagines that the humanities are essentially followed only by those who have their heads in the clouds, who are abstracted from 'reality' – i.e. the palpable endeavour of increasing productivity and material profit – the purely practical processes of developing one's wealth in concrete and quantifiable terms.

Thus far we have concentrated on the way in which reification affects the life of the individual in and through labour; the means by which the labourer produces and reproduces his or her own being at the level of economic existence and the way he or she is converted into an abstract and partial force of production therein. But the fact of having a mode of production which transforms the essence of the individual into a 'thing-like' entity inevitably bleeds into the field of social life more broadly. If we consider romance and sex, for example. In the modern period we have witnessed the rise of the dating agency to help facilitate these aspects of our lives, and this in itself is instructive. In an increasingly atomized and fragmented world, where one changes jobs, houses, counties and even countries often many times in the course of a single life, then the potential to form romantic connections which emerge from the context of a given community and which develop over time is considerably diminished. The dating agency replaces the organic connection which is facilitated by people meeting in a work context or a community context over a prolonged period – by an artificial database which draws strangers together according to a very different type of paradigm. When one signs up to the dating agency, the impulse is to make oneself as 'attractive' as possible by listing the series of attributes which make you more 'sellable' to the various anonymous individuals 'out there' who might come across your profile. This has a lot in common with the CV; that is, you are presenting yourself as a 'thing' with a series of positive qualities which can be accumulated and quantified in and through an advert. 'I have a good sense of humour', 'I have a great body', 'I am outgoing'. Of course, advertising yourself through a dating agency gives you much more leeway to promote your own personal interests than does a CV. But nevertheless, the dating agency model would have proved baffling to someone living even a century earlier, in as much as social relationships more generally – whether they were about work or life outside work – would have been formed in and through living encounters with people who were known to one another as members of the same community, and their interests and similarities would have emerged from that organic context.[5] I am not, by the way, suggesting that dating agencies are a 'bad thing'; indeed they perform a necessary role in the context of the anomie which pervades modernity, and many people have formed genuine and important relationships as a result of signing up to such services. But there is an element of reification to this, especially in the context of the latest dating apps like Tinder where the possibility of getting to know someone personally in and through the setting of the community more broadly is replaced by a situation in which you become simply another 'commodity' competing against hundreds or thousands of others in a vast, anonymous and virtual 'marketplace' whereby people are discarded almost instantaneously – in and through the swipe of a finger across a digital screen. And when encounters do take place they are often fleeting, arbitrary and random, before you are once again sucked into the market maelstrom of vast numbers of discrete and isolated Tinder profiles. It seems clear from something like Tinder that the ghostly power of a vast reified market is, in some way, redrawing human relationships and human interactions in its own image.

But while Tinder might not be best conducive to forming meaningful relationships over a longer period, it is just as likely to be fun, exciting and dynamic – as it is alienating, isolating and lonely. But there is a much darker side to the world of dating and sexual encounters when it comes to the means and modes of reification. I am thinking about the rash of what are euphemistically described as 'seduction seminars' which are offered by so-called dating gurus. These take the form of instruction manuals, group meetings and even weekend breaks which gather mostly young men together in order to receive tuition on how to manipulate young women into sex. Much of it is extremely unsavoury, some of it strays into the dark waters of rape culture, and virtually all of it is based on the unstated, underlying terror which is exhibited by the 'men's rights' movement' about the increasing level of agency and visibility expressed by modern, independent women in terms of both politics and culture. It is about rolling back the gains of the sexual revolution and feminism by repackaging a rather hackneyed stereotype in a modern form; that is, the idea of the woman as an essentially passive entity who can be controlled and swayed, this way or that, provided the man is prepared to step up and manifest raw masculinity and confidence. Investigative journalist Neil Strauss recorded some of the techniques in his book *The Game*. They involve things like telling pre-prepared and self-aggrandizing stories, using a set of distraction techniques to gradually increase the amount of physical contact, creating 'false time constraints' (the suggestion that you have somewhere much more important to be in order to make the woman feel she must make more effort with you) and also a manoeuvre called 'negging' which involves subtly undermining the woman's self-esteem, so that she becomes ever more under-confident, more desperate for approval and thus more easy to manipulate.

Of course, such attitudes – the view of the woman as a passive receptacle waiting to be shaped and determined by authentic masculine agency – have a seasoned lineage which extends far back in history, well beyond the capitalism of the modern period and the dualistic and reified reality it calls into being. Women have been quite literally treated as objects, i.e. as chattel to be exchanged in and through marriage as a way to cement property relations for millennia. But the logic which underpins these 'seduction seminars' has, in my view, a reified character which corresponds specifically to modern capitalism. Under capitalism the worker is 'free' in as much as she has the choice to sell her labour power to any one of many possible businesses, factories and workplaces, and yet, when she does so, more often than not, she is degraded into a simple abstract force of production which needs to be manipulated and tweaked by the capitalist or manager into yielding its optimum capacity. The seduction manual also treats the woman in the same way; that is, she is ostensibly free and has the capacity to move around, to 'choose' from a selection of men, but at the same time any particular man (if he is to be effective in his status as a man) must degrade her to the level of a physical thing which will respond positively to a carefully selected series of stimuli designed to achieve 'optimum productivity', or in this case yield full sex.

In an insightful piece on the issue, the journalist Jason Wilson noted how much in common these seduction seminars have with computer gaming: 'it conceives of the path to sexual intimacy as a kind of video game walkthrough, where if you learn to press the right buttons in the right sequence you're bound to "win"'.[6] The video game with its glittering graphics and luminous polygons, its pounding, high-octane soundtracks, and the rapid, flashing pace of its action provides a modern template by which a woman under capitalism becomes a reified entity, a technological puzzle to solve, a challenge to overcome, a level to complete – using ruthless ingenuity and concentration to press all the right buttons and eventually win your fantastic award. It is perhaps no coincidence that Neil Strauss, who became very involved in the 'seduction industry', chose to call his book *The Game*, nor is it a coincidence that, as Strauss noted, a disproportionately large number of men who sign up for this industry are computer programmers. It expresses the reification of a specifically human relation into a purely technological problem, set against the furore of market competition envisaged in and through a computer game where you, Player One, have the chance to dazzle and shine. Masculine sexuality in its antiquated and patriarchal guise reinvents itself in the light of capitalist modernity in and through the reification of woman as a technological dilemma which needs to be finessed in order to yield its 'productive' dividends. Again, as savagely misogynistic as pre-capitalist forms of society often could be, the idea of using some type of pseudo-scientific technical manual as a way of forming intimate social relationships would have been utterly baffling and incomprehensible to a male living in those earlier times.

Much of the 'seduction seminars' and indeed the rancid politics of the 'men's rights movement' more generally are carried online, through advertisements and videos which are proliferated and spread through social media. Social media is a particularly interesting issue for any investigation of reification. At first glance, it would seem that social media operates in the exact opposite fashion; that it facilitates social relationships between human beings who otherwise – given the fragmentation of modern existence and the sheer distances which open up between people – might never have the chance to come together and share interests. Of course, it is also fraught with bullying and trolling, which are phenomena that manifest a strong sense of alienation and fragmentation. In addition, a medium like Facebook is very commercially driven, funded by the revenues which are taken in through advertising and the selling on of the commercial and demographical information of its own users. So, from the outset, it is important to recognize that social media is fraught with contradictions, and is something of a contested terrain where different class tendencies crystallize and conflict.

I want to focus again on the way in which the reification of the labourer under conditions of modern industry creates a form of abstract labour which can be scientifically measured and rationalized in terms of the quantitative demands of the productive process. Facebook and Twitter, like anything else in the social realm, mediate qualitatively unique human experiences, but they do so in a very particular fashion. When someone posts a Facebook update, when one talks about an experience one has had, or posts a photo of a lovely place visited with friends – the unique, personal and qualitative aspect of the event is frozen in a type of digital stasis; the qualitative experience becomes objectified and ossified in a permanent physical form in and through the status update. Linked to this, most crucially, is the system of 'liking'. The 'like' button allows other users to 'like' the status and in this way the experience goes from being something which takes place in terms of a fluid, most often fleeting event experienced in real time usually with a limited number of people – to something which is permanantized as a digital memento whose 'value' can be measured in precise quantitative terms. Of course, the qualitative immediacy of the real experience isn't necessarily disrupted or negated by the digital preservation of it in a quantifiable form as a Facebook status update. But sometimes it can be. A friend of mine once relayed a story about a colleague and his wife. The colleague and wife were climbing a mountain in the Swiss Alps. The wife moaned and complained bitterly throughout the rather laborious and difficult trek, until they reached the summit. At which point she took out her phone, took a picture of them at the top waving and posted the picture on Facebook with the caption: 'Exhilarated! Sometimes in life you have to reach for the skies!'

The update, one assumes, probably received a good few 'likes'. What became most satisfying for the wife was not the qualitative experience itself – to revert to Marxist terminology it was not the immanent 'use value' of the experience which was most pertinent to her; but rather it was the quantitative value the event could command once it had been 'reified' in and through the Facebook forum; once it had been converted from a living, organic experience to a 'thing-like' entity whose value could be measured in 'likes' and the prestige which flowed from this. And again, this mirrors what happens with labour in the modern epoch; it goes from being a qualitative and organic process which flows from the depths of the being of the individual labourer to something which is ossified and congealed into a commodity form and the precise quantitative 'exchange-value' such a form commands. Of course, I am not saying that a Facebook status update is literally a commodity (it is not determined by the law of value as a commodity is) and for the same reason, Facebook is not a marketplace. And yet, in and through the reification of experience, status updates behave as commodities; that is to say they accrue a certain value which is measured and quantified – not in terms of socially necessary labour, but in terms of digital 'likes' – and furthermore these updates compete with one another in a virtual realm which behaves in some ways like a vast marketplace; that is, those status updates which receive most 'likes' amplify their given status, and are given more visibility, more attention. For this reason Facebook users are automatically pulled into a market-like competition in which they are pressured to accrue as many likes as possible to make sure their own updates remain visible and appreciated.

Eventually the 'exchange value' of the experience, the need to get a given number of 'likes' can become the 'end' of the experience itself. You can be on a Valentine's date with your partner, having a candlelit dinner, and you might feel a creeping sense of unease, something is missing. The only way to remedy this is to take a picture of the meal in front of you, in all its culinary perfection, upload it to Facebook and make a comment about how Valentine's Day is the most wonderful time of the year. You check your phone to see how much the post has been liked as the meal commences, but the experience itself has now fragmented into two component parts – that of the organic, intimate and shared time you and your partner are spending in the restaurant, and that which can be objectified and materialized in the digital realm and measured in terms of a broader quantified amount of 'social value'. There can come a point when the thing which really gives you the sense that the experience has been worthwhile and satisfying – is no longer the experience itself – but only its reified expression manifested in and through social media. In the case of the wife climbing the mountain, she actually hated the experience – i.e. its 'use value' was negligible and even negative to her, but in terms of its 'exchange value', in terms of its reified aspect, it was at once enjoyed as something overwhelmingly positive.

I am not saying, by the way, that everybody who posts photos and comments on Facebook or Twitter is necessarily allowing a reified experience to overcome an authentic one. Sometimes people post because they had a particular experience which was moving and lovely for them, and they simply wish to share that with genuine friends and loved ones – their social media being a convenient means by which this can be achieved. But what I am saying is that the forms and structures of capitalist social existence – particularly what Marx called the 'cell' of capitalism, the commodity form itself – are stamped with the dual aspect of use value and exchange value, and that this fundamental dualism is not only embodied in the conflict at the level of economic existence between the reified character of labour power in its commodity form over and against the living and authentic being of the worker as human being, but that such a dichotomy also bleeds into the realm of culture – and that here the power of exchange value, the power of reification, has a warping gravity which bends a lot of our cultural experiences in its own direction. Not everyone using Facebook is transfiguring their lived experience into reified 'exchange value', of course, but there is a certain compulsion to move in this direction. With regard to my own experiences as a journalist and writer, sometimes when I put up a particularly witty status update, or post an article I have written which carries a pertinent political point – even though I am satisfied with what I have written, when it receives only a limited number of 'likes' (as most of my posts do) I often feel a sense of demoralization and have the feeling that what I have said is a little worthless in the broader scheme of things. Sometimes, on the back of those type of feelings, I consider ways to 'censor' my writing, or to tweak it in such ways that it might be softer and nicer and more appealing to a broader demographic – the broader number of strangers who are described as 'friends' on my Facebook account. And I have to actively resist this impulse.

Up until this point we have been considering a key aspect of reification; that is, at the economic level industrial capitalism breaks down and fragments the unified and organic labour operation into a series of single abstract and quantifiable forces, and we have looked at how that abstract quantification has a bearing on the way we experience culture. This is clearly one of the most important aspects of reification, but perhaps the most important aspect of all is how the reification of social relationships under modern capitalism actually renders invisible the way in which the extraction of surplus product takes place. Let's recall that every society based on a division of class requires the ruling class to be able to extract a 'surplus product' from the direct producers who produce the economic means by which everyone is able to live. This surplus product supports their own status and power as a privileged group who are not tied into the immediate and direct labour which is necessary to produce and reproduce social existence. In antiquity, the appropriation of surplus product enacted by slave owners against slaves, for example, was a naked act of visible brutality and repression. In capitalism, however, the act of appropriation is rendered invisible. For it appears to be a simple exchange of equivalent 'things' which opens up between employer and employee, i.e. an exchange of a designated period of labouring time for its equivalent as a cash sum.

But what Marx came to understand was that the commodity labour power has an aspect to it which differentiates it from other commodities. A diamond, for instance, has a high exchange value because – in bringing it to market – a complex and painstaking series of labour operations are required: it needs to be mined, the ore needs to be extracted, the diamond needs to be transported, shaped and polished; its value, therefore, is equivalent to the level of socially necessary labour which is embodied in it. Labour-power as a commodity is also measured in the same fashion, i.e. the socially necessary labour required to feed, shelter and clothe the worker so that she can bring her labour power to market to be sold for a given period of time. What Marx noted in particular was that labour power as a commodity has the unique property of being able to create value over and above this – a surplus value. If the worker's needs for food, clothing and shelter in any given day are equivalent to four hours of labour – the capitalist can cover this in the wage they provide, but at the same time the worker has the capacity to work beyond those four hours; they could instead work for eight hours, thereby providing a value over and above the value of their labour power as an equivalent. It is this value which the capitalist accrues as profit.

Thus, the surplus labour which the capitalist is able to accrue from the labourer in the form of profit – the essence of the social relationship of exploitation which opens up between them – is rendered invisible by the appearance, i.e. what appears to be a simple transaction of equivalent 'things' – a given quantity of labour for a given quantity of money. Or to say the same thing, at the level of appearance, the 'thing' is foregrounded while the actual social relationships seem to fade away into nothingness. Vulgar bourgeois economics absolutizes the appearance, fetishizes the 'thing'; people are not categorized into the classes whose central social relationship takes the form of the appropriation of surplus labour by capital; rather they are described as discrete, individual and generic actors; buyers and sellers who exchange the commodities they have in a never-ending flux mediated by the market, but how they have come by those commodities – how their respective wealth or poverty, their capacity to sell or buy has been constituted in historical terms – is never interrogated. The unending exchange of things between a complex of generic and ahistorical individuals attains a ghostly and independent life over and above the underlying social relationships which set the basis for it; indeed, this becomes the precondition for many branches of modern economics such as Game Theory which employs modelling to predict outcomes based on the rational interests of generic individuals whose interests are set into conflict with one another, interests which are, furthermore, measured almost exclusively in quantitative terms of loss or gain. But to the individual capitalist, reality does take place on this basis, i.e. on the rational and quantifiable set of calculations and adjustments he performs on the various elements of production. Marx writes, 'it is precisely wages, interest and rent that go into this production as limiting and governing amounts of price. These, therefore appear to him as the elements determining the price of his commodities.'[7] In other words, the capitalist, of necessity, perceives 'the cost of his inputs as the basis of commodity prices (rather than beginning from the concept of the value of commodities)'.[8] He experiences reality in this way because he perceives it from the purview of the individual; hence, the 'qualitative' nature of profit as something which is generated in and through the social relationship of exploitation which opens up between classes remains, of necessity, occluded. For the individual capitalist, the essential nature of social reality appears merely as the series of quantitative adjustments he or she must make to the various ossified elements of production, thus generating either a profit or a loss. Game Theory (and many other branches of modern economics), therefore, represents the faithful translation of the reified appearance from the purview of the individual and generic economic actor into a theoretical guise.

Of course, the critique of bourgeois economics from the point of view of reification, baldly stated above, has been covered in much more depth and profundity by thinkers like Isaac Rubin, Georg

Lukács and Michael Lebowitz, to name just a few. But it is not only economics as a subject which in some sense encompasses the reified appearance while allowing the social relations which set the basis for it to vanish into oblivion. In her excellent book *Marxist Literary Criticism Today*, Barbara Foley talks about the notion of 'art for art's sake'. This is the idea that one should not analyse art from the broader historical context; one should not try to see in it something 'political', i.e. something which carries either a radical or reactionary flavour in the context of the social struggles of a given era. This point of view has, quite naturally, found great favour in the universities and colleges as opposed to what is seen as the 'narrow, dogmatic, political' interpretation of art. Foley notes this sense that the artwork should have a kind of stand-alone 'autonomy' and not be hitched to the wagon of any particular set of social or political interests – was also extended to literature under the New Criticism movement during the Cold War. These New Critics increasingly put forward the doctrine that 'extra-textual considerations – biography, history, economics, conditions of production and reception – are irrelevant (indeed deleterious) to textual analyses: the critic should remain focussed on matters of technique'.[9] As Foley notes, the ability to regard an aesthetic entity as an autonomous cultural product which is utterly divorced from the social relations and processes which set the basis for it is itself an echo of the commodity fetishism which the capitalist mode of production generates: 'Somewhat ironically, for all its pretentions to be liberated from history, this aesthetic doctrine recapitulates in the realm of literary theory the fetishism of commodities in the realm of economics, in so far as both present the appearance of a given entity – whether commodity or poem – as self-generating, divorced from the social relationships from which it has arisen.'[10]

In historiography too, something similar occurs. The Scottish historian and essayist Thomas Carlyle cultivated the 'great man' theory of history, famously arguing that '[t]he history of the world is but the biography of great men'.[11] But as Herbert Spencer would write so tellingly of Carlyle's 'great man' – '[b]efore he can remake his society, society must make him'.[12] In other words, Carlyle's notion of the great man allowed for the world-making individual to become divorced from the social relationships and processes which set the basis for him, and thus he leaps into the pages of the history books like Athena leaping from

Zeus' head, fully formed and completely autonomous. This autonomy insulates a generic individual as a given 'thing' from the social and historical processes which infuse genuine individuality, and it constitutes a form of reification therein. It is no coincidence that this approach to historiography was developed in the nineteenth century, the time when industrial capitalism was consolidated in some of the most powerful countries across the globe. The need to look at the individual as a generic entity divorced from social conditions (and therefore abstracted from both class interests and class conflict) received a particularly concentrated expression in accordance with the development of a society which manifested its fundamental socio-economic relationships in the guise of the constant exchange of 'things', but such a political purview also had useful implications for ruling class power in a more explicit and mendacious fashion.

I recall a debate from some years back between Noam Chomsky and Christopher Hitchens about the events of September 11th and the attack on the Twin Towers. Chomsky was, in the rather laborious, dogged and fact-rich way of a serious academic, trying to draw attention to the way in which the processes of American and European imperial intervention in the Middle East had helped create the conditions for the attacks on the Twin Towers. He would argue Osama Bin Laden was partially formed with US backing, i.e. the support of the United States in training Mujahedeen troops to fight their Soviet rivals in Afghanistan, part of a bigger bi-polar conflict between contending superpowers, and that the continued support of the Israeli war machine as a proxy for American imperialism and the means by which the interests of independent Arab states could be held in check (along with the ongoing decimation of the Palestinian people) – all of this provided fuel for the fundamentalist fire, and the background from which the horrific crimes of the Al Qaeda terrorists could be contextualized.

Hitchens averred. For him, any attempt to rationally understand the social oppressions in the Middle East itself through the context of a history of imperial intervention and invasion was simply to justify the actions of the awful fanatics who committed their crimes on that September morning. He argued that not only did the social context more generally have no bearing on the crimes themselves – 'Does anyone suppose that an Israeli withdrawal from Gaza would have forestalled the slaughter in Manhattan? It would take a moral cretin to suggest anything of the sort'[13] – but furthermore that any attempt to see the situation in such a light was the same as saying the innocent men and women who were incinerated in the Twin Towers had somehow brought it on themselves, that it was the equivalent to talk of 'chickens coming home to roost'.[14] How did Hitchens explain what had happened? Abstracting from all social and historical process, he described Osama Bin Laden as 'a near-flawless personification … [of] … evil'.[15] In other words, Hitchens had reverted to a more atavistic paradigm; the reified category of the 'great man' – bereft of social process or origination – was, by him, reformulated in terms of the 'evil man'. Of course the moral category of 'evil' predates capitalist society by a good deal but what must be noted here is how easily it is slotted in to become a key ideological component of a reified world which works to split irrevocably organic social relations from generic entities or things as a mode through which historical events can be 'explained'.

The 'autonomy' of the generic entity divorced from social processes, understood as an enclosed, self-sufficient 'thing', is, therefore, a form of reification which pervades the humanities and social sciences and informs an analysis of history, economics, art, literature and politics. But that sense of the individual ego as an autonomous and abstract 'thing' reaches well beyond the academy. We find one of its most concentrated theoretical expressions in the self-help industry, a gargantuan money-spinning endeavour which has launched a fleet of books, seminars, podcasts and gurus, and which is very popular with large numbers of people outside the university world. A recent example of the genre is Chloe Brotheridge's *Brave New Girl*. This book is not without good intentions. It aims for the empowerment of women. It quite correctly recognizes that women, on average, are paid less than men in the workplace for the same job roles, and it also recognizes the different modes of acculturalization which apply to girls and boys; specifically that boys are most often taught they have the real potential to act upon the world, to radically transform it, whereas girls are most often taught that they must first change themselves, that moulding their physical appearance into something pleasing and attractive becomes the defining feature of who they are. Brotheridge quotes a survey carried out by Girl Guiding in which a third of the female respondents said 'people made them feel as though the way they look is the most important thing about them'.[16] As Brotheridge also says, women are most often 'raised to be nurturers and given dolls and Sylvanian Families to play with'.[17]

But while Brotheridge's book raises very clearly the way in which women are disadvantaged and unvoiced by patriarchal power both economically and culturally, the solutions she proposes to this issue are a lot less persuasive. They involve a combination of trite pragmatism, 'visual realization' and 'positive thinking'. To achieve her goals, the individual woman must first visualize her own personal 'ladder of bravery'. 'All you have to do is keep moving, inch by inch, up the ladder of bravery towards your end goal of confidence in every situation … In fact, in any area where fear holds you back, you can create a ladder of bravery. The ladder shows you the manageable steps toward ultimate bravery.'[18] The issue of women's oppression is fundamentally socio-historical in nature. Forms of patriarchal oppression which take shape through millennia are brought to bear on the objective social structures of capitalist society, channelled through the world of employment and the nature of the family – ensuring that women are not only paid less on average, but enjoy less political and cultural representation and also end up doing more unpaid labour in the home. Beyond the obvious ridiculousness of it, Brotheridge's incitement to the individual woman to picture in her head 'a ladder of bravery' is a form of thinking which poses an explicitly individual and abstract solution to a problem which is fundamentally structural and socio-historical by definition, i.e. to economic inequality which is structural in nature and can only be challenged and transformed by broader social movements and organizations – Brotheridge opposes the abstract self-sufficient individual who can overcome all injustice simply by putting her mind to it: 'Remember, you are a brave warrior woman and are capable of doing anything you set your heart on.'[19]

The rallying cry, that you 'are capable of doing anything you set your heart on', is not only trite but also silly. I'd like to become the heavyweight champion of the world, but there are certain objective realities which mean this is unlikely to work out for me. But there is something more at work here than simply geeing people up, motivating them, giving them a burst of confidence even if the root source of that confidence is a mirage, an illusion, a castle in the sky. The 'warrior woman' in question is every woman, the generic woman – the woman who is abstracted from any socio-historical content, a transcendental template of womanhood per se. She can do anything because, bereft of any concrete socio-historical determinations, there is only ever the abstract question of whether you are confident or not, whether you are committed or not, whether you are brave or not. And all you need to do – if you are an unconfident person – is simply read the correct self-help book which will allow you to reverse the poles and become a confident person. So, when Brotheridge comes to address the question of women at work, she gives employees several tips which flow from mastering their inner confidence and powers: 'Stand up to dinosaur managers', 'Pushing through the fear is better than suffering in silence', 'Don't assume managers will refuse your request', 'Challenge expectations about old ways of working'.[20]

Of course, finding the courage to stick up for yourself can be important in many different situations, but nevertheless this always takes place against a backdrop of highly concrete social and historical factors. You can't afford to 'stand up to dinosaur managers' if you have seven children and you are working in sweat shop conditions for less than a dollar a day. That is an extreme example, for sure, but the majority of working women do end up in more precarious and lower-paid jobs than their male counterparts and thus enter into more highly skewered power relations with their employers. They have less ability to simply 'stand up' to managers, not because they lack in courage or conviction, but because of objective social circumstances, the realities of job insecurity, the knowledge that you are replaceable and the fact that you are often on the edge of a ravening poverty. The real buttress against these kinds of vulnerabilities is collective action; an employer can easily dismiss or mistreat one (woman) worker, but it is much harder to dismiss a whole factory of them. The development of bargaining power through the creation of trade unions is thus a key route into creating better job conditions and evening out wage discrepancies. Brotheridge, however, never even touches on the issue of trade unions or political and economic representation more generally – precisely because, for her, the concrete categories and hierarchies of the social world fade before the inner power and untapped resources of the generic individual.

I suspect this is partly to do with Brotheridge's own experience of work. University educated, from a middle-class background, having her own medical practice in London, specializing as a clinical hypnotherapist, and now working as a highly successful author too. While her life might well have been filled with real hardship and tragedy, I am willing to bet she has nearly always been in the type of jobs where standing up to a boss is a much more viable thing to do in terms of the context, the legal and financial support someone in her position would have access to, and the kind of opportunities which would still be available to a person with her qualifications even if she left this or that particular workplace. If one lives a relatively privileged existence, the determinate successes of one's working life can become much more a question of the confidence you are able to exude, the will to success you demonstrate and so on; these things all accord with a capitalist work ethic of improvement and achievement which particularly resonates with the aspirant middle-class and its glittering fleet of young, dynamic entrepreneurs – a good few of whom have made a lucrative career for themselves in the self-help industry. Brotheridge enjoins her reader to 'give yourself permission to be confident, to fake it until you make it, and most importantly of all, give yourself permission to risk failing because it will be absolutely worth it'.[21] For Brotheridge, in terms of her own trajectory, this is undoubtedly true. She has made 'a lot of my goals a reality. My first book *The Anxiety Solution* was a bestseller on Amazon, it was featured in the *Daily Mail* several times and I was invited to speak at events I'd always wanted to speak at.'[22] For the uninitiated, the *Daily Mail* newspaper is perhaps the most reactionary paper in Britain's somewhat laughingly called 'free-press';[23] it is unstintingly pro-capitalist and works to justify the position of the rich and powerful on the basis of generic individuality and the sense that they happen to have been more 'brave', more 'dynamic', more 'intelligent', more 'hardworking', more 'determined' than the rest. They have realized their 'potential' in a way that the vast majority of others have failed to do. It is perhaps no great surprise that the same paper is a staunch advocate of self-help manuals.

In Jane McGonigal's self-help book *SuperBetter* the process of reification reaches its zenith. Like all self-help manuals *SuperBetter* begins by raising the individual up, separating them out from any concrete socio-historical determinations and rendering the inward untapped potential of the generic ego absolute: 'You are stronger than you know ... You are the hero of your own story.'[24] But, just as with some of the 'seduction manuals' which developed out of the whole 'men's rights movement', *SuperBetter* reiterates the 'goal' (in this case recovery from trauma and depression) in the fashion of a video game in which – given the right technical moves and adjustments – success is to be had; specifically 'victory' can be assured by 'finding allies' and collecting motivational 'power-ups'.[25] Metaphysical qualities such as optimism, creativity, courage and determination all become elements you can accrue in and through 'playing' the game (life) correctly; that is, they become quantified and tangible 'things' which can be possessed, logged and utilized given the correct level of technical finesse the player is prepared to exhibit. Again this is the logic which underpins the tweaking and optimization of the factory machine, but channelled into human relationships which are divorced from their qualitative and social content, and reimagined in the guise of a video game-style competition between generic individuals in which the goal is to accrue more 'things' to yourself and thus to ensure triumph. As Alexandra Schwartz comments in a particularly insightful article for *The New Yorker*, the 'fuzzy wishful thinking' of the self-help books of yesteryear has increasingly 'yielded to the hard doctrine of personal optimization'.[26] More and more do self-help gurus show a commitment to the science of quantification: 'What they're selling is metrics. It's no longer enough to imagine our way to a better state of body or mind. We must now chart our progress, count our steps, log our sleep rhythms, tweak our diets, record our negative thoughts – then analyze the data, recalibrate, and repeat.'[27]

Of course, the sense that our relationships and our experiences are becoming increasingly reified is something which the vast majority of us feel or intuit on some level, and those who are the overseers of the capitalist mode of production – the employers, the managers, the advertisers – are alive to the same sensibilities. That the prosaic mechanics of exchange value rationalize and petrify the use value of organic human experience converting it into an optimum series of quantifiable and never-ending 'things' generated on the production line is something which creates a more generalized malaise throughout society – a sense of profound inauthenticity, the loss of the truly human experience – and such a loss is something which even the capitalists themselves can pick up on. When we consider advertising, for example, we realize that it very often attempts to describe the reified productions of 'exchange' in terms of the living traditions and social relationships which operate across the terrain of 'use'. So, take the average TV advert for pasta sauce. Typically, you will be presented with a multi-generational

Italian family; they are gathered around an old oak table in the garden under the pouring light of the afternoon sun, to a backdrop of rolling fields flecked with hazy yellows and russet browns. Grandparents, parents and children are all speaking animatedly, gesticulating with their hands, laughing, when suddenly they are interrupted by the rotund figure of the Italian mother who brings a large steaming pan of her sauce out onto the table. As the rich, ruby-red sauce is dolloped over fine lines of perfect pasta, the voice-over might well inform you in luxurious, dulcet tones that the secret recipe for this sauce has been in the family for generations, handed down from mother to daughter.

It is, of course, a simple lie. But what does the lie – what does the presentation of these idyllic rustic conditions of community life – seek to disguise? The answer is a series of exhausted, dead-eyed workers, dressed in synthetic grey uniforms and hairnets, working against the backdrop of rattling, clacking machinery, shuffling endless numbers of generic jars of sauce further down the factory conveyer belt. The capitalists and advertisers do not and cannot understand the processes of reification from a scientific point of view – i.e. they cannot identify the point at which the conversion of a portion of surplus value into profit as a social relation of exploitation is manifested as the mere exchange of things or services, and that this process eventually sets the basis for the quantification and rationalization of labour as an abstract, inhuman force on an industrial and society-wide basis. But they nevertheless intuit (as most of us do) that there is something profoundly inauthentic and dehumanizing about capitalist production which requires the use of the 'lie'. They sense that human beings (or as they know them, 'consumers') are in some way alienated by the processes which generate their encounter with the 'thing' (the product); and the advert is more often than not the attempt to 'dereify' the product, to allow the consumer's encounter with the product to feel like an authentic living experience rather than a cold hard exchange underpinned by the cash nexus and the relentless gears of an impersonal, vast and alien market machine.

And it is not just with advertising. The term 'emotional labour' was coined in 1983 by American sociologist Arlie Hochschild in her book, *The Managed Heart*. She defined it as the need to 'induce or suppress feeling in order to sustain the outward countenance that produces the proper state of mind in others'.[28] In particular, she looked at how this 'emotional labour' was deployed in industry, specifically bill collecting and flight attendants. The flight attendant's job is to deliver a service and create further demand for it, to enhance the status of the customer and be 'nicer than natural'.[29] I would go further; I would say it's not just about flattering the customer or appealing to his or her ego (though this is often part of it) but more importantly it marks the attempt to 'dereify' the transaction, to suggest that what is really taking place is not so much a simple exchange of things (money for product) but a true meeting of personalities in the form of an authentic social experience. When you go and eat in a posh restaurant, select a specific wine, and the waiter or waitress looks at you and murmurs in a soft voice of appreciation 'very good, Sir, very good indeed!' – it is not just a compliment in isolation; rather the suggestion is that you are something of a connoisseur, that the waiter or waitress is acknowledging and appreciating your taste, your understanding of wine.

But in making such an appreciation, the waiter is crossing from the realm of exchange – i.e. the bald, practical elements of exactly what you require as a customer – to the realm of use; that is, he or she is showing some appreciation for a talent or hobby which belongs to the authentic realm of your personhood, something you have cultivated in terms of a private interest which corresponds to your own personal history. Of course, the artificial transition from exchange (the realm of commerce) to use (the realm of genuine personality and interest) simply cannot be made; the waiter or waitress knows nothing about your real personality, and they make the same noises of appreciation to virtually all their customers no matter what type of wine they select. But the point here is to notice the necessity for the 'lie'; how, in an increasingly reified world in which the prerogatives of exchange have sunk so deeply into our social realities – the desire to recover that which is authentically human, the need to encounter others as more than just the bearers of 'things', to meet them in terms of social relationships which are premised on the recognition of the living personality of each; such a need is more than a need, it can manifest as a yearning. And it is this yearning which capital in its unconscious transpersonal way is tapping into when it compels its labourers in the service industry to perform such 'emotional labour', or in the advertising industry when it provides the image of more traditional and nostalgic forms of social gatherings.

Of course, not only is the attempt doomed to failure; in a certain way it reproduces what it seeks to repress with a redoubled intensity. For most people (provided they are not braying bankers or noxious hedge-fund managers), the experience of having a waiter or waitress fawn over you – telling you what a wonderful choice you have made by pointing to a particular wine on the menu – is a vaguely uncomfortable one, precisely because it feels forced somehow, artificial. You don't by any means feel connected to them. You don't really know what to say in response. Likewise, while watching the advert for pasta sauce, the majority of us are not going to feel genuinely warmed by the family having lunch. Watching them gathered around the table, laughing and talking, does not provoke a sense of nostalgia or happiness which comes from the thought of meals shared with family and friends. For, while the depiction of the people on screen is, ostensibly, one of organic communal and familial life, in another way there is a hollowness and artificiality to it which is carried by the plastic grins and glassy eyes of the actors.

For when actual families gather for dinner it is nothing like this. In real life there are tensions and awkwardness along with happiness and pleasure, the myriad of social contradictions which have evolved out of a lifetime of shared experiences, problems and joys. But the family on-screen seem bereft of any living substance; their smiles are the synthetic smiles of automatons, their laughter – a toneless, tinkering and artificial sound cast into the void. There is an eeriness to the performance of human life funnelled through the prism of capital which is why – when you look closely enough – the family portrayed on the advert do not seem fully alive. The force that animates them is not one of authentic social relations, but rather something alien and implacable; the interminable, ghostly movement of capital expansion is what flickers behind the eyes of those gathered around the table, going through the motions with their rictus, lifeless grins. For this reason, the people depicted are more Stepford Wives than Happy Families. Capital's endeavour to disguise the ossified interminability of its own ghastly and lifeless mechanics is reproduced with a strange and spectral intensity; the attempt to portray an authentic human experience yields its opposite – the robotic motions of artificial beings, forever happy, forever delighted, reflected back at you from behind the mirror, moving through their artificial world, timeless and strange.

But capital can't live without the performance; like Pinocchio, its lies are endemic, but also like the famous puppet, it longs to be 'a real boy'. Early in this chapter I talked about reification in the context of applying for a job; how the CV reduces the living personality to a series of 'things' to be better applied to the productive process by the employer. And yet, what I didn't note is that in the same moment employers often feel the need to create the illusion of a 'dereified' reality. When a potential worker goes to a typical job interview – let's say she wishes to get a position working on the factory floor of 'Smith's Paper Factory' – when she is interviewed by the manager, the manager asks that simple question which most of us have been asked many times: 'Why do you want this job?' Now the truthful answer is nearly always: 'Because I have bills to pay, and a family to support and this is the most expedient way of doing that!'

But although that is the simple truth of the situation, any interviewee who stated it thus would find their next destination at the unemployment office. What the interviewee is required to do is to feign interest in the company in question: 'Well for a long time I have admired Smith's Paper Factory for the consistent and excellent work it has done in the paper-making industry and I hoped that one day I could be a part of that process!' In other words, the interviewee is required to take part in a pantomime in which they are compelled to present a purely commercial interest in the company which is premised on their ability to realize their labour as an exchange value in and through a wage – in terms of a deeply authentic and human commitment to the company which grows from their own organic personhood, something which is premised on use value. Of course, both the interviewer and the interviewee are aware that it is highly unlikely the interviewee has developed a fascination with the paper-making industry in their spare time over some years, and yet the spectral power of capital creates its compulsions almost behind the back of the people having the conversation. It is perhaps the ultimate testament to the ghostly life of capital, the way in which it generates this strange, otherworldly and lifeless parody of the very real, authentic, flesh-and-blood human relations which are submerged beneath the reified world.

Chapter 5
Literary Theory and the loss of the historical totality

Literary Theory is almost as old as ancient Greek philosophy itself and goes back to Aristotle at least where, in his *Poetics*, he formulated aesthetic principles of comedy and tragedy. In the twentieth century, however – co-extensive with the rise of universities and the type of education which would facilitate a wider demographic than the elite bastions of old – the shape and contours of a new type of Literary Theory began to attain definition. It drew sustenance from the Russian formalism which developed in the context of the 1917 revolution, but perhaps the strongest impetus to modern-day Literary Theory came from the structuralist linguistics of the 1950s (influenced by Ferdinand de Saussure) and the structuralist anthropology of Lévi-Strauss, along with their post-structuralist and post-modernist successors such as Derrida and Bathes, and also the increasingly fashionable psychoanalytic theory of figures like Freud and Lacan.[1]

This threadbare summary might briefly be supplemented by pointing out that Literary Theory and its components were often evolved out of the need to destroy the 'grand narrative', the type of theories which tried to form a totalizing and coherent picture of the historical process as a whole, with its own necessary and immanent logic, and to draw political and aesthetic conclusions within the light of that overarching 'objectivist' framework. In the febrile environment of the early seventies, as the Civil Rights movements went into retreat, as neoliberalism secured its first substantial foothold in the bloody laboratory of Chile, and as the beginnings of a great and sweeping process of de-industrialization set in across the First World countries, the sense of radical political possibility felt increasingly illusory. Where once the clash of classes and the struggle for revolution held sway, now such living social categories had been supplanted in favour of a strange and eerie terrain in which reality was 'decentred', causes had become 'absent', and 'signifiers', rather mysteriously, tended to 'float'.

A more detailed analysis of Literary Theory is beyond the scope of this chapter, but what I want to look at here is how two thinkers who locate themselves in the Marxist tradition have sought to fuse Marxism with some of the main strands of Literary Theory. In so doing they have managed to propel themselves into incredibly prominent positions as celebrity intellectuals who sell millions of books and are invited to make speeches across the globe. I want to examine these thinkers as a way of demonstrating how the trends they mobilize in Literary Theory are, in fact, anti-Marxist. Again I am not trying to give an assessment of these thinkers as a whole; I do not propose to provide an overview of their body of work and their place in Literary Theory more broadly – something I am less than qualified to do.

What I aim to achieve is to once more focus on that very specific question of class and its role in the Marxist theory of history: how – in adopting some of the most fashionable trends in Literary Theory and continental philosophy more generally – these thinkers remove the focus from a coherent class analysis which unfolds historically, replacing it with a series of formalistic categories which operate in an abstract and transcendental realm, thus divorcing the art object from the historical and social conditions which gave birth to it. The thinkers I wish to consider both identify as Literary Theorists and they both identify as Marxists. They are Terry Eagleton and Fredric Jameson.

Terry Eagleton is probably best known for his work *Literary Theory: An Introduction* which has sold over 750,000 copies since its release in 1981. In that book, Eagleton elucidates his attitude to a Marxist approach to literature as well as the aspects of Literary Theory and continental philosophy which inform his approach. To begin with the first. Eagleton alights on one of the most significant problems with regard to any Marxist interpretation of literature – i.e. that of historical objectivism. In other words, why, for example, do ancient forms of myth, art and epic poetry continue to move us when the conditions of life which set the basis for them have long since perished? As Siegbert Salomon Prawer wrote in his monumental study of Marx's relationship to literature 'once gunpowder and shot have been invented, one cannot introduce a hero like Achilles into the modern world; *The Iliad* represents an oral form threatened by the invention of the hand-press and even more by that of machine-printing'.[2] And yet herein lies the paradox, for we are still compelled by the great hero's travails even today.

Eagleton is unable to get to grips with the *aporia*, and for this reason his analysis collapses into a form of relativism. He first asks the question: 'Karl Marx was troubled by the question of why ancient Greek art retained an "eternal charm", even though the social conditions which produced it had long passed; but how do we know that it will remain "eternally" charming, since history has not yet ended?'[3] He then reflects on the grounds for aesthetic taste in the first place: 'Just as people may treat a work as philosophy in one century and as literature in the next, or vice versa, so they may change their minds about what writing they consider valuable. They may even change their minds about the grounds they use for judging what is valuable and what is not.'[4] Returning to the subject of Greek myth he is able to hypothesize:

> Let us imagine … we discovered a great deal more about what ancient Greek tragedy actually meant to its original audiences … We might come to see that we had enjoyed them previously because we were unwittingly reading them in the light of our own preoccupations; once this became less possible, the drama might cease to speak at all significantly to us.[5]

In speculating in this fashion, Eagleton is bringing out the idea that our aesthetic standards are always in flux, always relative to what has gone before, and in some sense there must open up an insuperable gulf between the past and the present in which the latter cannot objectively apprehend the former because, in looking back, we are always blinded by 'the light of our own preoccupations' in our own time. For the same reason, '[t]here is no such thing as a literary work or tradition which is valuable in itself, regardless of what anyone might have said or come to say about it. "Value" is a transitive term: it means whatever is valued by certain people in specific situations, according to particular criteria and in the light of given purposes'.[6] Thus Eagleton is able to imagine a future which produces a society 'which is unable to get anything at all out of Shakespeare. His works might simply seem desperately alien, full of styles of thought and feeling which such a society found limited or irrelevant'.[7] And this is not simply because such a society has grown decadent or spiritually impoverished such that it is incapable of appreciating 'great art' but rather such a society might have undergone such 'a general human enrichment',[8] that human taste would have superseded all its limitations in the here and now and the beauty of Shakespeare would seem pale and pallid compared with the aesthetic of the future.

I wanted to elucidate Eagleton's thoughts on this in detail because I think it is so important to understanding the direction he takes. He is unable to rise to the level of an objectivist theory of history at least with regard to his analysis of the aesthetic. What does this mean specifically? The Marxist theory of history involves an ontology of labour which maps the changing forms of social organization which mediate human labour with nature and the underlying contradictions and tensions which drive such changes. The various changes are, ultimately, classified in terms of stages, of modes of production – i.e. the particular forms of social organization which mobilize labour in and through the tools and the technology which generate that labour's product. So Marx talks of the 'feudal mode of production' or the 'capitalist mode of production' and indeed endeavours to distil these different forms of social organization into their logical essences as concepts, but as Goethe would remark, if theory is grey then reality is most definitely green, and while such logical concepts can exist as independent and pristine abstractions in the realm of thought, in the context of the broader reality, things prove to be a lot more contradictory and messy. A given society often has several economic modes of production at work within it at any one time, all jostling for supremacy. The late Roman Empire, for instance, was characterized primarily as a slave mode of production with pockets of concentrated private property developing on its Western periphery which spoke of a certain level of 'proto-capitalist' investment especially in the cities, while in the same moment, centred around Constantinople in the East, one encounters what might be described as a 'tributary' mode of production as the central form of economic organization.

The issue becomes richer and more complex still when one considers that the supersession of one mode of production by another does not involve a hard and fast break. Marx regards any future communism as the antithesis of capitalism, but from a particularly Hegelian viewpoint, in as much as what has gone before is preserved as well as negated; it is, in the Hegelian terminology, 'sublated'. In revolutionizing feudal productive relations, mercantile – and later industrial-capital – helped sever the direct producer from the land reconstituting labour in a socialized form, lots of proletarians working together in collective workplaces, but while communism was to abolish the capital – labour-power relation it would at the same time preserve the socialized character of labour which had reached fruition with the development of industrial capitalism. The collective workplace would continue to exist, but it would be under the political and economic control of the working class itself.

In other words, even though Marxism described historical evolution in terms of its fundamental outlines in and through a series of stages by which the lower were eventually revolutionized by the higher, nevertheless, it is always true to say that the earlier forms of society were not only negated by their successors, but were also in some sense fundamentally preserved, much like in the animal kingdom – a higher species contains in itself the ghostly outline of all those which came before encoded in its DNA.

The Hegelian concept of 'sublation' – to both preserve and negate – is one which Eagleton is tone-deaf to. His conception of the way in which aesthetic standards develop in a given historical soil is abstract precisely because it tends to emphasize the moment of 'negation' in isolation, whereas any genuinely Marxist account of the aesthetic must fuse the objective and the relative within the corpus of its own historical unfolding. No matter how different, how distant, one historical epoch might be from another; no matter how relative the nature of its specific historical character to the next, there is a universality in which all historical stages in the life of mankind must partake. That is, each and every one of them involves the struggle to develop slumbering potentials, to actualize the possibilities of human freedom which are latent and implicit in the forms of social organization of any given epoch.

For the majority of human history, such a struggle has taken shape exclusively against natural barriers. But once society attains a class character and begins to develop along class lines the struggle for freedom becomes about developing those progressive social agents which are forged in the crucible of class conflict and class oppression and have the capacity to radically alter the dimensions of the social order, thus bringing to the fore new possibilities and forms of human freedom. The difference, the relativism, of the various historical stages is itself nothing more than the expression of the ever-changing moments in which new forms of freedom are posited. In this, the Marxist account, the moments of the objective and the relative are held together in a dialectical unity, and this also provides us with the solution of the problem of the 'aesthetic' – the solution to the problem as to why we are still moved by earlier and more 'primitive' forms of art.

For if one acknowledges the teleological component of historical development – the notion that historical progression is at the same time premised on the broader unfolding of human potentiality as freedom – then any Hegelian or Marxist analysis of the aesthetic can take wing from this fact. Art effectively becomes one of the cultural mediations of this process, one of the ways in which the longing for more concrete freedoms and potentialities is expressed – the way in which a future image of ourselves can be illuminated but only ever in vague outline, only ever in a profoundly mystified, individualized and, more often than not, unconscious fashion. I don't say, for example, that Tolstoy was aware of the historical character of Russian feudalism in the nineteenth century according to a precise and self-conscious sociological analysis, and the central protagonist of his greatest novel, Anna Karenina, is in no wise depicted as someone with any particular political leanings – certainly she least resembles a radical or revolutionary struggling for broader forms of social freedom through a conscious political programme.

And yet the tragic depiction of Anna – an aristocratic woman whose potentials to love and create from within the context of her own existence – are very much limited and suppressed by the objectivities of the patriarchal and feudal world in which she is situated – in this tragic depiction Tolstoy is able to show Anna's courageousness in seeking to love whom she wishes to love, to bring out the most authentic aspects of her personhood in and through a struggle for self-determination, while at the same time throwing into relief the callousness and brutality by which such burgeoning freedoms are crushed. It is precisely the tragic tenor of Anna Karenina – the revelation of the best and most authentic aspects of her personality and the possibilities of a better future for her which are then crushed on the rocks of the present – which awakens for us, the readers, a hunger for her freedom and the preciousness of the struggle to achieve our own, even if we ourselves are no longer languishing in conditions of feudal backwardness. Anna moves us not because we are as she is, not because we are situated in the same patriarchal-feudal world, but because, despite the difference and the relativity which opens up between our epoch of life and that of Tolstoy's, we are bound together in the same historical whole, the same totalizing process by which humanity is able to unfurl its slumbering powers and potentials – the universal struggle to awaken in itself the conditions of life that will better facilitate its own sublime self-expression.

We can see that a Hegelian-Marxist account of literature depends on its ability to unify the objective and subjective in the unfolding trajectory of history as whole, what Georg Lukács described as a 'mediated totality'. Totality, in this sense, refers to a series of historical or logical moments which only reach their fruition and meaning as a result of their mediation with one another as part and parcel of a totalized unfolding. In the great preface to *Hegel's Phenomenology of Mind* the maestro talks about a fruit-bearing plant, which seems to immediacy to be a rather stable and given thing which does not require much thought to fix in our mind. We can recognize it, and verify our recognition by reaching out, plucking an apple and sinking our teeth into its moist crispness. But in actual fact, when considered dialectically, the fruit is an example of a Hegelian totality which is comprised of a series of moments which are unfolded, each to be both transcended and preserved in a greater and complete unity. The significance of each is to be fully gleaned in and through its membership to the whole:

The bud disappears when the blossom breaks through, and we might say that the former is refuted by the latter; in the same way when the fruit comes, the blossom may be explained to be a false form of the plant's existence, for the fruit appears as its true nature in the place of the blossom. These stages are not merely differentiated; they supplant one another as being incompatible with one another. But the ceaseless activity of their own inherent nature makes them at the same time moments of an organic unity, where they not merely do not contradict one another, but where one is as necessary as the other; and this equal necessity of all moments constitutes alone and thereby the life of the whole.[9]

It is in this sense too, where one can look at history dialectically, one can recognize how the various historical stages – which in some sense do oppose, contradict and annul one another as different and separate entities – nevertheless reveal their 'organic unity' when taken as part of the overriding process of the whole. And yet this is precisely what Eagleton is incapable of doing. Indeed he mounts an attack on both Hegel and Marx for their propensity to read historical development as a mediated totality and therefore to recognize in it some broader and universal purpose which reaches its fruition in and through the historical and social transformations which the collective subject passes through – i.e. a progressive actualization of the possibilities of human freedom as its underlying *raison d'être*. For example (*vis-à-vis* Hegel) in one of his early books Eagleton berates his one-time mentor Raymond Williams for a 'dangerous', 'teleological' and 'historicist' approach which ends up 'reducing the social formation to a "circular" Hegelian totality and striking political strategy dead at birth'.[10] Why using the Hegelian, Marxist and Lukácsian conception of totality would strike 'political strategy dead at birth' or what conceivable relation Raymond Williams – a most un-Hegelian thinker – actually has to Hegel in the first place are questions on which Eagleton doesn't choose to linger. But in case one feels that his attack on totality is part of an early formative phase in his thinking (the book in question is from 1974) then it is worth noting that several decades later the same anti-Hegelian (and the current writer would argue anti-Marx) motif is in effect.

In a 1999 review of the book *Marxism and Human Nature* Eagleton describes the author Sean Sayers rather witheringly as 'a full-bloodedly Hegelian Marxist'.[11] He attacks Sayers on the basis that Sayers provides an objectivist and thoroughly determinist view of historical development, a 'Hegelian-Marxist motorway of historical progress'[12] in which 'an ordered, rational series of stages, each of which slumbers immanent in the previous one ... will necessarily culminate in the historical "destiny" of socialism'.[13] Ultimately, Eagleton is able to conclude, 'Sayers is in fact a full-blooded teleologist.'[14] I don't think Eagleton understands what the word 'teleology' actually means nor does he have any feel for its resonance in Aristotelian and Hegelian philosophy, important in this context. But *what he takes it to mean* is the type of insult which can be flung at anyone who treats history in a highly deterministic fashion – i.e. those who allow the objective, universal moment to override everything else, subsuming the rich, relativistic nature of an infinite variety of persons and populations in the grinding cogs of an all-encompassing mechanics which eventually generates a finished historical product – 'socialism'.[15] Again, Eagleton identifies the notion of 'totality' as an integral part of 'Hegelian historicism' – an all-encompassing 'determinism' – when Eagleton writes how, for Sayers, 'human nature' becomes 'the totality of these historically evolving powers'.[16]

What is particularly illuminating in this review is that Eagleton attacks Marx himself on a similar basis. According to Eagleton there are two versions of Marx: there is the 'Hegelian', 'teleological', 'totalizing' and 'deterministic' Marx, but there is also a 'non-teleological Marx'. For Eagleton, 'Sayers is in fact a full-blooded teleologist. So was Marx, at least from time to time; but there are indeed sufficient grounds in his and Engels's work on which to construct a non-teleological theory of history as well.'[17] Of course, what Eagleton is saying is not in the least bit true; the reason why he bifurcates Marx into a 'teleologist' on the one hand and 'non-teleologist' on the other is simply the result of the fact that Eagleton is unable to rise to the level of dialectical thinking (part and parcel of Hegelian teleology by the way) in which the objective and the relative moments enter into an 'organic unity' as part of the broader historical unfolding of the whole. But once Eagleton has severed Marx in this fashion, it is very clear which Marx he prefers and which Marx he wishes to oust; the Hegelian Marx who describes history in terms of an objective and unfolding totality must be vanquished by the 'more defensible version of Marx ... S.H. Rigby's Marxism and History valuably distinguishes these two competing texts within Marx's work, and amply demonstrated the untenability, both theoretically and empirically, of the teleological model'.[18]

At this point we are able to understand, I think, at the metabolic level, exactly why Eagleton is unable to bridge the gap between epochs, between the ancients of the Homeric period, and the here and now; for him, aesthetic value must always remain a 'transitive term'; the art of the past cannot be classified according to a true aesthetic objectivity precisely because we cannot view it except through the distorting prism of 'our own preoccupations' – i.e. the social and historical conditions of the present. To think otherwise would be to open oneself up to the type of 'historical determinism' which, for Eagleton, is part and parcel of the Hegelian concept of the unfolding totality, a concept he feels is repeated in the worst aspect (teleology) of Marx's own thought.

We are also now in a position to see why Eagleton gravitates towards various stands of the philosophies which inform much of Literary Theory – because these tendencies are very much about striking out against the vision of the totality, the historical development which crystallizes an objective and universal purpose in its unfolding – and more concretely the way in which the literary work in some sense mediates this. From the Hegelian-Marxist point of view, the great work of literature itself has to in some way carry the semblance of the whole; that is, it must depict the clashing of social agents as part of the ongoing trajectory of a totalized historical development – albeit at the more abstract and fantastical level of individual character and destiny. For this reason the great literary work must, in some vague, individualized and unconscious fashion, provide a distant image of the totality and the forces and contradictions which drive its development in order to reveal those qualities at the level of individual destiny which in some way express the power and potentials of human development at the level of the historical whole.

Again I think we can see the image of a totalized and historically constituted society whose logic seeps into the lives of the protagonists in something like *Anna Karenina*, and of course, this is exactly how Marx and Engels understood the great strength of Balzac's novels, while the same approach informed Lukács' analysis of the 'historical novel' – the great totalizing works which begin with Walter Scott and reached their apotheosis in the late nineteenth century. Lukács writes that the demand for totality is something which connects the individual lives of the characters in an epic or a novel with the totalizing social forces which are at work in social life more broadly. The demand for totality 'is essentially a demand for an artistic image of human society which produces and reproduces itself in the same way as the daily process of life ... aims at a total embodiment of the life-process'[19] but at the same time such a totality is expressed indirectly and in a deeply unconscious fashion – expressed in and through 'the dramatic collision' of a series of individual characters whose 'human aspirations ... in their mutual conflict ... participate in this central collision'.

Because of his inability to conceive a totalizing and dialectical theory of history which unites the objective and the subjective, the universal and the relative within its remit, Eagleton is also compelled to attack the concept of totality as a historical unfolding when it appears as the central precondition of Marxist aesthetic analysis: 'Both Lukács and Goldman inherit from Hegel a belief that the literary work should form a unified totality ... Lukács sees the work as a *constructed* totality.'[20] The idea of understanding a literary work according to the Hegelian notion of 'totality' is something which Eagleton maligns as 'close to a conventional position in non-Marxist criticism'[21] and to it Eagleton counterposes the approach of Pierre Macherey (another Literary Theorist heavily grounded in continental philosophy and post-structuralism) which argues that

> a work is tied to ideology not so much by what it says as by what it does not say. It is in the significant silences of a text, in its gaps and absences, that the presence of ideology can be most positively felt. It is these silences which the critic must make 'speak'. The text is, as it were, ideologically forbidden to say certain things.[22]

(One wonders if, for Macherey and co, the text might best be revealed with all its words removed!) But Eagleton goes on; because, for Macherey, the text has gaps, silences, the subjects on which it does not speak, it is therefore 'always incomplete. Far from constituting a rounded, coherent whole, it displays a conflict and contradiction of meanings; and the significance of the work lies in the difference rather than unity between these meanings ... there is no central essence to it'.[23]

Again one can see how the conceptualization of the whole as a historical unfolding which is comprehended as an identity in difference – the objective unity of a series of relative and antagonistic historical moments – can be replaced by an account which absolutizes the moment of the relative, the moment of difference – 'the significance of the work lies in the difference'. And once the historical totality is sundered and fragmented, once the moment of 'difference' is absolutized, then the collapse into relativism on Eagleton's part is quite inevitable; just as he understands that there is no 'objective' standard of aesthetic judgement, so too does he understand that one cannot talk of the 'central essence' of any literary work, for the idea of a work having any kind of universal or objective essence is itself an impossibility. In his most famous work Eagleton informs us that '[t]here is no "essence" of literature whatsoever'.[24] In fact, according to Eagleton, anything which is put to page can be considered to be literature; for, bereft of any 'central essence', it is ultimately shaped on a relativistic basis by the subjective feelings and thoughts of the person doing the reading: 'If I pore over the railway timetable not to discover a train connection but to stimulate in myself general reflections on the speed and complexity of modern existence, then I might be said to be reading it as literature.'[25] Of course, this is taken from his bestselling book *Literary Theory: An Introduction*, which was written in the earlier part of Eagleton's career, so one might imagine that this kind of philosophical naivety doesn't categorize his later thinking – except for the fact that in his 2013 book, *The Event of Literature*, the same relativist and subjectivist perspective is relayed almost verbatim. In that work he argues that a handbook on fish-breeding or a plumber's manual might be read as examples of literature providing they are 'magnificently written' and that the person who reads them uses them 'as an occasion for reflections which range beyond their evident functions'.[26]

Once one has lost touch with an overarching objectivity which is crystallized in and through the historical process, the fundamental social and class struggles which are fought out and which, ultimately, determine the possibilities and limits of human freedom – once one has lost touch with this process and the fluid social categories and relationships which underpin it – one must inevitably relegate aesthetic meaning to some secondary and partial sphere which is then separated out from the life of the historical whole (from the totality) and assumes a fixed and fetishized existence over and against it. So, for example, the meaning of a given work of literature arises not from the social world in which the political and aesthetic consciousness of the author are shaped but rather is to be discovered in the way in which linguistic structures relate to one another in a self-contained and transcendental realm. An alien and surreal landscape populated by the never-ending production of 'signs' or 'signifiers' trailing back indefinitely like the refractions in a broken mirror. And if one is able to decipher such strange and mysterious semiotic coding, then one is able to access the hidden secrets of the text – though of course there really are no such secrets for 'truth' itself is simply another sign, another signifier set into motion, full of sound and fury, and yet *signifying* nothing.

The sense that there can be anything outside the linguistic realm, the idea of an objective reality which language itself flows from and mediates, becomes ever more blurry and wan like the image of something glimpsed through a windowpane running with rainwater on the darkest of nights. 'Truth', 'meaning' and 'objectivity' all eventually fade away, deconstructed by the esoteric excesses of portentous figures like Jacques Derrida, or they perish before the linguistic structures of power and discourse evoked by such fashionable celebrity intellectuals as Michel Foucault. Of course, much of this is cod-philosophy of the highest order, and Eagleton has absorbed just enough of Marx to make him rightfully critical of some aspects of it, on the odd occasion. So despite the many positive comments he makes on structuralism, he also retains enough savvy to declare: 'Structuralism, in a word, was hair-raisingly unhistorical: the laws of the mind it claimed to isolate – parallelisms, oppositions, inversions and the rest – moved at a level of generality quite remote from the concrete differences of human history.'[27]

And yet, as we are about to see, the lacuna in Eagleton's own methodology – his inability to conceive the totality as a genuine historical unfolding – means that he can't help but collapse back into relativism, and this, in turn, makes him particularly vulnerable to those philosophies which seek to strike out at the whole, at historical objectivity per se. This is particularly clear in his book *Criticism and Ideology*. Here in particular we see the influence of Althusserian structuralism in and through Althusser's concept of 'Ideology', along with the notion of an unknowable and ahistorical reality which is irrevocably masked by 'Ideology' and cannot be encountered by rational thought (i.e. some type of variant on the Lacanian 'real'). So 'the text itself privileges ideology as a dominant structure',[28] and such 'ideology', just as with Althusser, manages to separate irrevocably the subject from 'the real' which is the unknowable precondition behind the creation of the structures of 'ideology' in the first place: 'it is precisely in this absence of the particular real … the text gives us such ideology without its real history alongside it … it is unconstrained by the necessity to produce any particular real'.[29] In the same work we see how these moments combine in order to obliterate living historical process and, therefore, to set the basis for describing literature in purely formalistic, transcendental and lifeless terms. Here is Eagleton writing about the 'text' and the various elements which shape it.

> The 'disturbance' of relation between signifier and signified in the 'prototypical' literary discourse is an effect of the relation between that discourse as a whole and ideology. It is because the text's materials are ideological rather than historical – because as it were, the text exists in the 'hollow' it has scooped out between itself and history – that it lacks a real particular referent, and displays that lack in the relative autonomy of its structuration. The 'poetic' text displays it also in its disproportioning of signifier and signified, whereby the absence of a concrete historical object is proclaimed, made manifest, the very predominance of the signifying process over the 'pseudo real'.
>
> We need, however, to be more precise both about the ideology which the text works, and the process of that working. To formulate the issue in this way is already to risk falsification, for the text, as I shall argue later, does not simply 'take' ideological materials which are extrinsic to it. Ideology pre-exists the text; but the ideology of the text defines, operates and constitutes that ideology in ways unpremeditated, so to speak, by ideology itself. The particular production of ideology which we may term the 'ideology of the text' has no pre-existence: it is identical with the text itself. What is in question here, indeed, is a double relation – not only the objectively determinable relation between the text and ideology, but also (and simultaneously) that relation as 'subjectively' flaunted, concealed, intimated or mystified by the text itself.[30]

My own take on this is that it is little more than errant nonsense. The way Eagleton keeps putting words in 'quotation marks' as though he is wanting to be incredibly careful about what he is saying, about the concepts he is deploying, making sure they are read in just the right fashion, is immensely annoying, while at the same time the chaotic and pretentious language simply rambles on and on – its high-faluting and portentous tone failing to disguise the dirge-like repetition of certain stock-in-trade phrases from the structuralist and semiotic projects and the utter meaningless which lies behind them. It doesn't even make sense on its own terms. 'Ideology pre-exists the text' and the text 'constitutes that ideology' (which pre-exists it) while simultaneously, '"the ideology of the text" has no pre-existence: it is identical with the text itself'. It is a blatant and muddled self-contradiction but perhaps that is not so surprising if all the concepts you are using are bereft of any genuine meaning in the first place. It is not so much that Eagleton is some kind of charlatan, but more that he genuinely believes he is a cutting-edge savant 'freewheeling' the type of profound and esoteric concepts of the intellectual elite, and the sheer opaqueness and confusion which are wrought by these kinds of streams of consciousness only confirm the genius of the person who is unleashing them. More fool him, but aside from wasting his readers' time, is this really the worst thing in the world?

Undoubtedly not, but there is a more serious consideration here. We can quite clearly see behind the clouds of hot air and confusion; there is something more going on. The divorce, the separation, from historical process – from the life of history itself – is repeatedly emphasized. We are told that the 'text's materials are ideological rather than historical'. For a Marxist (though not an Althusserian) such a statement is nonsensical as ideology springs from history and is part and parcel of it. We are told that the text lacks a 'real particular referent' because it exists in some kind of 'hollow' (whatever that means) which separates it from history. The 'poetic text' too is bereft of any 'concrete historical object'. But most vital of all, there is no mention of the interplay of social classes and groups, relations of exploitation, forms of oppression, the existence of states, governments and nations – all of which are forms of the process wherein human beings produce and reproduce their social reality and through which the aesthetic consciousness is filtered.

Instead such living categories are annulled in favour of the mysterious 'autonomy of structuration', the cryptic relation between 'signifier and signified', the clash of something called 'ideology' and something called 'discourse' – all of which play out on an abstract and alien terrain where concepts and structures seem to exist independently and autonomously over and above the human world which gave birth to them. What I think Eagleton's torturous paragraph provides (and numerous others which pepper his awful book) is the creation of a fetish, the raising up of a mystical and alien conceptual realm which is then worshipped by those who feel themselves to be its gatekeepers – to have privileged access to its mysteries and secrets – but at the same time they have only ever succeeded in prostrating themselves before what is, in essence, a lifeless, ossified 'thing'. Or to say the same, what Eagleton has succeeded in doing is to take the living fluid categories of historical development in Marxist thought and transmute them into the fixed and petrified forms of the structures which pervade Althusserian 'Ideology' and Foucauldian 'discourse'; that is, he has transfigured those same living social and historical categories into dead 'things'. His thought performs a comprehensive act of reification, even if it is one which he remains oblivious to.

Once more, one could argue that this is an example snatched from an early section of Eagleton's career and is not representative therein. But again, returning to his 2013 book, that same rather bizarre and jarring combination of discourse theory, Althusserian structuralism, semiotics and Lacanian psychoanalysis, is on display when it comes to the task of describing what literature is and what it does. Let's take a paragraph which explicitly addresses this question. On page 83 Eagleton writes:

A lyrical poem or realist novel presents what is meant to be an irreducibly specific reality; but because the signs it uses are only signs because they are iterable, capable of being deployed in other contexts, any particular literary statement packs a wealth of general connotations into itself. It is thus that the singular comes to behave as a microcosm, condensing whole possible worlds in its slim compass. The more texts are fashioned and framed to display this duality, the more they conventionally approach the condition of literature. Literary texts typically exploit the double nature of discourse by portraying irreducibly specific situations which are at the same time, by the very nature of language, of more general import.[31]

Here we have many of the same motifs, the semiotics, the discourse theory, the arid and brittle formalism, the verbose language, the grandiose delivery – 'condensing whole possible worlds'. The mood is one of an Eagleton in flight, a superstar intellectual soaring across the stratosphere buoyed up on the world-historic concepts of the great and the good, dazzling us with the firework display of his own blazing erudition. But it all has the tone and feeling of a conjurer's trick. For when you actually go behind the weighty intellectualism of the exhibition, what is actually being relayed here? What do you really learn? We are told how the work of literature presents what is meant to be a 'specific reality' but it does so through 'signs' – signs which are capable of being deployed in other contexts – so any 'literary statement packs a wealth of general connotations into itself'. For this reason, any literary statement exhibits a 'duality' between the universal and particular.

But is it only a 'literary statement' which behaves this way? What about a sentence from a property surveyor's report? Or a court summons? If you receive a letter through the door stating 'You are due to stand trial on the 14th', that refers to a specific person in a specific situation (i.e. yourself), but at the same time, the possibility of holding a trial is part of a broader and more universal legal framework which is not limited to this or that individual in isolation. It can apply to everyone and anyone. You understand what the letter is referring to – even if you, yourself, have never had the experience of being on trial before – precisely because the 'trial' concept is a general one. The court summons, therefore, refers to 'an irreducibly specific reality' (you are being prosecuted because you stole that bag of crisps from this branch of Marks and Spencer) but at the same time it 'packs a wealth of general connotations into itself'.

In fact, one might go further. Is there any word that doesn't display this duality of the general and the particular? When I point out how beautiful that particular red rose over there is, shining in the light, you understand exactly what I mean because you are possessed of the more general concepts of 'beauty', 'red' and rosiness'; the particular, therefore, only ever reveals itself in the light of the universal. With the exception of proper nouns, there are no words which don't reflect this duality. No words which don't, of necessity, refer to something which is both universal and particular. It is not just 'literary texts' or 'literary statements' which work this way. All language works this way. So when Eagleton – through the mystical rhetoric of 'discourse' and 'whole possible worlds' and 'signs' and 'microcosms' – eventually exhausts a paragraph packed with dense, exotic phrases and concepts, what we are left with is the revolutionary and stunning proposition that *literature is in fact constituted by language*. When you unpack everything Eagleton has said, what remains is the most banal of truisms.

And whatever else, this reveals the incredibly formalistic nature of the concepts on offer here – the fact that, when you go behind the scenes, they are not telling you much of anything at all. The ultimate meaning is an empty one. And this is due to the concepts themselves – 'structures' 'discourses', 'signs' and so on – being abstracted from social realities. Concepts which are opaque, nebulous and lost in space precisely because they have been separated from the very life processes of humanity which confer meaning. When one tries to press Eagleton's account to find out exactly what he means when he talks about something like 'discourse', one receives the indelible impression that he isn't quite sure himself. He lurches between the inscrutable and the most flagrant self-contradiction. In one chapter Eagleton defines discourse as 'the use of language for strategic ends in practical situations'[32] but in the very next Eagleton writes that literary works are 'snatches of "discourse"' as opposed to 'specimens of "language"'[33] blithely unaware that he is contradicting the definition he has set up only pages before.

And if these are your methodological 'building blocks', to so speak – that is, if you can't manage to provide the basic concepts of your theory with any type of internal coherence – then the analysis which is developed on the back of them becomes ever more vague and unintelligible. If Eagleton doesn't really know what he himself means when he wields the concept of 'discourse', he has even less of a chance of getting to grips with other concepts which he uses the notion of 'discourse' to inform. A case in point. 'Ideology' is another big player in the Eagleton oeuvre and he uses the concept of 'discourse' to illuminate it. Eagleton writes: 'Ideology is the neuralgic point where power impacts discourse and bends it out of true.'[34] God only knows why the word 'neuralgic' is employed here as it involves short sharp stabbing pains to a nerve (though people who have had to read a good deal of Eagleton's prose might have some level of familiarity with the concept). More importantly, though, the statement is simply gobbledegook.

Of course one might argue that the current writer – lacking the world-historic genius of a figure like Eagleton – simply doesn't have the brain power to get to the bottom of it. All well and good, but it doesn't explain the fact that at a different place in the book 'ideology' is no longer something which is drawn into contradiction with discourse – 'bending it out of true' (whatever that might mean) – rather 'ideology' and 'discourse' now become synonymous as when Eagleton describes the writer's unconscious motivations as manifesting in terms of 'ideological discourse'.[35] In another book, Eagleton informs us that 'ideology' is that of which 'discourse is the product'[36] but in the same chapter of that book Eagleton also explains 'ideological construction' is '*contingent*' to the nature of 'discourse'.[37] Such flagrant contradictions are at work all the time, ultimately working towards the complete dissolution of meaning.

Occasionally, however, Eagleton treats ideology in the classical Marxist sense – i.e. a political and cultural conception of the world which expresses given social and class interests. And when he treats it in this way what he has to say becomes at once more interesting, freed from the drudgery and burden of the dead weight of Althusserian structuralist categories; he has, for instance, some very interesting things to say about the ideological standpoint of the poet T. S. Eliot. Eliot, for Eagleton, is particularly attuned to the fragmentation of capitalist life which was brought to fruition by the First World War because he was in some way 'disinherited … by industrial capitalist America', preferring to look back in time, raising up an *ideological* vision of '"blood", breeding and "organic" regionalism' expressed by the 'right-wing neo-agrarian movement in Virginia'.[38] T. S. Eliot's ability to conjure up the fragmentation of post-First World War capitalism was a product of his roots in a more agrarian society which was tightly bonded in a more organic cohesion by patriarchal tradition and an explicitly racial division of labour – it was from a conservative-traditionalist standpoint, therefore, that Eliot was able to level his beautiful and poetic critique of the modern world.

But in a different chapter in the same book, Eagleton is back to describing 'ideology' in a purely ahistorical and Althusserian fashion when he writes:

The literary work appears free – self producing and self-determining … but this freedom simply conceals its more fundamental determination by the constituents of its ideological matrix … The pseudo-real of the literary text is the product of the ideologically saturated demands of its modes of representation … The text is a tissue of meanings, perceptions and responses which inhere in the first place in that imaginary production of the real which is ideology.[39]

The fluidity and clarity of the short section on Eliot where Eagleton mobilizes the categories of living history – i.e. the social and economic character of the American South – is thrown into relief by the type of dead, dense language which underpins his retreat back into the most fashionable forms of structuralism and Lacanian psychoanalysis. Again we find the same bereavement of meaning, again the same physical, brittle lexicon to describe something which is actually metaphysical and social in essence – note how the text has an 'ideological matrix', how it forms in a 'tissue' of meaning. But, most of all, note the rather clumsy contradiction which is set smack bang in the middle of his ramblings – 'the literary text is the product of … ideologically saturated demands' while in the next instance the text is responsible for 'the imaginary production of the real which is ideology'. In the first moment 'ideology' is seen as the source for 'the real'; in the second it is the other way round.

The concept of 'the real' is one that Eagleton draws upon too in an utterly haphazard and contradictory manner. Sometimes he seems to use 'the real' to refer to the social and historical backdrop to the text – he talks about something called 'the historical real',[40] sometimes he talks about a 'political real' (though how that is different from a historical real is never to be discovered), there is a 'textual real'[41] and a 'pseudo real'[42] and so on, and Eagleton flits between all these definitions in a rather random and devil-may-care fashion, but his utter disregard for meaning and consistency means that he once again generates the most flagrant of contradictions from within the midst of his own rambling diatribes. For example, on page 69 we discover that '[i]deology … produces and constructs the real' whereas a couple of pages after we discover that the opposite is true when Eagleton reveals that 'ideological character' is rather determined by 'the real'.[43] But more than anything else, Eagleton tends to use the concept of 'the real' as a Lacanian alternative to historical development. The 'real' is something which possesses us before we enter into the world of language;[44] according to Lacan, it demarks the state of initial harmony and purity which all human beings encounter before they are pulled into the realm of language (and social relationships), and in this sense the real is a transcendental condition which is prior to historical development. Eagleton writes that '[t]o enter language is to be severed from what Lacan calls the "real", that inaccessible realm which is always beyond the reach of signification, always outside the symbolic order' and yet 'we will spend all of our lives hunting for it'.[45]

In *The Event of Literature*, Eagleton has already provided continuity with much of his early work by describing literature in the purely formalistic terms of the structuralist concepts of 'ideology' and 'discourse', but to the formalist critique is added a given content. The *raison d'être* of literature, according to Eagleton, does not depend on in some way capturing the unfolding life of the historical whole, the process of generations and generations of human beings making and remaking their world; rather 'literature would seem to depend for its existence on a certain loss or distancing of the real, and this absence is vitally constitutive of its presence ... the work seeks to compensate for this loss of the real'.[46] With one final contrary flourish – 'this absence is vitally constitutive of its presence' – Eagleton's abandonment of Marxism and the method of historical materialism is complete. The living historical process is irrevocably displaced by the transcendental category of the 'thing'. Reification reaches its fruition.

In an incisive and penetrating essay – albeit one which is penned from a highly conservative viewpoint – the sharp American art critic Roger Kimball also honed in on Eagleton's propensity to flit between various and contradictory definitions of an array of concepts: 'Professor Eagleton's primary weapons against the charge of vulgar Marxism are words like "hegemony," "ideology," and "aesthetic," all of which in his hands have the wonderful property of meaning any of about six different and conflicting things.'[47] The reverence and deference the current left tends to grant towards its 'superstar' intellectuals means it often falls to the intelligent right-wing critic to point out the simple inconsistencies, flagrant errors and the ridiculousness of much of what is on offer – he or she being the only one to actually exclaim with a gasp of exasperation – 'hey that guy isn't wearing any clothes!' But beyond his wry lampooning of Eagleton's grad school pretentiousness, Kimball's article has hit upon a genuine, fundamental feature of Eagleton's oeuvre – that is, the sheer eclecticism which runs through it, which seems to deflect any single interpretation or any level of coherency and objectivity.

Kimball, it seems, has had his rather sardonic gaze focused on such figures and such trends in 'Marxist' Literary Theory for some time, for he also provides a pithy but telling overview of the work of Eagleton's colleague and comrade-in-arms, and perhaps the most influential living literary theorist writing today – Fredric Jameson. In another witty and cutting article, Kimball goes to work satirizing some of Jameson's more ridiculous pronouncements, but along with the acidity of his irony, Kimball is able to pinpoint the same methodological tendency as he unearthed in Eagleton; that is, the vast body of work which constitutes Jameson's immense output is underpinned by a similar insoluble mix of often conflicting and contradictory positions – a sporadic and haphazard eclecticism which works against the grain of any cohesive historical unfolding driven by the type of class conflict which is at work in the whole:

> It's rare that you find him arguing for economic determinism or the proletariat or the revolution in any straightforward way … He regularly updates, supplements, massages ideas culled from Marx while mixing and matching interpretive categories drawn from later Marxist and quasi-Marxist thinkers. If this makes for rather a thick stew, so be it. In the end, it is not Marxism so much as a generalized left-leaning radicalism – what the critic Frederick Crews aptly summed up as Left Eclecticism – that informs Professor Jameson's critical enterprise. Marxism itself functions as a reservoir of slogans and political animus, but its fundamental tenets are often neglected in favor of other more recherché critical approaches and attitudes.[48]

In what is perhaps his most famous work, *The Political Unconscious*, Jameson himself affirms his fidelity to a 'Marxist' approach to understanding literature, but when he begins to lay out his stall we actually discover several different and clashing methodological trends. First off, Jameson draws upon the Lacanian roots of Althusser's 'philosophy' to provide his own account of the relationship between history and the text: 'history is not a text, not a narrative, master or otherwise, but that as an absent cause, it is inaccessible to us except in textual form, and that our approach to it and to the Real itself necessarily passes through its prior textualization, its narrativization in the political unconscious'. Again we find a depressingly familiar scenario. There is the tortuous and mangled language which seems to hint at great revelation, but when you actually break it down it doesn't reveal all that much at all. For example, how many of us are shocked into surprise when we are treated to the epiphany that 'history is not a text'? Indeed it is not – neither is it a letter, or a name, or a rose, or a dog named Barney. In addition, there is the loose conglomeration of concepts which often seem contradictory and self-refuting. We are told that the Lacanian real is somehow translated into the 'political unconscious' in and through 'narrativization' but how does that actually happen? Aside from everything else, the process of narration is a conscious and deliberate endeavour. How can it take place in an 'unconscious' – political or otherwise?

But primarily we encounter the same abiding theme – history as something which is unknowable in the rationalist sense, 'an absent cause', to use the Althusserian term, and we can only encounter it through 'the text'. Why that is so is anyone's guess. Don't we in some way encounter history when we go to the polling station to vote, when we have an argument about whether or not women are good drivers, when we attend a protest and pull down a statue or when we refuse to answer the door to a Jehovah's witness, when we look upon a Rembrandt painting or superstitiously step around a ladder to avoid walking underneath it? Don't we encounter history and its forms and traditions in a thousand and one myriad ways every day of our lives? Why on earth do we 'encounter' history only through 'the text'? Of course, when you are a top-flight intellectual in the mould of an Eagleton or Jameson, providing the answers to such simple and piffling questions is beneath you – if indeed you trifle to consider them at all. But once more we are made witness to the type of methodological operation which sees the historical moment narrowed down – 'an absent cause' – and ultimately vanquished in favour of some transcendental category (in this case the Lacanian 'Real' yet again).

Moving from Althusser and Lacan, Jameson turns to the highly formal approach of semiotics, particularly that of Algirdas Julien Greimas. For Jameson, Greimas's work can be repurposed through a Marxist lens but when Jameson outlines the way in which this is achieved, one again comes to understand that any Marxist theory of objective historical development has long since been nullified. Jameson argues that one of Greimas's more central (and surreal) concepts – that of the 'semiotic rectangle' – becomes 'a vital instrument for exploring the semantic and ideological intricacies of the text'[49] though why a 'semiotic triangle' or a 'semiotic octagon' or 'semiotic giraffe' might not do the job equally well is never quite explained. Nevertheless, Jameson's dalliance with the ridiculous is only getting started, as from there he proceeds to lay out Greimas's approach in broader terms:

Greimas' scheme, constructed by means of purely logical or analytical negations, by its very exhaustiveness, opens up a place for the practise of a more genuinely dialectical negation in the tension between the realised and unrealised terms; what for Greimas is to be formulated as a structural homology between the various levels on which the semiotic rectangle reproduces itself, for us, on the contrary, becomes powerfully restructured into a relationship of tension between presence and absence, a relationship that can be mapped according to the various dynamic possibilities (generation, projection, compensation, repression, displacement) ... So the literary structure, far from being completely realized on any one of its levels tilts powerfully into the underside or *impense or nondit*, in short, into the very political unconscious of the text, such that the latter's dispersed semes – when reconstructed according to this model of ideological closure – themselves then insistently direct us to the informing power of forces or contradictions which the text seeks in vain to wholly control or master ... Thus, by means of a radically historicizing reappropriation, the ideal of logical closure which initially seems incompatible with dialectical thinking, now proves to be an indispensable instrument for revealing those logical and ideological centres a particular historical text fails to realise, or on the contrary seeks desperately to repress.[50]

Again we hear the claxon blasts of the same grandiose trumpeting – Jameson working on the furthest frontiers of thought, revolutionizing all that has gone before in 'a radically historicizing reappropration', presenting his readers with 'the practise of a more genuinely dialectical negation', opening up new and 'dynamic possibilities'. And behind all the wind and hot air of these swirling and verbose sentences, the reader is once more implicated in the never-ending struggle to extract anything vaguely resembling sense or meaning. The 'literary structure' 'tilts' into the 'political unconscious of the text' and the text then disperses its 'semes'[51] (like a dandelion its seeds?), but those 'semes' are now somehow 'reconstructed' (by what?) according to a 'model of ideological closure' (whatever that means) which then directs us towards 'forces and contradictions' (of what?) which the text 'seeks in vain to wholly control or master' (can a text 'seek in vain'?).

Again one is confronted by an entirely reified reality. It is not the human mind which possesses an 'unconscious' but rather 'the text' itself; it is not social classes, groups or individuals which are possessed of life and movement, but rather a 'literary structure' which somehow manages to 'tilt' into the 'unconscious of the text'; it is not people, societies, plants or cells which have the ability to reproduce, rather it is those 'semiotic rectangles'; and last but not least, it is not human beings embroiled in history's flux, seeking to master the forces and contradictions which open up from within their own social and economic forms of organization, rather such 'forces and contradictions' are displaced onto some independent and autonomous realm which the text itself 'seeks in vain to wholly control or master'.

Jameson has accrued considerable acclaim and a wide readership writing in precisely this way, no doubts because his legions of fans believe that the sheer complexity of the sentences which fissure into implacable, impenetrable and labyrinthine convolutions must, by virtue of their very opaqueness, signify the sheer depth and profundity of the mind which is generating them. And in reading someone of such utter world-historic brilliance, his acolytes no doubts believe that such brightness is refracted back onto them. Debating with such people is always going to be a thankless task, but to anyone who comes to Jameson and is bedazzled by the density of the language and the opaqueness of the concepts, I would ask them simply this: the 'semiotic rectangle' or the 'Lacanian Real' or 'the political unconscious of the text' or Althusser's 'absent cause' – take any one of these concepts and try to apply them to an actual text. To Dostoyevsky's *The Idiot*, to Hesiod's *Theogony* or to J.K. Rowling's *Harry Potter*. Take a few moments to reflect on what that 'semiotic rectangle' or that 'absent cause' has actually helped you to understand about the text in question and the world in which it was written. And if, ultimately, you draw a blank, then know it is fine to say just that – that the first step to a worthwhile analysis is taken when we are able to look at pretentious and preposterous figures like Fredric Jameson with the clear and empowering recognition: *they are simply not wearing any clothes*.

Kimball, with no small degree of astuteness, has described the sheer eclecticism of the Jameson project as a 'thick stew'. And to this murky brew of Althusserian, Lacanian and semiotic methodologies, Jameson now puts forward his 'historical' approach, one which he describes as 'Marxist'. He identifies three different layers to his approach:

> [S]uch semantic enrichment and enlargement of the inert givens and materials of a particular text must take place within three concentric frameworks, which mark a widening out of the sense of the social ground of the text through the notions, first, of political history, in the narrow sense of punctual event and a chronicle-like sequence of happenings in time; then of society, in the already less diachronic and time-bound sense of a constitutive tension and struggle between social classes; and ultimately, of history now conceived in its vastest sense of the sequence of modes of production and the succession and destiny of the various human social formations, from prehistoric life to whatever far future history has in store for us.[52]

This is mechanical and clumsy, to say the least, perhaps because Jameson has such little feel for living history – by the standards of the author more generally, however, it is remarkably clear and coherent. And he brings into the analysis the role of social classes. Unfortunately when he goes into more detail on the issue we experience yet another reversion to a more reified paradigm; Jameson tells us that when it comes to class 'our object of study will prove to be the ideologeme, that is the smallest intelligible unit of the essentially antagonistic collective discourses of social classes'.[53] The use of 'ideologeme' is telling here, the conversion of 'meaning' into a quantified, reified physical thing – i.e. a 'unit' – and telling too is the use of 'discourse' which in Foucauldian and post-Marxist theory works as a stand in for the notion of class as a social relation to the means of production in the true Marxist sense.

But more generally the separation between the second 'framework' and the third is problematic. The second relates to the 'struggle between social classes' while the third relates to the 'sequence of modes of production' but anyone with the slightest acquaintance with Marxism would understand that the 'sequence of modes of production' is driven precisely by the class struggle. Treating these two moments in a discrete fashion allows Jameson to treat the mode of production as something almost independent of historical formation driven by living class conflict; in other words, it allows Jameson to treat a mode of production not as a social relation but as a purely given 'thing'. It allows Jameson to once again reify class.

And we can see this very clearly in terms of his analysis of Lukács which forms a chapter of another one of his most well-known books, *Marxism and Form*. Here Jameson ponders Lukács' conception of reification, and he goes into the question of why, for Lukács, the consciousness of the bourgeoisie is unable to transcend a reified perspective, whereas from the standpoint of the proletariat, reification can be overcome. Jameson begins by summarizing Lukács' account of Kantianism:

> According to Kant, the mind can understand everything about external reality except the incomprehensible and contingent fact of its existence in the first place: it can deal exhaustively with its own perceptions of reality without ever being able to come to terms with noumena, or things-in-themselves. For Lukács, however, this dilemma of classical philosophy, to which Kant's system is a monument, derives from an even more fundamental, prephilosophical attitude toward the world which is ultimately socio-economic in character.[54]

I have never heard Kant's system being described as 'prephilosophical' but that's a minor quibble; otherwise what we have here is an accurate summary, for Lukács believed that Kantianism – as the pinnacle of bourgeois thought – carried in its philosophical form the limitations of the bourgeoisie as a class at the level of 'socio-economic' existence. But what about these limitations? Jameson explains that the 'life experiences of the middle classes in the economic and social realm'[55] mean that they are compelled to understand 'the objects that they produce ... the commodities, the factories, the very structure of capitalism itself'[56] in a purely contemplative fashion.

> The middle classes understand our relationship to external objects (and consequently our knowledge of those objects) in static and contemplative fashion. It is as though our primary relationship to the things of the outside world were not one of making or use, but rather that of a motionless gaze, in a moment of time suspended, across a gap which it subsequently becomes impossible for thought to bridge.[57]

Again we get a similar array of sweeping grandiose pronouncements, the same purple prose – that 'motionless gaze', that 'time suspended'.

But once you set aside the 'epic majesty' of the rhetoric, you once again realize that Jameson has got this all wrong. He says that the middle classes, by virtue of their socio-economic position, cannot conceive of a relationship to the outside world which is 'about making or use' but that is simply ridiculous. What factory owner doesn't try to make use of his or her workers, the technology they invest in, the land they purchase – as much as they possibly can with an eye to securing profit? Indeed any commodity a capitalist (or anyone else) purchases must first manifest as a 'use value' in order to eventually be realized as an exchange value. All Jameson would have had to do was familiarize himself with the first chapter of Karl Marx's masterwork when the great German revolutionist noted exactly this in a prose a little simpler and direct than Jameson's own.

More importantly still, it is not Lukács' attitude in the slightest either. For Lukács, the capitalist remains sundered in a 'reified' consciousness, because the social-economic forms of reality appear in a reified manner which confirms in the capitalist his own ability to make and remake the outside world. Capital appropriates a portion of surplus value which the commodity labour power generates, and this is key to the profit of the capitalist, but such a relationship of exploitation is obscured by the reifying effect of what appears to be a mere exchange of things – i.e. a day's wage in return for a day's labour. Because the true source of his profit is obscured by the effects of reification, the capitalist experiences profit creation as something emanating from his own activities *vis-à-vis* the productive process; that is, the true form of productivity and profit creation appears to him as the result of the ingenuity and guile he deploys in order to invest in wages, technology and property, or as Lukács puts it, for the capitalist profit creation 'necessarily appears as an activity … [whose] … effects emanate from himself'.[58] Far from creating a purely 'static and contemplative' attitude to the world, the reification process actually bolsters in the capitalist his sense of determining and shaping the forms and structures of his own reality. He is, to put it in the Marxian refrain, 'at home in his alienation'.

Jameson's analysis of the position of the proletarian – according to a Lukácsian framework – is equally wrong-headed and incompetent. Jameson begins by arguing how, according to Lukács, the worker is able to overcome a reified consciousness by winning through to a 'knowledge of himself as an object, toward self-consciousness. Yet this self-consciousness, because it is initially knowledge of an object (himself, his own labor as a commodity, his life force which he is under the obligation to sell), permits him more genuine knowledge of the commodity nature of the outside world than is granted to middle-class "objectivity."'[59] Jameson's opening gambit is abstract but unobjectionable; it is very true that, for Lukács, the worker is in some sense a living commodity and that the ability to recognize this is in somewise tied to the ability of the working class, by virtue of its economic position at the level of social existence, to go beyond the reified appearance. But the worker's knowledge of herself as a 'living commodity' is not the knowledge of just any commodity under capitalism. It is the knowledge of a very specific commodity – i.e. that of labour power. It is true that Jameson mentions this fleetingly – 'his own labour as a commodity' – but this is not carried through to the body of the analysis. Instead Jameson states:

> The worker, on the other hand, knows the finished product as little more than a moment in the process of production itself: his attitude toward the outside world will thereby be significantly altered. For he will see the objects around him in terms of change, rather than in the timeless 'natural' present of the middle class universe (with its corresponding emphasis on man as a universal).[60]

In this paragraph we can see the decisive critical manoeuvre; Jameson moves away from 'his own labour as a commodity' and towards 'the finished product' as being the decisive category in terms of informing the worker's 'attitude toward the outside world'. This might seem like a trivial or inconsequential issue but, in fact, it is critical. Reification, for Lukács, is not simply about any society where there is a high level of commodity production; rather it involves a society where labour power appears in its commodity form as the general social relation of exploitation (capitalism). In other words, reification (and the worker's ability to overcome it) is based on the social relationship of exploitation which opens up between labour-power and capital. But when Jameson shifts the focus from 'labour as a commodity' to 'the finished product' – i.e. when he shifts the focus from a relationship of exploitation to the generic commodity – he is at the same time performing a reifying act; that is, he is converting a social relationship into a 'thing'. In Jameson's account the worker, being part of the productive process, now watches the 'product' being shaped and finished – i.e. she sees a particular product on the factory line in a process of flux, and thus Jameson is able to conclude that the same worker will be able to recognize 'all objects around her in terms of change', even history itself.

This is, of course, naive and idealist in the extreme. A millionaire financier might spend his days watching the never-ending fluctuations of stocks and share prices on a giant screen on the Wall Street Stock Exchange floor, but despite his awareness of such movement, one might still question his ability to develop a revolutionary approach to historical change and to overcome in consciousness the forms and modes of a reified reality. But again the real issue here is what a decisive break Jameson makes with Lukács himself while purporting to outline the theory of the latter. In Lukács' view, the worker is able to transcend a reified consciousness precisely because she is the bearer of the commodity form as labour power. When the capitalist seeks to exploit the labour power of the proletarian, he – the capitalist – is compelled to treat the worker in a purely reified fashion, i.e. as one more motive force – one more 'thing' in the productive process. The capitalist can only relate to the worker in this way, as a quantifiable element whose productive capacity the capitalist seeks to optimize – just like any ordinary piece of machinery.

In this way, the capitalist (depending on circumstances) may adjust the worker's pay or their hours or work rate – all of which are quantitative calculations designed, in the last analysis, to maximize the overall profit margins of the company as a whole. For this reason the capitalist, by virtue of his social position, cannot pierce the reified veil in which social relationships appear in the guise of the exchange of things. The capitalist cannot perceive in profit creation the exploitation of living labour by capital in and through the appropriation of surplus value. When he sees the worker in the production process the capitalist does not perceive the social relationship which makes of the worker a worker but is compelled only to see the 'thing', only to see one more quantifiable element in the production process which can be adjusted and tweaked – to relate to the worker on that basis, depressing wages, increasing working hours and so forth.

But those same sets of adjustments which, from the purview of capital, take place in a purely quantified way impact the worker as a qualitative determinant of her existence more broadly; they determine whether she can take her children on holiday, or they determine the type of education her children receive or in many cases they will even work to determine the duration of her lifespan. Lukács describes how '[t]he quantitative differences in exploitation which appear to the capitalist in the form of quantitative determinants of the objects of his calculation, must appear to the worker as the decisive, qualitative categories of … [her] … whole physical, mental and moral existence'.[61]

The worker, then, has the potential to better comprehend the use value, the living social existence which underpins the reified, quantified realm of exchange value precisely because she contains within herself both moments embodied in the commodity form as labour power. It is labour power in its dual aspect as use and exchange which underpins her ability to recognize that capital is an alien and alienating form, but to understand that it is simultaneously underpinned by the mental and physical productions of her own essential being set into motion by a given social relationship: 'The special nature of labour as a commodity … [t]he specific nature of this kind of commodity had consisted in the fact that beneath the cloak of the thing lay a relation between men, that beneath the quantifying crust, there was a qualitative, living core.'[62]

Ultimately, the worker's ability to achieve genuine self-determination and control over the human powers she sets into motion depends on her capacity to relieve the forms of labour her activity calls into being of their alienated character. To possess them in a self-conscious way, to return them to herself. Not only to perceive the cleavage which opens up in her existence between use and exchange, between the qualitative aspect of her authentic existence and the reified aspect of her working life which is embodied in capital, but having once acquired this knowledge, to then act upon it in order to change it. But what shape would such action, such change, take?

In order to answer that question we are once again returned to the Marxist-Hegelian notion of totality. We have already seen how, for Hegel, totality involves a series of moments which are drawn together in the unfolding whole. Marx gives us an example of Hegelian totality when he describes how an initial moment – a situation in which the individual peasant proprietor controls a small plot – is eventually superseded when the great mass of direct producers are severed from their properties on the land and converted into landless wage labourers who are concentrated in great hubs of socialized production which are at the same time the private property of a few capitalist owners. But this again sets the basis by which a higher moment can be called into being: 'Centralisation of the means of production and socialisation of labour at last reach a point where they become incompatible with their capitalist integument. This integument is burst asunder. The knell of capitalist private property sounds. The expropriators are expropriated.'[63] By taking control of the means of production, the proletariat 'does not re-establish private property for the producer, but gives him individual property based on the acquisition of the capitalist era: i.e., on cooperation and the possession in common of the land and of the means of production'.[64]

But in taking control of the means of production, the proletariat also takes control of the whole, of the unfolding process which yielded the feudal and capitalist moments – moments which reach their historical fruition by shaping the basis of a 'universal' class which has the ability to take control of the fundamental means by which all human life is created and recreated in the democratic interests of collective humanity. And this is why the role of the 'soviets' or the 'workers' councils' is so essential. For the Lukács of *History and Class Consciousness*, the workers' councils are the means by which the workers achieve and regulate self-consciously the means of production in accordance – not with the prerogatives of exchange value and capital expansion – but with the richness and qualitative needs of the authentic human existence. The overcoming of reification, for Lukács therefore, is a product of the ability of the working class to theoretically and self-consciously apprehend the historical nature of the capitalist social system and its own position within it by virtue of the fact that the proletarian is the living embodiment of use and exchange value as a bearer of labour power in its commoditized form; moreover this theoretical consciousness is capable of being translated into revolutionary action by the fact that the proletariat – by virtue of its structural position and collective sweep – has the ability to place *the totality* of society's economic organs under its collective control and determine economic output in accordance with authentic human need. In this way, the proletariat abolishes reification, for it ends the social relationship of exploitation which undergirds the capitalist system – the exploitation of labour by capital – and thus ends in practice the very process which allows social relationships to appear in the guise of an exchange of things. In this way, the proletariat abolishes itself as a class. Lukács writes:

> The revolutionary workers' council … is one of the forms which the consciousness of the proletariat has striven to create ever since its inception. The fact that it exists and is constantly developing shows that the proletariat already stands on the threshold of its own consciousness and hence on the threshold of victory. The workers' council spells the political and economic defeat of reification. In the period following the dictatorship [of the proletariat] it will eliminate the bourgeois separation of the legislature, administration and judiciary … this situation can be explained on the basis of the Marxist theory of class struggle and class consciousness. The proletariat only perfects itself by annihilating and transcending itself, by creating the classless society through the successful conclusion of its own class struggle.[65]

For Lukács, therefore, Marxism of necessity is the description of the totality unfolded as a series of unified historical moments – precisely because the proletariat as a class contains the ability to submit the totality to itself at the level of practical existence in and through the creation of workers' councils and the self-conscious control of the means of production determined in line with the needs of the majority. In the Hegelian-Marxist-Lukácsian philosophy we can now see how the concept of the totality is bound to the class position of the proletariat as the culmination of a historical unfolding which involves a unity of theory (the ability of the proletariat to see beyond the reified veil and penetrate the 'mystery' of surplus value) and practice (the ability of the proletariat to act on that knowledge, to organize the totality of human production in accordance with the totality of human needs).

Jameson has understood virtually none of this. Because he traduces Lukács so pitifully – because he makes the lynchpin of Lukács' concept of reification – not labour power in its commodity form, but the generic commodity itself. The worker simply sees the commodity rolled out as a 'finished product' and therefore identifies it as a moment in the generic process of production, and from this, Jameson argues, the worker is then able to see all things in their guise as aspects of historical change, developing the possibility of a more revolutionary perspective therein. But in arguing that the proletarian develops the possibility of a revolutionary consciousness in and through her experience of the way in which a generic commodity is produced, Jameson abnegates Lukács' actual analysis which insists that the possibility of a revolutionary consciousness is premised on the material fact of the worker being a bearer of a particular commodity, *that of labour power* – i.e. that commodity which embodies both use and exchange values at the level of the worker's social existence and which allows that worker to make the transition in consciousness from the reified appearance to the recognition of the social relation of exploitation that lies at the basis of that appearance.

This, in turn, informs the possibility of revolutionary practice and the need to take control of the means of production. But because Jameson himself reifies the Lukácsian account, because he replaces the centrality of the commodity labour power (and the social relationship of exploitation which constitutes it) with the account of a 'thing' – i.e. any generic, mechanically produced commodity on the factory line – he also removes the rationale for the way in which the worker's own social existence, embodied as the commodity labour power, allows her to make the transition from the reified appearance to the social essence in consciousness. In so doing, he (Jameson) removes the possibility of the revolutionary practice which follows from this. Such revolutionary practice is itself grounded in the ability of the proletariat to conceive the historical unfolding of the totality in theory (Marxism) before realizing it at the level of practical existence in and through its revolutionary seizure of the means of production in terms of the social whole. The Marxist category of 'totality', therefore, is bound to the social existence of the proletarian as uniquely structured around the commodity labour power; the ability to conceive the totality as a historical unfolding can only be achieved from the perspective of the proletariat which as a class – as the living bearer of the commodity labour power – has the propensity to bring the totality to its self-conscious fruition.

Jameson understands next to nothing of this. For him the worker has the potential for revolutionary consciousness not as a consequence of the social relation of exploitation she is in thrall to but because she 'knows the finished product as little more than a moment in the process of production itself'. And for this reason, any understanding of totality as the historical unfolding which culminates in the ability to take control of the means of production on the part of the working class and the capacity to raise that same totality in conscious thought – i.e. a unity of theory and practice – is annulled in favour of a conception of totality which is static, abstract and purely conceptual, bereft of historical life therein. Jameson describes how 'inasmuch as he knows the interrelationship of tools and equipment to each other, [the worker] ... will come to see the outside world not as a collection of separate, unrelated things, but as a totality in which everything depends on everything else'.[66] So the worker's consciousness of the totality is simply an aggregate image of an organic whole in which 'everything depends on everything else' and she gains this understanding because she realizes there is an 'interrelationship of tools and equipment to each other' in the workplace.

To use this as the basis for revolutionary consciousness is not only idealistic in the purest sense, it is patently ridiculous. In the Roman manufactory workshops of old, slaves would also have been confronted by the 'interrelationship of tools and equipment to each other', but the idea that they could have approached the philosophical conception of totality which is the province of Marxism and ultimately underpins the revolutionary consciousness of the modern working class and its historical trajectory is simply absurd. The conception of the whole being shaped by the interrelation of the parts is an important one, philosophically speaking, but it is difficult to say how such a conception of totality is any different from the philosophical conceptions of a Spinoza or certain conceptions of the totality discoverable in religious thought like Hinduism or Buddhism.

What's more, by reverting to a pre-Hegelian concept of the totality, by focusing on the purely physical features of the workplace – 'interrelationship of tools and equipment to each other' – Jameson detaches revolutionary consciousness from its necessary basis in a social relationship of exploitation which is mobilized in and through the commodity labour power. The worker's ability to develop a revolutionary understanding of capitalism is grounded in their class position at the level of social existence, because this, in turn, is bound to their capacity to fundamentally transform the social mode of production in practice. But when one removes revolutionary consciousness from its necessary grounding in social being – as Jameson does when he asserts that it is because the worker sees the 'interrelationship of tools and equipment to each other' that she is able to develop a notion of totality therein – one is also tempted to respond; well, so what?

For if the worker or any other person (let's say a bio-chemist who is studying microscopic organisms and is constantly being confronted by the way in which the whole is the sum of the parts) becomes aware that the social world comprises a totality in which the different sections are enmeshed, why should they act in a practical and revolutionary way? There is nothing in this knowledge in and of itself that will tend that person, of necessity, towards a more radical politics. They could well gravitate in that direction, of course, but equally they might end up taking a purely contemplative attitude towards the social whole. Because Jameson's vision of totality isn't developed from the proletarian's social existence as embodied in the commodity labour power it can never extend beyond a purely contemplative and idealistic posture; it is a conception which dooms theory to be forever divorced from practice, precisely because Jameson has succeeded in splitting the social consciousness of the proletariat from its grounding in social being. He does this in the name of Lukács but in so doing Jameson reveals his complete ignorance of Lukács' theory of reification and the Marxist-Hegelian philosophy which underpins it.

It might seem odd to devote so much time to Jameson on Lukács and the latter's theory of reification, but I do so for a reason. I think it clearly shows that Jameson, just as with Eagleton, simply doesn't understand what the concept of the totality entails from a Marxist point of view – that is, he doesn't comprehend it as a historical unfolding as a mediated whole. Jameson's comprehension of the 'totality' in terms of the sum total of a lifeless aggregate of different elements provides yet another way in which he is able to reify the Marxist conception of that same concept, transforming it from a living historical development into the strange and static interplay of 'thing-like' entities which manifest in almost purely structural, physical terms. In his 2016 book *Raymond Chandler: The Detections of Totality*, Jameson exemplifies this when he makes his notion of 'totality' the lynchpin of his analysis of the noir novelist's crime writing oeuvre.

According to Jameson, there are two central ways in which Chandler works to create a fictional image of the whole: 'the vaster totality of the natural landscape to the … purely logical systemization of the social order'.[67] To begin, how is the social order to be totalized? Jameson suggests that this happens primarily through the way in which Chandler sets up the opposition between the private and the public realms. Jameson argues that the private and the public realms the novelist depicts also represent an opposition between the authentic and inauthentic which opens up in social life. Jameson writes:

> What happens, however, is that the private 'unpresentable' areas behind the official reception rooms and 'fronts' come to be considered little by little as more 'real' than the areas designed for public appearance: it is in the backrooms then, and behind the scenes, that some more authentic activity takes place: and it is felt that only those who know such operations 'from the inside', that is to say, who know what goes on behind the counter and in the backroom, have any genuine knowledge (or know how) ... [this] serves to confirm the ideological opposition between authentic and inauthentic, serves therefore in a quasi-metaphysical way to reconfirm the idea of 'reality' itself.[68]

In looking at Chandler's fictional world in and through the opposition between the private and the public, the authentic and the inauthentic, Jameson poses the issue of the totality in a fascinating and significant way. There is this opposition in Chandler and it is a pronounced one. The sense of there being two worlds: the world of the public appearance – the politician grandstanding on the podium, the millionaire philanthropist, the oil tycoon who lives in a great mansion, the powerful police chief announcing a new crime initiative, the small town bigwig. And then there is the other world: the netherworld which operates behind the scenes – the call girls, the assassins, the gigolos and the grifters, the drunks and the dissolute, the lowly hotel concierge, the chauffeur driver; all the people who remain below the radar swathed in shadow.

Of course, one can only explain the first world by recourse to the second. It is the secret underworld of a vast underclass which can be used to reveal the endemic corruption at work behind the scenes and which gives life to the seedy activities of the dodgy politician or corrupt judge. And this is a class opposition too – the lives of the rich and privileged are in some sense parasitic on the darker underbelly of the life of the city. And it is from this perspective that the character of Philip Marlowe begins to make sense; he is in some way able to mediate both the 'public' facade and the 'private' essence. Marlowe himself is from the underclass; he himself is canny and shrewd, practical and ruthless; and he knows how to speak the language of the streets. This hardboiled P.I. becomes the means by which the two realms are mediated; often Marlowe is hired by someone 'respectable' and wealthy – someone very much in and of the 'public' realm, but in order to solve the mystery, Marlowe must penetrate the appearance and go to the social essence, using his underworld contacts and all his plebeian toughness and guile to figure out the complex network of social relationships and connections which led to the single 'event' of the crime itself.

And here we are presented with an unfolding totality; Marlowe becomes mediating factor in the process by which the first moment – the inauthentic appearance – is then drawn into relation with the 'authentic' backroom essence, and it is the unity of these moments which eventually culminates in the resolution of the case. This is an unfolding totality in the true Hegelian sense and in the same moment it also speaks to reification; the murder or the blackmail appears in the first instance to be an isolated and random and senseless 'thing', but Marlowe's job is to unpack and exhibit the living set of social contradictions and relationships which of necessity give rise to it, solving the mystery and relieving the crime of its 'reified' character therein.

Again Jameson manages to miss virtually all of this. And again, this is not accidental. His inability to conceive of the totality as a historical unfolding – but instead to see in it the lifeless aggregate of a series of ossified and often transcendental categories – means that he interprets the totality encompassed by the inauthentic 'public' realm and the authentic 'private' realm in a way which robs Chandler's work of all its living socio-historical content. Thus the opposition between the 'public' and the 'private' for Jameson is no longer underpinned by the social contradictions which open up between the different class layers, between the reified appearance and the social essence – rather the opposition allows us to understand

> the two-fold merit of grasping hermeneutic activity (whether that of the textual interpreter or that of Marlowe and other detectives) 1) as a ritual, as an activity whose connotative meaning confirms and secures an ideology which greatly transcends its immediate denotative intent (the immediate solution to the enigma or problem);

and 2) as a spatial form, that is, as an activity whose fundamental material organisation is to be found in space (rather than in cognitive categories)[69]

Of course, it is up to the reader to decide what type of meaning, if any, can be gleaned from an explanation such as this. But what I would hope is abundantly clear at this point, is that, whatever else, it has nothing in common with a Marxist analysis. And one should also note the element of reification underpinning what Jameson has written; again meaning is not to be discoverable in socio-historical forms but rather the way in which a 'fundamental material organisation is to be found in space' – i.e. the metaphysical *milieu* of social life is reduced to the purely physical and lifeless aspect of matter – 'to be found in space'.

In Jameson's second description of the type of totality which underpins Chandler's fictional world, something similar is on display. Here Jameson argues that totality, as the 'unifying mechanism of these novels',[70] reaches its most 'concrete expression' not in terms of the 'plots themselves' but rather in terms of the 'evolution of the weather'.[71] The weather, according to Jameson, 'holds together the otherwise random or even centrifugal tendency of the episodes to drift apart from one another',[72] and the 'projection of the axis of geography or nature onto that of society ... allows for the transfer of closure as such from the vaster totality of the natural landscape'.[73] Again we encounter the reifying motif *par excellence* – the resolution ('closure') of the novels is not a product of the way the lives of their main characters interrelate and evolve – i.e. the 'plots themselves' – but rather the socio-historical moment is subsumed by 'the projection of the axis of geography or nature onto that of society'. What is socio-historical in essence – i.e. character interrelation and development – is annulled in favour of the physical thing, 'geography' or 'nature' as the force which underpins a totality which is profoundly static and lifeless precisely because it has been made bereft of the human existence which breathes life into it. And nowhere do we see this more 'clearly' than when Jameson reveals his methodological approach to reading Raymond Chandler (and literature more generally). He writes:

But 'space' must be read; unless conventional modes of reading are presupposed (conventions being themselves everywhere in crisis in this society), the reader may expect to pass through an initial period of programmation, through some inaugural entry chamber in which the appropriate decoding techniques are taught and learned. Even as far as the category of space itself is concerned, it cannot be assumed to pre-exist the text either, but must be projected by the latter as that 'code' of space which the reader must learn to read.[74]

Here the aspect of reification once again reaches its zenith; 'space' itself attains a strange, spectral life, and it is only by passing through the mystical, mysterious 'inaugural entry chamber' whereby you attain the sacred 'decoding techniques' which will allow the secrets of 'space' to be revealed. And it is there where Fredric Jameson stands, at the gate of the 'entry chamber', the guardian of the temple if you will – whose esoteric brilliance proffers the promise of revelation, but only if you are prepared to leave your wits at the door. It seems to me that the passage is not only convoluted and lifeless like so much of Jameson's writing, but that it would be more at home in the pages of a Scientology leaflet rather than a book which purports to engage with Chandler and literature from a Marxist perspective. It is not that the book has no value whatsoever; there are places where Jameson occasionally threatens to say something interesting. His observations on the blood-soaked origins of California and how these cast a shadow across the Sternwood Mansion (the setting of the first chapter in *The Big Sleep*) are not without interest or insight; like Eagleton, glimpses and flashes of historical analysis pepper a broader eclectic mix which is why, in a certain sense, Jameson's work, and the formidable number of books which comprise it, is often quite illusive and difficult to pin down.

But I hope this chapter has managed to point towards a general trend. Lukács' theory of reification has a certain aesthetic beauty to it; it recognizes as its necessary corollary proletarian revolution and the Marxist theory of history as that of the totality, of the unfolding whole. It unites within its remit the oppositions between use and exchange, being and consciousness, theory and practice, the quantitative and the qualitative drawing them into a dialectical and conscious harmony as part of this totality, as part of this unfolding whole. But when Jameson reads the concept of totality in a purely physical structural sense, the moments which are reconciled within the historical whole fall asunder once more into lonely and isolated oppositions; social being remains forever severed from social consciousness, theory from practice. For Jameson, reification is transformed from being the expression of the social relation of exploitation which opens up between capital and labour power to being the expression of the way in which any commodity is physically produced on the factory line and the purely contemplative attitude which arises from this in consciousness.

The irony is that such a transformation is itself a reifying one; Jameson reifies the Marxist conception of the proletariat as a living historical process, and he does so in the exact same way as his Frankfurt School predecessors by shifting the focus from the commodity labour power and the social relation of exploitation which underpins it to the consideration of the commodity as a mechanically produced 'thing' bereft of socio-historical substance. Once the Marxist conception has been denuded of the social and class relationships which drive it, once the totality is no longer read as a historical unfolding, it is natural and inevitable that Jameson's analysis of literature becomes drained of its socio-historical content, and in the aftermath we are left with the rigid ossified forms and categories of structuralism and semiotics, like a set of skeletal bones washed up on the sand, baking in the acrid sun. The loss of meaning which arises from such a vacuum is perhaps best expressed by the fetishism of emptiness; the key to Jameson's analysis – along with those 'semiotic rectangles', the Althusserian 'absent causes' and the Lacanian 'reals' – becomes emptiness itself expressed in terms of the category of 'space'. In Jameson's strange and surreal oeuvre the true key to meaning becomes 'decoding' its loss – 'mapping space' – decoding the absence which lingers in a reified and alien terrain once the obliteration of the true human content has been achieved.

Like Jameson, Eagleton has never come to terms with the Marxist concept of totality – by and large because he has never understood the roots of it in Hegelian philosophy which emerged as a response to the problem of the Kantian thing-in-itself (a problem 'thinkers' like Lacan and Althusser constantly reintroduce into their thought without even being in the slightest bit aware of it). For his part, Eagleton regards the Marxist concept of totality in terms of an absolute and mechanical determinism which overwhelms individual subjectivity, and to compensate for this Eagleton is pulled towards those same fashionable strands in continental philosophy which seek to strike out at the image of the social and historical whole. He mobilizes

Althusserian structuralism, Foucauldian discourse theory, semiotics and Lacanian psychoanalysis among others and in so doing brings to bear the essential ingredients in Literary Theory which are perfectly calibrated to transform the richness of socio-historical development into the formal and lifeless categories of a reified and transcendental realm – most prominently when it comes to the issue of literature itself. For both thinkers, for both Eagleton and Jameson, the historical whole is dissipated, broken down, dissolved – and when the unfolding totality is lost and only emptiness abides – it is at that point when they project the illusory and holographic image of a reified world out across the void.

Chapter 6
Stephen King's *IT* and the proletariat as identical subject-object of the historical process

In one of the earliest scenes in Stephen King's *IT* the writer takes us to a festival in the small rural town of Derry. The Canal Days Festival, the residents agree, is a 'rousing success',[1] and something which marks the boom years the town enjoyed after the opening of its canal some decades before. But as with a lot of Stephen King scenarios there is something which is not quite right, something a little off kilter, something askew which, at first, you can't quite put your finger on. In order to spruce Derry up, all sorts of little acts of maintenance are conducted. Potholes which have gone unattended for years are now filled in and smoothed over, town buildings are refurbished and repainted, and graffiti is removed. But what was written on those walls which so desperately required erasure? 'KILL ALL QUEERS' and 'AIDS FROM GOD YOU HELLBOUND HOMOS!' The festival is designed to commemorate the town's history; the old, venerable patrician families donate their antique treasures to be displayed before the gawping dazzled eyes of curious museum goers; and yet the flesh-and-blood of the real, visceral history of the town is likewise evacuated and erased. The Tramp Chair which the local council once used to cage vagrants so that they could be placed in the main square and subjected to the jeers and abuse of passers-by would not be on display for the festival-goers. Nor would they see black-and-white pictures which depicted the bullet-riddled cadavers of the Bradley Gang after a notorious shootout. One receives the impression of a festival which is conducted in the open before bright light and big blue skies and yet everywhere the shadows are creeping from the backstreets and the corners, just on the edge of your vision.

The sense that something sinister is at work behind the happy façade grows stronger until King graduates it into a moment of explicit horror. But the horror, at this point, is still not of the supernatural kind. We are introduced to a couple, Adrian Mellon and Don Haggerty, enjoying the 'happiest summer'[2] of their lives. The older, more cynical Haggerty is uneasy in Derry, for he is aware of the graffiti which has sprouted up and the pulsing current of homophobic hatred which runs through it. And yet he is persuaded to linger here by the more idealistic, youthful and vulnerable Mellon who believes that something of genuine charm and value is to be found in the small-town community over and against the vast looming anonymity of the big city. Mellon is still full of dreams; the young man is penning his first novel, and Haggarty is both compelled by and frightened for his big-hearted sense of innocence.

At the end of the festival, as the parades are winding down, and the shadows grow longer, the couple are attacked. King has worked so softly on the meticulous, tender details of their love, and this helps throw into relief the utter horror and tragedy of what happens to them. Mellon is seen holding hands and kissing his partner, and these gentle flirtations along with the camp hat the young man is sporting attract the attention of several embittered homophobes, their humanity numbed by a sense of dull aggression. The encounter culminates in a night-time attack which sees Mellon beaten half to death before being tossed over a bridge in a scene which smacks of a gut-wrenching realism, exhibiting with great artistic integrity the affection between the two men and the nature of the dull, listless prejudice and hatred which mobilize their assailants. Of course, at this point, the supernatural element is very much in the background; we are dealing with concrete social relations of power and the violence which those who are in some way disempowered, exploited or marginalized on the edges of social life are made to endure. King's description of homophobic hate is acute and the condition of the victims is described with great poignancy but the situation itself is unremarkable and not unusual for '80s small town Americana with all its rural conservatism. But King goes on to make the point that there is something different about Derry: these outbreaks of violence have a murderous intensity which goes beyond the norm, and more than this, they are also concentrated into short cyclical bursts, with the murder rate spiking every twenty or so years. One of the important elements in *IT* the novel is just how King elaborates the *longue durée* of Derry's town history.

Long before Mellon and Haggarty take their fateful walk by the bridge, King describes another atrocity buried deep in Derry's historical past. One of his central characters, Mike Hanlon, is told a story by his father who is terminally ill in hospital. The child leans in to the wizened, withered figure of a once strong father who has been eaten away by cancer and in the gloom of the hospital room the old man tells the boy about what happened in Derry many years before. His father tells him how he was one of the Black GIs stationed at an army base at a time of extreme segregation. The Black soldiers, like Mike's father, were not expected to frequent white establishments in their free time, especially those afterhours drinking or dinner clubs which the town elite attended. Instead, Mike's father, William Hanlon, along with a couple of friends, makes a trip to a more raffish and disreputable establishment (Wally's Spa) where the clientele were of a different sort: 'The men … were pulp-cutters in those big red-and-black-checked lumberman's jackets, scars and scabs all over their hands, some of em missing eyes or fingers, all of em missing most of their teeth, all of them smellin like woodchips and sawdust and sap … They smelled big, Mikey, and they walked big, and they talked big. They *were* big.'[3] Mike's father is approached by such a man and the young Black soldier feels no small degree of trepidation; 'he was dead drunk, and he smelled as high as a basket of month-old peaches. If he'd stepped out of his clothes, I think they would have stood up alone. He looks at me and says, "Mister, I gonna ast you sumpin, me. Are you be a Negro?"' Mike's father responds affirmatively and in as friendly manner as possible, and the dirt-poor lumberman follows up with 'a grin so big I saw all four of his teeth. "I knew you was, me! Hey! I seen one in a book once! Had the same – " and he couldn't think how to say what was on his mind, so he reaches out and flaps at my mouth. "Big lips," I says. "Yeah, yeah!" he says, laughin like a kid. "Beeg Leeps! … Gonna buy you a beer, me!"'

On the one hand there is a clear racial element to the exchange, the fetishization and fascination with lip-size which comes to denote an 'other', someone who is conceived almost as of being a member of a different species – 'I seen one in a book once!' At the same time there is a childlike sense of curiosity and wonder in the lumberman's approach; that most human of impulses, to discover someone new, to find out about them, and despite the racially charged language there is no sense that the lumberman feels Mike's father to be in some way inherently inferior to himself. His tone is, indeed, one of friendship and comradery. King handles the scene deftly; the context is racialized and he does not shy away from the fact that the poor whites partake in what are typical racist tropes. At the same time he shows the possibility of a broader solidarity, both the young Black soldiers and the hefty, older, white labourers regard one another with a certain curious interest and wry amusement. The Black soldiers find a place drinking with their poor white counterparts.

Of course this does not sit very well with the privileged white elite who have a vested interest in preserving a racial hierarchy which also helps maintain the oppressive economic pecking order. The town council wants 'to make sure that none of those barbags or peavey-swingers got polluted by the Blacks of Company E'[4] – i.e. they want to make sure that any political solidarity which might develop between the poor whites and poor Blacks was curtailed in advance. King's writing here is just splendid; not simply because of his mastery of slang – the dialogue which so expertly and authentically conveys the mood of the Black GIs and the rural white workers – but also because the scene and the story exhibit the way in which racism operates at a systematic and community-wide level and exposes the true interests of those who benefit from it therein. And yet there is nothing didactic or idealistic in the exposition, and it flows easily and naturally, tapering towards its tragic conclusion. In the end it is decided by the local council members to segregate the Blacks by giving them a small ramshackle hut in a desolate field, in this way offering the slightest of concessions to be rid of the problem. But the Black soldiers come together, pooling their limited resources, and turn the task of refurbishing the shack into a labour of love.

The floor was still dirt, but we kept it oiled down nice. Trev and Pop Snopes ran in a lectric line – more Midnight Requisitions, I imagine.

By July, you could go in there any Saturday night and sit down and have a cola and a hamburger – or a slaw dog. It was nice … a way of thumbing our noses at Fuller and Mueller and the Town Council. But I guess we knew it was ours when Ev McCaslin and I put up a sign one Friday night that said THE BLACK SPOT, and just below that, COMPANY E AND GUESTS. Like we were exclusive you know![5]

In addition, company E find they have:

a pretty decent jazz-band among us … Martin Devereaux, who was a corporal, played drums. Ace Stevenson played cornet, Pop Snopes played a pretty decent barrelhouse piano. He wasn't great, but he was no slouch … by the end of that August, there was a pretty hot little Dixieland combo playing Friday and Saturday nights at the Black Spot … And the next thing you know, people from town started to show up at our club. Even some of the white soldiers from the base … At first those white faces looked like sprinkles of salt in a pepperpot, but more and more of them turned up as time went by.[6]

Again there is something of great authenticity in this; the simple truth about poverty and the poor, that they have very little but their own resources and guile and solidarity to draw upon. In mobilizing these, the members of Company E are able to create and work a club which is not only a bustling success but which also in some way transcends the racial divide. The councilmen having failed in their initial gambit to thwart such solidarity now resort to a more terminal tactic. One night, when the Black Spot is in full swing, a group of hired thugs wielding flaming torches surround the club chanting 'Come out, niggers! Come out, niggers! Come out, niggers!'[7] They then proceed to set the building alight. The scene is an extremely harrowing one, the fear and pain of the human beings inside the club are chronicled by King in an unflinching fashion, and yet at the same time the pathos is drawn out not only from the violence and the loss of life, but also from the loss of what these people had managed to build, together. It represents a profound description of injustice and a truly humane portrayal of the struggle for freedom and solidarity, and when King writes like this, delivering both hope and pathos, one is reminded most of all of Steinbeck.

In both the scene with the gay couple and the Blacks and whites who come together in the Black Spot the authentic horror is conveyed, not by the presence of some supernatural force, but by social relationships of power and oppression. And yet, almost as an afterthought, when Mellon is pushed off the bridge by his homophobic assailants, something is waiting for him in the shadows below – the creepy, murderous, supernatural spectre of Pennywise the Clown, surely one of King's most perturbing and inventive creations. In the case of the Black Spot, as the building is burning and the people are screaming, Mike's father sees a vast sinister bird which is, surreally enough, suspended in the air by a number of balloons which have been strung around it, almost like a clown's party trick. In both scenes the spectre of Pennywise looms large; King is able to deftly and expertly intertwine the real and realist horror of race hate, misogyny, homophobia and the oppression of the outsider, with the supernatural force which Pennywise represents. For the clown is merely the avatar of a much deeper, subterranean and ancient entity; one whose true essence is occluded by geography and time, something so old and so distant as to defy human cognition; hence the moniker 'IT'. Pennywise is recorded in the annuls of the town's history, he is referenced in old journals, he appears in faded black-and-white photos from years before, and he appears against the backdrop of historical atrocities and real-world injustices.

So the novel achieves two significant things. Firstly, it fuses supernatural horror with real and authentically drawn themes of social exploitation and oppression. IT becomes stronger, draws power from human ignorance and oppression, and likewise IT helps galvanize those tendencies in the social world. Secondly, the novel calls into being a profoundly dualistic reality. One the one hand, the small town of Derry seems to exist in an eternal present; the small town of parades and festivals, of quaint little shops and sun-drenched parks, the normalcy and the routine of the everyday. And then that other reality; the reality of the darkness of the historical past – the persecution, apartheid and murder. In a sense the present attempts to mask the past; the town council wiping off the graffiti before a parade and, more generally, the whitewashing of injustice and oppression on the part of the townsfolk who no longer care to remember the bloody details of the town's history. None of that history is on display during the Canal Days Festival and it is almost as if the town is in the grip of a collective amnesia; they are not alive to the forces of historical darkness which are at work below the façade and routine of everyday life. And in a sense this is the very essence of IT, embodied; IT is a spectral, supernatural and infinitely malevolent presence which lurks beneath the surface of town life; IT lives behind the drains in the dank dark tunnels of the sewer system – it lurks in the forests on the periphery, it hides in the old, crumbling house which is on the edge of town. So, in a certain way, the fundamental question of the novel becomes this: What social agency within the township is capable of seeing beyond the surface appearance and penetrating to the depths, the depths of history, the depths of the physical geography, in order to recognize the truth which lies beneath?

King's answer to the riddle is, of course, children. In a very real way children are closer to the earliest origins of our own historical past; they fear the dark in the way our ancient ancestors might have done, hunched close to a smouldering fire, aware that just beyond the frail periphery of the light lurks the shapes and shadows of dangerous predators, their eyes glowing in the blackness. Whereas for early hominins such threat would have come from the undergrowth or from the thick darkness of the forests, or the rustling high grass, for the young child the danger comes from the shadows which are gathered underneath the bed or the darkness which lives in the depths of the wardrobe. For that is where the monster lives. There is, therefore, some parity between the primitive prehistoric fears of our most distant ancestors and the elemental anxieties of young children who want to keep the door open and the light on in the hall, after they have been kissed goodnight. Young children tend to be alive to the notion of a world within a world – a world of monsters, fairies, changelings, sprites, genies, ghosts and so on, that we adults can no longer see; as we grow up, as we become acculturated and accustomed to the routines and structures of social life, our childhood fears of monsters lurking in the darkness tend to be replaced by the more prosaic and real-world worries which surround issues like unemployment, disease, poverty and death.

For this reason, it is the children of Derry who are in a particularly effective position to recognize and come to terms with the presence of IT. The children of Derry are able to register the dualistic nature of the small town they live in; they are able to penetrate the façade of the ordinary and see deeper into the horror which lives under the surface. When some of their number are murdered, the adults are baffled and perplexed by what seems to them to be a tragic aberration, and only the children are able to register the nature of the supernatural force which is at work beneath the radar. But the group of kids who gather to fight IT are not just ordinary children in the context of the small town where they live. Bill, whose young brother has been murdered by the entity, has a pronounced stutter. Ben is heavily overweight, Mike is Black, Stanley is Jewish, and so on. They are all in some way outsiders, exiles from the cultural mainstream, often mistreated or neglected by their own parents, and viciously bullied by other, older kids precisely because they are in some way different. Each of these children in some sense feels fundamentally alone. IT appears to them individually in the guise of their worst fears. For the leader of the group, the bright, stuttering Bill Denbrough, IT appears in the form of his murdered brother, Georgie. For the germophobe and hypochondriac Eddie, IT appears as a leper whose suppurating wounds ooze blood and pus, and so on. Each of the children doubt themselves, not only in terms of the visions they experience *vis-à-vis* IT, but also because they themselves are marginalized and outcast.

But the guiding thread of the novel is one of solidarity. By coming together, by forming the group which they dub 'the Losers', each of the children has access to a friendship and a collective which is bigger than themselves. The fact that they are all different, all maligned; the fact that they don't fit in is precisely what binds them together, a true negation of negation in Hegelian terms. And this is another one of King's supreme strengths as a writer; he demonstrates with delicate and blushing artistry a coming-of-age tale in which the tentative friendships and puppy loves of a group of children on the cusp of adolescence bloom against a darker background of supernatural threat. The children – through their solidarity, friendship and trust – are able to graduate the understanding of their own subjective fears and isolation into a broader and shared understanding of the evil which does exist, the spectre of Pennywise, and the realization they are the only ones who are capable of resisting it. How is this done? The children are able to comprehend IT, in part, because they are children, because they are still alive to the supernatural world. But as we have already seen, IT's power isn't exclusively supernatural, or rather the supernatural is drawn into a symbiotic relationship with social realities of oppression and exploitation. The unmasking of IT, therefore, becomes not just a supernatural question: i.e. a question of whether to use garlic against it, or silver bullets, or curses or incantations. Nor is it just a question of discovering the places where IT resides. As well as these things, the key to understanding IT becomes, of necessity, a historical question. In order to comprehend IT's true essence, the Losers have to come to terms with the very real events and injustices which have been perpetrated during the town's history, socio-historical events which are bound up with the supernatural malevolence IT exudes. The Losers have to do what the townsfolk cannot; they have to recover their own historical past. Through old photos, through newspaper accounts, through the disjointed memories of the adults, through library research and various other means – the Losers begin to build up a historical depiction of IT which reveals (in the faded images or accounts where the presence of the clown is in effect) that every twenty-seven years the town experiences a series of terrible events or tragedies; these correspond to the fact that IT has awoken from its slumber and is now ready to feed.

Because the Losers become aware that IT awakens for only a short period, they understand they have to act at once. This they do by homing in on IT's location, by using certain 'supernatural' aids like silver, but more importantly – the more they understand what IT is, the less they become afraid of it. The key to the defeat of IT lies in the apprehension of the historical past. In and through the rational understanding of the process of development which underpins IT, the Losers are more and more able to shed their individual fears and inadequacies and come together as a group whose collective action is capable of defeating the monster. Though the book is saturated with supernatural horror, there is also a seam of rationalism which runs through the plot and is key to the resolution. IT is rationally apprehended by the Losers as a historical process, and such a rational awareness becomes, in the book, the pre-condition for human praxis. It really is remarkable how such a literary plot dovetails with a Hegelian or even Marxist set of politics; that is to say, the rational apprehension of historical development becomes the pre-condition for self-conscious and collective social transformation. In terms of Marxist politics, one might argue that the single most important task of the revolutionary party is to act as a repository for the historical memory of the class – to help recover past periods of revolutionary action, to help awaken the revolutionary awareness of the proletariat in and through the recollection of past revolutionary moments and the realization of the role the class is destined to play. In recalling the past, both the successes and failures of the revolutionary struggle, the proletariat becomes rationally armed with the awareness of its own historical destiny and thus the necessity of its own political action. In times of ebb and downturn, in times of relative affluence or abject defeat, the possibility of political struggle can *sometimes* seem either utopian or remote. The deeds of the past fade and there only seems the likelihood of a dismal reconciliation with the here and now. Political activity wanes. The class is separated from the struggles of the past by way of a collective amnesia. By becoming the repository of the successes and defeats of the revolutionary past, the party or tendency becomes the means by which such amnesia can be overcome, by which the most important revolutionary principles developed in and through the crucible of past struggles can be preserved, ready to be drawn upon, and better translated into action once the moment is ripe and the class struggle reaches its zenith once more.

Of course, *IT* is a world away from such directly and explicitly political themes. *IT* is not about political parties, radical left organizations, Marxism or any of those things. But *IT* is about a struggle for freedom and the rational recognition of the historical means by which that can be achieved. *IT* is about the recovery of what has been lost as a prerequisite to collective action in and through the solidarity of the marginalized and oppressed. *IT* is about how we come to recognize the struggles and contradictions of the historical past which are at work beneath the façade of a seemingly eternal present. And *IT* is also about the struggle against the historical amnesia which occludes what has gone before. How so? When the Losers figure out Pennywise's historical *modus operands,* when they are able to rationally comprehend the means by which IT can be defeated, when they finally achieve a victory against IT through their collective action, forcing IT back into its decades-long hibernation – what then happens? The answer is that the Losers themselves begin to forget. The further they are from their childhood encounter with IT, the more their lives taper away into adulthood – the more the outlines of the past blur and fade to the point at which they have not just forgotten the memory of IT but have even forgone the memories of one another. They go on to inhabit their adult lives, and King's point is wonderfully made; adulthood itself implies a certain type of amnesia. Becoming an adult implies shedding an array of childhood fears and memories in favour of the necessities of the present and a more stabilized and structured social routine. King writes about the Losers:

> They would no longer imagine that there were piranha in the Kenduskeag or that if you stepped on a crack you might really break your mother's back or that if you killed a ladybug which lit on your shirt your house would catch fire that night. Instead, they would believe in wine with dinner – something nice but not too pretentious, like a Pouilly-Fuissé '83, and let that breathe, waiter, would you? Instead they would believe that Rolaids consume forty-seven times their own weight in excess stomach acid. Instead, they would believe in public television, Gary Hart, running to prevent heart attacks, giving up red meat to prevent colon cancer … As each year passed their dreams would grow smaller.[8]

The collective amnesia which the Losers experience demarks the movement from childhood to adulthood more generally. Their task, as adults, is to recover their memories, to confront their childhood fears, to come to terms with their own historical past – in order to once again do battle with the entity. As adults who have become serious people with independent lives, people who are integrated into the routines and conventions of the 'ordinary' world – for the Losers to delve back into their histories, to remember, is a horrifying prospect, for they are acknowledging that those early elemental childhood fears are not credulous superstitions cultivated by immature minds but were real all along. The monster has always been in the closet, shrouded in darkness, waiting for its time to come. The scene which most exemplifies this is when the Losers, as adults, gather in Derry again. They meet at a Chinese restaurant – a meeting organized by Mike Hanlon. Mike is a vital character for he becomes a cipher for the concept of memory itself. He works as a librarian and is intimately acquainted with the real history of Derry through the books, the same history which involves the disappearances, murders, disasters and oppressions which feed IT. Mike, unlike his comrades, does not leave Derry; thus, he is the only one in the group to have remembered what happened to them as children, and he never fully relinquishes the awareness of the threat IT poses. The meeting in the restaurant is conveyed effectively; the tension between people who have not seen each other for a long time gradually melts as – from within the hot aromas of the sizzling food, the gentle haze of the warm light – the Losers talk and laugh and gently rediscover one another. At the same time outside, the shadows of night creep closer. When it comes to the end of the meal each opens a fortune cookie, and it is then when IT makes its presence known, allowing horrific creatures to slither forth from the packet, playing upon the individual fears of the Losers once more.

This leads, of course, towards the denouement of the novel, whereby the Losers recover their collective memories and comprehend the nature of the force that is arrayed against them in order to battle Pennywise in the catacombs one last time. The ending is, by far and away, the weakest part of the novel. When the Losers finally manage to overcome their fears – avoid succumbing to IT's various manifestations – when they finally manage to see beyond the façade and comprehend the true nature of IT which lies behind the various illusions and disguises the entity throws up, what they discover is anything but credible. In an ending which seems hastily and haphazardly improvised, King reveals that IT is actually an ancient, giant cosmic spider which was around at the dawn of the universe. Alongside IT is another equally old entity; a gigantic turtle called Maturin who vomited up the mainstream universe after a particularly bad belly ache. Maturin gives Bill Denbrough the ability to destroy IT once and for all in and through something called the 'Ritual of Chud', the unleashing of a psychic battle which takes place in a realm known as the 'Macroverse'. The ending is bad, almost goofy, especially considering the exceptional work and writing which have already been done. One can see what King is trying to do; he is trying to create the type of cosmological mythology, the kind of origin myth, which can undergird a whole universe much in the manner of someone like Tolkien and his Middle Earth epics. The problem, however, is that King relegates such an endeavour to a relatively tiny part of his novel by way of the conclusion. Some of the elements are briefly hinted at beforehand, it is true. But because the relationship between the turtle and IT is laid out so briefly at the end almost as an afterthought, the work required to fully create an alternative universe with all its complexities remains woefully underdone. It feels as though the ending is tied up in a haphazard, artificial and rather facile way.

But there is another way by which the ending is inherently bad, another aspect of it which is very different from what has gone before. Most fundamentally, IT's horror is fused with the social world more broadly; that is, IT draws its power from genuinely human forms of oppression and misery and its spectral-like existence, its lurking evil, attains its true tenor in this context, for it is also an evil which lurks in the hearts of men waiting to be awakened. But the ending detaches the entity IT from its grounding in the social world. When IT is drawn into battle with the gigantic cosmological turtle *vis-à-vis* Bill Denbrough, the whole guiding thread of IT is displaced onto a completely separate and artificial realm. IT the entity is no longer in some sense the representation of the spirit of Derry itself, the accretion and accumulation of the historic ills of the town materialized in the evil figure of the clown. Instead IT becomes something purely mystical, abstracted from the social realties in which it takes shape, projected outward onto some rather cheesy and transcendental realm whose vacuous mysticism becomes almost unintentionally comic. By revealing IT in the manner he does, King denudes and drains the entity of all its sinisterism, and it becomes simply just another gaudy and ridiculous monster set against the backdrop of a rather superficial and psychedelic realm.

The ending is bad, of necessity. And this has both aesthetic and ontological implications. In his combination of autobiography and horror story analysis, *Danse Macabre*, Stephen King draws out the fundamental problem of all horror writing. It is something King himself first heard expressed by the horror, fantasy and sci-fi writer William F Nolan at a fantasy convention. Nolan, King recalls, posed the problem in terms of the monster behind the door:

Nothing is so frightening as what's behind the closed door, Nolan said. You approach the door in the old, deserted house, and you hear something scratching at it. The audience holds its breath along with the protagonist as she/he (more often she) approaches that door. The protagonist throws it open, and there is a ten-foot-tall bug. The audience screams, but this particular scream has an oddly relieved sound to it. 'A bug ten feet tall is pretty horrible', the audience thinks, 'but I can deal with a ten-foot-tall bug. I was afraid it might be a hundred feet tall'.[9]

In one way the point is quite an obvious one. There can be nothing more frightening than the unknown. When you don't know what is behind the door, your imagination is free to run riot. When we finally see the monster revealed, when it becomes a 'real' object with a particular set of dimensions, it loses its metaphysical edge; it becomes just another 'material' object which sits along all the other material objects of the world and is thereby subject to human power; something which can be transformed, effaced, and perhaps even vanquished. When the indefinite 'thing' which lurks in the darkness of one's imagination is eventually defined, provided with a corporeal form, rationally exhibited – it loses its spectral power; it passes from that which is unlimited precisely because it is undefined, to that which is limited and finite (in philosophical terms, of course, this is very much the transition from the Kantian noumenal to the phenomenal). Its mystique and its implacability cease to pertain. And sometimes this can be quite jarring. In the excellent film *Jaws*, directed by Steven Spielberg, the shark is rarely seen; instead, at the opening of the film, you see a young woman swimming in the early hours of the morning and you have a sense of the vastness of the ocean below her – a great, dark enigmatic and infinite space upon which she floats as a mere speck. And then, just like that, she is gone. We know, of course, that there is a shark, but the shark is almost never seen; instead it becomes a cypher for the absolute vastness, the dark infinity, of the sea itself. But when Chief-of-Police Brody and the others hunt down the shark, when the shark actually launches itself at the boat containing the people who are hunting it – at once an element of absurdity is introduced. On the one hand this has to do with 1970s effects; you can see the jaws of the shark opening and shutting rather mechanically on their hinges and in comparison to the size and girth of the trawler the shark itself no longer seems all that substantial. But the dissipation of one's fear is about more than just cheesy special effects. It is about the way in which the spectral horror of the infinite unknown expanse becomes materialized in a finite entity and the way in which the terror of one's imagination gives way before one's reason and rationality. The monster behind the door is finally unveiled.

Something similar happens in *IT*. For the majority of the novel we never truly know what lies behind the façade of the clown and the other sinister spectres – except that there is this lurking and undisclosed evil which inhabits a subterranean netherworld. Once, however, the Losers confront IT for the final time, and we are given the image of a great big spider much of the spectral horror is vanquished. Of course, this poses a key question. Is it possible for any horror writer to overcome this, the monster behind the door paradox? In a broader sense the answer to this question becomes a question of philosophy more broadly, specifically the subject-object contradiction. When rendered as a palpable and external object (shark, giant spider etc.) the horror ceases to be bound up with the subject in the most meaningful way; that is, it ceases to be part and parcel of the terror which is formed deep within the subject's own psyche, the terror which is generated by the subject's most intimate nature – a product of his or her own imagination. When the horror is rendered as a 'real' world object it is inexorably separated out from the essence of the subject's innermost life and the historical past of the individual on which the life of the psyche rests. The solution, therefore, in philosophical terms is for the horror novel/film not to allow the absolute separation of subject from object which pertains once the 'monster behind the door' is revealed. The solution is to somehow stop the terror from being externalized and rendered as an object which is completely separate to the subject's innermost nature. The solution is to achieve some form of subject-object identity in the final flourish, the ultimate denouement of the tale.

Perhaps that sounds a little convoluted or esoteric but in actual fact subject-object identity is something that some of the world's greatest scary films do demonstrate. I would like to turn to a couple of these. The first is M. Night Shyamalan's film _The Sixth Sense_. The story runs as follows. Malcolm Crowe, a child psychologist, is working with a sensitive and troubled young boy (Cole) who famously purports to see 'dead people', ghosts who are wandering the world around him and who do not understand that they are actually dead. In the course of his sessions with Cole, Crowe eventually comes to realize that the young boy is actually telling the truth. Crowe then helps Cole to understand his predicament and to be able to better deal with it. He ascertains that Cole is supposed to help the ghosts by helping resolve the injustices which have led to their demise, thereby providing the ghosts with the realization they are in fact dead. This, in turn, allows them to leave their earthly limbo thus laying their souls to rest. But, in the provocative conclusion, the 'objective' dilemma with which Cole and Crowe are faced, the endeavour to deal with the supernatural horror in a realm which is outside their own subjectivity – this is then radically subverted. For Crowe, in a scene which is both horrifying and poignant, realizes that the reason why he has been working with the young boy, the reason why he has been pulled into the young boy's remit – is because he, Crowe, is one of those dead people the young boy can see. It is one of the most provocative and powerful revelations in the history of horror, and its power relies on the fact that the horror of the external object – the supernatural entities which Cole perceives – is identical with the nature of the subject itself, i.e. Crowe, who is himself revealed to be deceased. In and through subject-object identity the true horror is not dissipated on some external object which is indifferent to ourselves; rather the horror of the external other is simultaneously bound up with the nature of ourselves. In this respect *The Sixth Sense* is a perfect horror film.

Another film in which the same ontological unity is achieved is the film *Psycho*. Here the issue is admittedly a little more complicated; the film isn't a horror in the traditional sense, for there is no element of the supernatural which intrudes. In addition, Norman Bates, the serial killer of the piece, isn't what you might call the protagonist; the protagonist is Marion Crane who is stabbed to death half way through the film in the infamous shower scene. But exempting these factors for a moment, the operation here is very much the same. Norman Bates is beholden to some awful mother figure who, in a rather 'Freudian' sense, has shaped his own degenerate, psychotic behaviour through her cloying and overbearing oppression. But we don't actually see the mother as a real person. For the majority of the film we see only a sinister shadow through a window rocking back and forward in her chair. We experience her through Norman's eyes in as much as we can tell that he is clearly terrified and oppressed by her but we do not experience her as a being with a set of particular dimensions and a personality that we encounter as a given fact in the real world; rather her presence remains spectral and intangible. We experience her as an 'object' out there through the subjectivity (the terror and awe he feels for his mother) of Norman Bates himself. But when that crucial reveal takes place, when the mother goes from being an ominous, horrific but undefined presence to an actual palpable real-life monster – we are confronted by the presence of Bates himself, dressed in his mother's clothes, speaking in her high-pitched voice, shrill and insane. It is revealed that he has murdered his mother many years before and unable to bear the realization of this, has somehow recreated her in and through his own mind as an alternate personality. Again we have an example of subject-object identity which in some way manages to preserve the 'horror' of what has taken place. Now imagine if *Psycho* had concluded in a more traditional way; if the subject-object duality had been preserved, if after Norman Bates had been subdued, police then found the way into his mother's room and were then set upon by a real shrieking old lady with a knife, his mother as she was in life. The sheer horror would not have been maintained; in fact, the spectacle would have been much more abjectly pathetic or even vaguely comical.

To return to Stephen King's *IT*, we now have a better sense of why the novel is so good, and yet the ending is so poor. Who is the subject in *IT*? Foremostly, it is Bill Denbrough and the other Losers. But it is also the historical subject, the town of Derry itself, its people. The evil of IT is filtered through that history like rushing water through rocks, an intangible and indefinable supernatural evil commingled with a very real set of social evils. The Losers are able to defeat IT in their first battle because they apprehend the essence and development of IT as an objective force in and through the historical development of their own social subject, i.e. the society from which they themselves have arisen. When King unveils IT as a gigantic flesh-chomping spider, in philosophical terms subject-object unity is irrevocably sundered; what we now encounter is a form of dualism in the aesthetic: on the one hand we have the subject, the Losers, their social world and the set of contradictions and conflicts which underpin it – on the other, we have the vague and hastily contrived image of a transcendental and hallucinogenic realm – the Macroverse – which King throws together in the last few pages of his epic novel. In order to defeat IT, Bill Denbrough pops into the Macroverse, communes with the giant turtle, vanquishes IT, and then returns to Derry in time to save his movie-star girlfriend, Audra Phillips – herself a rather glamorous but threadbare character, and in the scheme of things little more than a prop. The reason why there is an almost comic absurdity to Denbrough's final charge against the entity IT is because Denbrough has been yanked out of the social conditions in which his battle has thus far been located and grafted onto a woefully underdeveloped and artificial landscape which has nothing in common, no true point of contact, with the world which King has so successfully weaved hitherto. Subject and object are drawn into an irreconcilable division. Stylistically, the writing is still King's. But it also reads like the worst examples of experimental fiction which are grounded in hippie-esque notions of a skewered form of liberal individualism which sees art and emancipation to be the products of one's own journey into the solipsistic depths of the soul through the 'magical' and transcendental properties of certain hallucinogenic drugs. There is simply no other way to say it, it is just really bad. But again, to press home the point, it is bad for a reason. It is bad because the ontological structure of the novel previous has been so violently breached, and subject and object come to be held in irrevocable and irreconcilable opposition.

The subject-object contradiction is, more generally, the most important issue in all philosophy and forms the cornerstone and crux of Marxist philosophical thought in particular. The thinker who brought this most clearly into the light was the great Hungarian Marxist philosopher Georg Lukács in his brilliant but fragmented collection of essays from the 1920s, *History and Class Consciousness*. In fact, it is in this work where Lukács (quite correctly in my view) criticizes Engels' elucidation of the Marxist dialectic for not having placed emphasis on the role of the relationship between the subject and object in the philosophical and historical process. But what is most interesting about Lukács' discussion is the way in which he utilizes Kant. Lukács draws attention to the way in which Kant's system presupposed its famous irreconcilable contradiction between subject and object, phenomena and noumena; the contradiction by which the activity of pure reason is limited to the finite sphere and therefore the true object can never be penetrated rationally: 'pure reason is unable to make the least leap towards the synthesis and the definition of an object'.[10] But the irrationalism which is the ultimate consequence of the dualism which fissures through Kantian ontology – the contradiction between subject and object, phenomena and noumenal – is itself grounded in the forms and structures of social being:

> For the contradiction does not lie in the inability of the philosophers to give a definitive analysis … It is rather the intellectual expression of the objective situation itself … [t]hat is to say, the contradiction that appears here between subjectivity and objectivity … the conflict between their nature as systems created by 'us' and their fatalistic

necessity distant from and alien to man is nothing but the logical and systematic formulation of the modern state of society.[11]

For bourgeois thought the split between subject and object becomes 'its outermost barrier, one which cannot be crossed'[12] largely because the same contradiction is nestled at the heart of the social existence of the bourgeoisie itself. The existence of the capitalist class as a subject is predicated on its encounter with an object which exists forever 'out there', something which is not the manifestation of its own immanent productions, but is instead to be arrogated from an external power (proletariat) which exists in irreconcilable contradiction to itself. Capital is the social relation of exploitation which opens up between bourgeoisie and proletariat; it is the portion of labour power which is generated by the working class and which is then appropriated by the bourgeoisie for the purposes of investment and capital expansion. The object of appropriation which becomes capital is simultaneously the product of another; it is the alienated labour power of the proletariat brought within the remit of the bourgeoisie *vis-à-vis* production. The dualism of subject and object is thus built into the social existence of the bourgeoisie as something fundamentally irreconcilable; most significantly, the bourgeoisie itself cannot 'rationally' apprehend the nature of the contradiction – i.e. that its social existence is predicated on the alienation and expropriation of the labour of an other – for were it to do so, the conscious awareness of its own parasitical role in the productive process would impinge on its ability to facilitate that process in and through the creation of its own ideological hegemony.

For the bourgeoisie, the true secret of production then – the capacity of labour power to create new value, a surplus which can then be appropriated – remains an undisclosed and indecipherable object which cannot be rationally and historically apprehended by virtue of the bourgeoisie's own social position. Instead bourgeois thought tends to comprehend what the bourgeoisie as a class actually is in its abstract immediacy; because it sets capital into motion through its relationship to waged labour, the bourgeoisie imagines itself as the true wellspring of production, the social agency which through its discrimination, effort and guile is able to direct the productive process via its organization of the workers and its investment in technique and ideas. It therefore experiences itself as the prime mover of the productive process, the true source of value creation – in terms of the creation of jobs (which it contracts and designates), the creation of profit (which it is then able to control with an eye for reinvestment). Indeed the very idea that the capitalist class is the true source of value creation is a prejudice which is built into the very fabric of the language we use; who hasn't heard it said about some entrepreneur that they 'made 6 billion' therefore rendering oblique the labour of the workers in factories and workplaces across the board which truly creates that value.

With this in mind, the Kantian philosophy is revealed in a new light. The Kantian philosophy is also one of production; specifically, the subject as ego brings the forms and the categories of the understanding to bear, and in and through this process, generates the objects of experience. But, just as with the bourgeois subject, the Kantian subject is not as self-sufficient as it first seems; indeed its productive powers are predicated on an entity which exists forever 'outside'[13] itself. The forms and categories must first go to work on a 'thing' which is then formalized and categorized and it is the resultant synthesis which underpins and conditions the phenomenal universe. But though the noumenal provides the pre-condition of the productive capacities of the ego – the 'thing in itself', the object 'out there', which is absolutely necessary to the generation of experience – the subject itself can never comprehend this element which is such an integral part of its own productive process; the noumenal remains something unknown and unknowable from the conscious and rational purview of the individual transcendental ego. Kantianism then, in a philosophical and rarefied manner, raises the bourgeois class position and the contradiction which is inherent in it; that is, the noumenal becomes the idealized expression of the bourgeoisie's inability to penetrate rationally the historical genesis of value and therefore comprehend the nature of the object 'out there' on which its own class power is predicated.[14]

But with the proletariat, the situation is different. It is true that the proletariat as a class stands in an irrevocable and dualistic opposition to the bourgeoisie every bit as much as the bourgeoisie does to the proletariat. But the fundamental difference lies in this. For the proletariat, capital, the object 'out there' is not something which it appropriates; rather it is something which has been appropriated from it; capital is the labour power of the proletariat which has been alienated by the bourgeoisie. For the proletariat, the object 'out there' is not something which exists in inexorable difference to itself; rather capital is a product of the proletariat's most essential nature albeit one which is then manifested in an alien guise. For the bourgeoisie the subject-object distinction will always remain untraversable, for subject and object are antipodes; but for the proletariat, however, the object is, on the most fundamental level, identical with the subject; it is the production of the subject's essential nature. In selling her labour power, in taking part in the process by which her labour power is alienated as capital by the bourgeoisie, in selling her labour in its commodity form – the proletarian becomes what Lukács describes as a 'living commodity'. The bourgeoisie can never rationally penetrate its object, the object of appropriation, because the object will always stand as an extraneous 'other' at odds with its own immanent content, but for the proletariat the knowledge of the object of capitalist production becomes at the same time a knowledge of self: 'in the commodity the worker recognized himself and his own relations with capital … his consciousness is the self-consciousness of the commodity; or in other words it is the self-knowledge, the self-revelation of the capitalist society founded on the production and exchange of commodities'.[15]

The underlying identity of subject and object which is built into the proletariat by virtue of its socio-historical position at the level of practical existence is what creates the possibility for a self-conscious comprehension of the nature of capitalist production and from this flows the possibility for revolutionary action. Revolutionary action, just like revolutionary theory, is premised on the same dynamic – the proletariat as the identical subject-object of the historical process. The object 'out there', capital, the alienated labour power of the proletariat is not only manifested in the part of labour power which the capitalist class accrues in its immediacy as profit; also capital is embodied in the means of production, the tools, the machinery and the actual buildings and locations – the workplaces themselves. In the act of appropriating its own alienated labour, the proletariat must take a grass-roots democratic control over all the workplaces; in abolishing the wage-labour – capital relationship the working classes place the objective totality of society's economic organs under the subjectivity and self-conscious control of the proletariat itself in and through the creation of workers' councils. Thus from subject-object identity two elements inexorably flow – one, in rationally seeing itself as identical with the object the proletariat comes to understand itself as the true source of value creation; two, the knowledge of this helps supply the proletariat with both the awareness and the necessity of its historical mission, i.e. having realized the identity of subject and object in thought – the proletariat can then proceed to achieve the identity of subject with object at the level of social and practical existence in and through its revolutionary unfolding. It is often said that Marxism is the unity of theory and practice but if this is to mean something more than simple pragmatism then such an assertion must be grounded in an ontology of labour which outlines in theoretical terms the identity of subject and object as proletariat at the level of the forms and structures of social being; in this way alone, the possibility is truly set for the genuine synthesis of theory and practice.

Again, all this might seem very far away from something like *IT*. But it's not. The horror from *IT* flows from the fact that initially the entity IT appears 'out there', as something distinct, as something supernatural and utterly alien to the identity of the people who are confronting it. And yet, over time, the Losers and the reader themselves discover that, in fact, IT is bound up with the historical subject of Derry itself. IT's true horror lies in the fact that IT is fused with the social world and the subjectivity of the Losers themselves, the people around them, the town's history and so on. The key to understanding what IT is relies on the Losers' conscious awareness of this type of subject-object identity; furthermore, *such theoretical awareness also provides the impetus to the action* which they are able to take against IT. And in understanding this, the full glaring effect of the weakness of the conclusion to *IT* is thrown into relief. By raising up the 'Macroverse' and the character of the turtle and giant spider, the subject is suddenly forced into a completely artificial opposition from the object, an ontological separation which the majority of the novel previous has gone a good deal of the way to overcoming. It is this ontological break which causes the collapse in dramatic power and aesthetic integrity of the conclusion to *IT*. And so, providing a Marxist reading of *IT* then, is not about showing how the interests of the more 'proletarian' characters are exhibited, nor is it about trying to demonstrate the presence within the plotline of some kind of critique of capitalism as it applies to the town of Derry in a mechanical and didactic fashion. It is about showing how, in the larger philosophical sense, the broader struggles for freedom and against oppression are bound up with the character of the social world in which we live, and furthermore, that the possibility for radical action is premised on the rational awareness of how that same social world is something which is historically given – and therefore subject to historical change. Of course these truths are filtered through a broader supernatural conflict, but King's genius is conveyed by the fact that he is able to elucidate the shape and motion of broader social conflicts through the supernatural parameters he has laid out. For this same reason the conclusion violates the aesthetic necessity which the writer himself has called into being, a necessity which follows intuitively the central problem and contradiction of philosophy in the modern epoch and the fundamental forms and categories of social existence which underpin it.[16]

Chapter 7

The retreat from class: The theoretical fundaments of Moishe Postone's critique of Lukács

Moishe Postone considered himself to be a Marxist but one who had a radical new way of looking at Marxism. He argued that for a certain period of time something called 'traditional Marxism' had predominated and this traditional Marxism was based on a 'transhistorical – and commonsensical – understanding of labor'[1]. In the essay 'Lukács and the Dialectical Critique of Capitalism' Postone would go on to argue that Lukács' philosophy also presents as a type of 'traditional Marxism' in as much as it continues to frame its critique in 'traditional terms; that is, in terms of the proletariat and, relatedly, a social totality constituted by labor'. Postone then goes on to provide a critique of Lukács' theory of reification.

I always cringe slightly when any thinker or theorist announces they have managed to radically repurpose Marxism in this way – when they talk about a 'traditional' Marxism which they propose to update and modernize. Simply because I have found the language of 'modernization' in this context nearly always provides a euphemism for the retreat from class. Those dusty dinosaurs who still cleave to the idea of class conflict and the revolutionary act, of the proletariat being able to take power under its own auspices – surely that type of thinking is some kind of nineteenth-century relic which died out along with the spinning jenny and the coal mines of yore. Of course, such a posture is key to denuding the philosophy of its revolutionary impulse; if we are now living in a post-commodity, post-industrial world of 'immaterial labour' for instance[2] – then the possibility of the working classes re-appropriating their own alienated labour in and through control of the means of production becomes an increasingly futile one. According to the modernizers it is a solution for a bygone era and has been refuted in practice. Such 'updating' of Marxism to modern conditions, however, by removing any genuine revolutionary agency from contention also works neatly to blunt Marxism's revolutionary edge.

At the same time one has to acknowledge that the body of Marxist tradition is inflicted with a strong streak of sectarianism which relies on dogma and does little to encourage innovation and critical improvement. Many of the political sects treat the writings of the founders of Marxism in much the same way medieval priests treated the words of the Bible. Those who challenge the 'scripture' are often ostracized, treated as bitter political opponents even if the issue involves a relatively esoteric and anodyne point of theory. The mistakes and errors Marx, Engels, Lenin, Trotsky and others committed in their lifetimes and which have been revealed by subsequent historical experience are often papered over or simply disregarded completely.

So there is a fine line one must try to tread; between treating anyone who endeavours to critically develop the field as some kind of brazen heretic while at the same time trying to preserve the great discoveries that Marxism has won, and for the current writer at least, the sublime science of those discoveries is bound up with their revolutionary implications. I don't propose in any way an extensive examination of Postone's work; what I aim to do here is to interrogate his methodology and his conclusions when it comes to the role class plays in classical Marxism and the role class plays in Lukács' conception of reification. But in order to do this I want to begin with an examination of Postone's ideas about labour, nature and society more broadly. I have already referenced how the crux of Postone's critique is premised on the notion of something called 'traditional Marxism' which is 'transhistorical – and commonsensical'. How? Why? From the start Postone makes it clear that 'traditional Marxism' is something that places class at the heart of its project: it understands 'capitalism essentially in terms of class relations structured by a market economy and private ownership of the means of production. Relations of domination are understood primarily in terms of class domination and exploitation.'[3] But 'at the heart of this theory is a transhistorical – and commonsensical – understanding of labour as an activity mediating humans and nature that transforms matter in a goal-directed manner and is a condition of social life'.[4]

Postone throws around the word 'transhistorical' as a criticism – i.e. to posit labour as in some way being a transhistorical process is to fall into the dogmas of 'commonsensical' thought. And yet, at the most abstract level, there is a sense in which human labour really is 'transhistorical' – if by that we mean it has key characteristics which pertain to every social epoch and every human society regardless of the level of historical development they have achieved; that there are universal and binding characteristics to the labour process which apply as much to a tribe of hunter-gatherers as they do to a group of technicians working in a nuclear power plant. In fact, classical Marxism is pivoted on the recognition of this. For Marx, every society without exception experiences the need to be able to feed, clothe and shelter a substantial proportion of its population; that it must be able to produce and reproduce the material conditions by which the society could continue to exist in and through its labour – 'Every child knows a nation which ceased to work, I will not say for a year, but even for a few weeks, would perish.'[5]

But such ability to produce and reproduce the means of social existence depends on labour's mediation with nature and the forms of organization which facilitate this. Furthermore, the development of the division of labour in any given society depends on the forms of social organization by which different groups facilitate labour with nature; it might be simple and direct, as with hunter-gatherers picking berries from trees – it might also be incredibly complex and mediated, as with call centre workers ringing random homes to try to sell finished products which have been worked up in factories which synthesize the raw materials, raw materials which are, in the last analysis, mined, extracted and farmed in and through a more direct interaction with nature. The first – the case of the hunter-gatherer – applies to a simple and classless form of society in which a complex division of labour has not had the chance to develop – the second applies to a situation of great complexity and richness with many different labour operations, and also class stratification in and through the division of labour. But there is a transhistorical element which applies to both; that is, in both cases an original, elemental natural material is mediated in and through the social organization of labour – albeit that the form of such an organization has a very different character and is specific to the historical epoch in question: 'this necessity of the distribution of social labor in definite proportions cannot possibly be done away with .... What can change in historically different circumstances is only the form.'[6]

Indeed one might safely say that Marxism is the intellectual theorization of the process by which human beings create their own means of production in and through the organization of their social labour via its mediation with nature. Furthermore, it is in the tracing of that process – the evolution of more complex forms of social organization as an ontology of labour – which eventually allowed Marx to conceive in the modern epoch the true nature of socialized labour organized on an industrial basis in the form of the exploitation of labour by capital; subsequently Marx was able to recognize the social agency (proletariat) which has the capacity – by virtue of its number, concentration and class interests – to mould the forms and freedoms of a future society from the material of the present *vis-à-vis* its revolutionary ability to take control of the means of production. In this sense Marxism isn't something which urges us towards a more utopic future in terms of an abstract, idealized idea which floats above reality; rather it is an intellectual concept which is latent in the contradictions – the real forms and structures of social existence – which the organization of labour mediated with nature throws up.

I say this in order to make clear that when Postone writes how '[the] understanding of labour as an activity mediating humans and nature that transforms matter in a goal-directed manner and is a condition of social life ... [is] ... transhistorical – and commonsensical' – the first thing we should note is that this does not represent an attempt to 'update' Marxism, or to 'modernize' or 'adapt' or 'develop' it; rather it seeks to strike out at Marxism's most profound philosophical fundaments. Furthermore, if you deny the ontology of labour which is the essence of the Marxist theory of history, then – whether you wish it or not – you also lose its revolutionary implications; that is to say, the possibility of revolutionary overcoming is no longer tied to a concrete social agency which is itself evolved out of the broader development of the activity of human beings as they shape and reshape the world in and through their labour. Rather 'revolution' can only subsist as a purely moral postulate – a Kantian 'regulative ideal' to which moral individuals should aspire but which might never achieve any form of practical fruition. And this is absolutely vital. When Postone, in the same essay, talks about the supersession of the capitalist social system, we come to find that he does so in an abstract and nebulous language which works against the very notion of revolution in Marx.

For the classical position which Marx develops in *Capital* – the idea of the proletariat being the historical negation of capital at the level of social existence is effaced by Postone; 'the framework suggested by Marx's initial determination of the category of capital, such a theory does not constitute a critique of capitalism from the standpoint of its historical negation'.[7] What then remains in the aftermath? Because, according to Postone, 'capital and not the proletariat … is the total Subject' for Marx – the true historical negation of capitalism comes with 'the abolition of the totality'.[8] Notice here how we are moving away from a standpoint where, in and through revolutionary struggle the proletariat expropriates capital and takes over the means of production, abolishing the class relationship of exploitation therein – to a standpoint where what is abolished is not the nature of class society at all but an abstraction called 'the social totality'. In its way this is a fine example of the reification which Lukács worked to so meticulously diagnose – here the living social agencies of class conflict are transfigured into the dead and ossified formulation of a 'social totality', which – thing-like and bereft of living substance – becomes an abstraction which simply hangs in the air without rhyme or reason. Even on its own terms, what Postone is saying doesn't make any sense whatsoever. How on earth does one 'abolish' a 'social totality'? When would any society not persist as a totality, a social whole? One might as well try to abolish the 'social quantity' or the 'social substratum' or the 'social world' for all the good it would do you and all the sense it would make.

But to return to Postone's criticism of the 'transhistorical' and 'commonsensical' nature of the Marxist ontology of labour, what one has to ask oneself is simply this: Can there be any human society in which 'labour as an activity mediating humans and nature that transforms matter in a goal-directed manner and is a condition of social life' is not its prime condition? Can Postone provide an example of a society in the past which doesn't work this way? Can one even conceive in the imagination a society which doesn't produce and reproduce the conditions of its own existence in and through the self-conscious mediation of its labour with nature? When Postone dismisses such a postulation as 'commonsensical' he only reveals the fact that he simply hasn't understood the most elementary part of Marx's historical and philosophical thought. And all the guff about abolishing the 'social totality' flows from this fact.

If his understanding of Marxist theory is so compromised, his critique of Lukács, somewhat inevitably, is equally confused and unlettered. As already mentioned, for Postone, a genuine and authentic Marxist position is one which does not proceed from the standpoint of labour – but the standpoint of capital as 'the total subject'. According to Postone – Lukács' big error (and an expression of his dogmatic brand of 'traditional Marxism') lies in the fact that he, Lukács, does not treat capital as 'the total subject' (in the way Marx did) but rather Lukács begins from the standpoint of labour and the proletariat: for Lukács '"transhistorical labour," freed from the fetters of the market and private property, has openly emerged as the regulating principle of society. (This notion, of course, is bound to that of socialist revolution as the "self-realization" of the proletariat.)'[9] So again, most clearly we see how, for Postone, the idea of a class-based Marxism which is culminated by the proletariat taking power is not a genuine form of Marxism whatsoever; the authentic form of Marxism is one which jettisons such a 'transhistorical' and 'commonsensical' approach and treats 'capital' as 'the total subject'.

There are a few points to mention about Postone's 'capital' as the 'total subject' thesis. First off, in his masterwork, Marx does treat the concept of capital in a Hegelian fashion; that is he begins by treating it as a logical abstraction which contains within itself its own inner movement and development; the movement of capital (or more precisely the value-form) is analysed as an immanent logical unfolding as it passes through the initial abstract phases to the more concrete ones. As Chris Arthur says, Marx shows how capital as a logical concept 'builds itself up, moment by moment, into a self-actualising totality, an "Absolute"'.[10] But although Marx treats capital as a totalizing 'subject' – what Postone calls 'the total Subject' – he (Marx) does so in a precisely Hegelian sense; that is, for the purposes of the exhibition he is abstracting the logical concept of capital from its basis in the socio-historical determinations in the empirical world, specifically the labour power of the working classes. As Arthur also says, 'the movement of exchange, generating a system of *pure forms of value* … abstracted from the real material world … the form of value as such, which springs from exchange as a process of "abstraction" may be analysed regardless of any labour-content'.[11]

Of course, this in no way means that Marx has actually ceased to regard the development of society from the perspective of the proletariat – capital is, ultimately, the labour product of the latter in its alienated guise and from this springs the necessity of the proletariat's motion and trajectory; indeed Marx's historical and political analysis is predicated on that. But what Postone has done when he argues that Marx does not approach the development of capitalism from the standpoint of the proletariat is to conflate a necessary logical abstraction performed at a very early stage in Marx's overall exposition (and in the regions of 'pure thought') – with the much broader and overriding thrust of Marx's historical theory of classes; and the consequence is inevitable therein – Postone's brave new configuration of Marxism renders impossible 'socialist revolution as the "self-realization" of the proletariat'.

Postone's analysis, held together on such a thread-bare misconception, inevitably degrades into hopeless confusion. His criticism of Lukács rests on the fact that, like 'traditional Marxists' more broadly, he, Lukács, sees the 'social totality' from the purview of 'labour' whereas Marx in fact saw it from the purview of capital – capital as the 'total Subject'. And yet, later in the same essay Postone vividly contradicts this – his central criticism of the so-called 'traditional Marxist' position – when he writes that, for Lukács, capital as a historical subject is underpinned by 'the totality and the labour that constitutes it'.[12] So it turns out that Marx's position and that of Lukács are identical after all in as much as they both begin from the point of view of labour as the premise of capital.

But then Postone changes tacks again; now he says the difference lies in that, for Marx 'totality and the labour that constitutes [capital] …

become the objects of his critique'[13] whereas for Lukács (presumably) they are not. But what does it even mean to say that 'totality and labour' are the objects of Marx's critique? They are the objects of his analysis, for sure. But does he 'critique' labour? In fact, how would you go about doing that in the first place? How can you critique a concept which refers to the capacity of human beings to use their mental and physical powers to transform physical matter in ways which create and recreate the means for their own existence? You might as well provide a 'critique' of breathing, or a 'critique' of eyesight or a 'critique' of the colour green? It simply doesn't make any sense.

Perhaps when you know yourself to be an Important Intellectual Figure writing Important Intellectual Things you are free from the banal need to actually have people understand you; indeed the very opaqueness, self-contradiction and obscurity of your work are surely a sign of its profundity, of the labyrinthine complexity of your thought – the fact that only a tiny elite of the most gifted and precocious readers will be able to scale its dizzy heights. But, of course, this type of thing has little in common with Marxism and the profound democratic thrust of its revolutionary tenor. Marxism does not 'critique' labour (though one might certainly argue it critiques *the exploitation of labour*); rather the inverse is true. Socialized labour in its commodity form becomes the living critique of the capitalist social system because it has the ability to revolutionize it in practice – but again, and most crucially, this occurs through the culmination of *class struggle*.

Perhaps the clearest and cogent part of an otherwise convoluted piece of writing comes when Postone summarizes Lukács' attitude to the organization of labour under industrial capitalism; for Lukács, according to Postone, labour under capitalism is 'veiled by the fragmented and particularistic character of bourgeois social relations'.[14] Well, certainly a part of Lukács' understanding of the concept of reification does stem from a notion of 'fragmentation'. But once again the sheer self-contradiction in Postone's position abounds. Recall that Postone first accuses Lukács of developing an ontology of labour which is 'transhistorical' – it is this which he criticizes as a type of 'traditional Marxism'. And yet, in the next moment, he states categorically that Lukács' analysis of reification is premised on a highly specific historical category – '[the] particularistic character of bourgeois social relations'. The second description is simply incompatible with the thrust of Postone's broader critique, but he doesn't make any attempt to resolve or expand on it. But his analysis of Lukács and reification has significantly more troubling issues than inconsistency.

Postone talks about how, for Lukács, the processes of reification, 'rationalization and quantification that mould modern institutions are rooted in the commodity form'.[15] In the broadest and most abstract sense this is correct. But Lukács' great essay stipulates more than just this. I would argue that there are two absolutely vital criteria in Lukács' understanding of reification. The first centres around surplus appropriation: i.e. that the way in which the capitalist is able to extract some portion of labour power – surplus labour – which he or she does not compensate the worker for and is instead able to absorb as profit. Of course, surplus appropriation is again something common to all class societies, but in the relationship of capital to wage-labour the means by which one class expropriates the labour product of the other is rendered invisible.

In antique or medieval societies the means by which expropriation was carried out was visible to the naked eye; a feudal lord or slave master simply used his retinue and enforcers to confiscate the labour product or process of the serf, or the person of the slave. But in capitalism – the surplus product which is extracted from the class of direct producers by the ruling class – is actually disguised in terms of a contract which seems to entail the mere exchange of things or services for an equal amount; a fair day's work for a fair day's pay. Class exploitation and expropriation itself therefore appear in a reified guise as an exchange of 'things' – and consequently the portion of surplus product which the capitalist expropriates is rendered invisible. Hegemonically speaking, this has powerful implications; it allows for an illusion of equality and even freedom, whereby the generic seller, of his or her own volition, offers up a 'thing' or 'service' to a generic buyer; thus the forms and structures of broader class exploitation and oppression fade into the background.

The second fundamental aspect of Lukács' analysis of reification centres on the unique character of labour performed under industrial capitalism. This involves a particular type of abstract labour.[16] The medieval cobbler would make the shoes from scratch, shaping the raw materials into the finished product; he would be the overseer and impetus of the labour process in its totality. In an industrial factory, the workers making shoes would each perform a single operation in the overall process; one group of workers might be responsible for operating the machinery which presses the leather, for example, as the material crosses the factory conveyer belt. The point being that in the second instance the worker is no longer the motive power of production, no longer conceives the labour product as an intellectual ideal to be manifested in and through a self-conscious and imaginative strategy; rather the worker becomes merely one more component force in the processes of production themselves, exerting a physical force through the repetition of simple and automatic movements on the factory line; he or she becomes an abstract energy which is applied to the productive process, comparable with other energies such as electricity or fuel.

The labour of the worker under industrial conditions then is quite literally 'reified' – i.e. literally transformed into 'a thing', an abstract energy, a purely natural bodily force. When labour appears in its 'abstract' guise as a simple, untrammelled power of production, it also becomes quantifiable and commensurable. Two medieval cobblers would take very different lengths of time to cobble together any one pair of shoes, precisely because of their unique techniques and abilities. But the output of one worker performing the same mechanical action on the factory line will be roughly equivalent to that of any other worker in the same position over the same period of time.

Because of this, a factory manager can usually estimate with some accuracy just how many products a group of thirty workers would produce in a six-day week. The reification of labour itself crosses into the technique and strategy of labour management; because labour in its simplified abstraction can be quantified in this way, it can also be better rationalized – organized like any other force or component of production, such that it attains an optimal capacity; the labour of the worker can be precisely regulated according to clocking in cards and regimented breaks such that its output achieves its highest level. The development of Taylorism at the *fin de siècle* was the first coherent and self-conscious expression of this set into a theoretical prospectus.

Postone makes the case that, for Lukács, the processes of reification issue forth from his (Lukács') understanding of 'the commodity form as the basic structuring social form of capitalist society'.[17] But while this is true, it is also insufficient. The two main aspects of reification which are essential for Lukács are the way in which the expropriation of labour power by capital is rendered invisible and the way in which labour power in its industrialized form is manifested as an abstract force. The key to understanding Lukács' concept of reification, therefore, is not only through 'the commodity form as the basic structuring social form' (Postone) but more precisely through the commodity form in its specific guise as labour power. Lukács understands the processes of reification under industrial capitalism as arising most directly from the relationship of class exploitation which is situated around labour-power in its commodity form – i.e. reification is a necessary expression of the particular character of class relations which are historically evolved into the capitalist social system.

But while Postone emphasizes the role of the commodity form in Lukács' analysis, he abstracts it from the fact that we are in particular concerned with the commodity form as labour power. For this reason, reification ceases to be something which arises from the class struggle; rather it becomes something which is understood in terms of a more generic notion of 'modernity' which corresponds to the Weberian template of a rational bureaucracy: 'More specifically, Lukács adopts Weber's characterization of modernity in terms of processes of rationalization'.[18] But while containing great insight as to the character of modern bureaucracy, Weber's analysis has profoundly ahistorical roots; that is, he postulates an idea – specifically that of (Calvinist) Protestantism – which goes to work in the world creating the impetus to capitalist society; but as to why the idea arose when it did or the social conditions which were in place for it to evolve in the first place – for this, Weber can provide no type of coherent explanation. Protestantism simply comes into being – and thus created the conditions for modern capitalism premised on the idealistic impulses to hard work and investment that the religion promotes. The idea of reading the forms of consciousness from their basis in social existence, as in Marx, in Weber is inverted; consciousness simply bubbles into being from nothingness – pristine and fully realized in the Protestant theology – and then goes on to call forth the historical forms and structures of a new mode of production and its epoch.

By characterizing Lukács' theory of reification as a hybrid fusion of Marxism and Weberianism, Postone is able to dissolve its roots in the development of class struggle, instead reconfiguring it in the purely generic terms of a bureaucracy which is grounded in the category of the 'commodity form'. The issue of reification is no longer seen primarily as something which is pivoted on the extraction of labour power by capital in and through a relationship of class exploitation – rather the 'processes of rationalization and quantification that mould modern institutions'[19] spring from the structure of the commodity form per-se as a generic organizing principle – but one which is separate from the exploitation of labour power out of which a system of generalized commodity production grows.

As we have already seen, the character of 'rationalization and quantification' that the modern bureaucracy is stamped with develops out of the essence of capitalist labour in its fragmented, specialized and abstract form – i.e. labour manifested as partial and one-sided under industrial conditions – and therefore something which is quantifiable in precise terms, something to be rationalized in ever more precise ways. The reified character of modern bureaucracy, which was perceived quite correctly by Weber in several regards, was an expression of the way in which capital organized labour in the context of the developing industrial revolution – it was, therefore, a fundamental expression of class exploitation and appropriation. Indeed, there have been many pre-capitalist societies which have featured high levels of commodity production and yet the phenomenon of reification was barely extant.

What makes capitalism unique is that labour power itself has emerged in its commodity form and as the predominating form of labour within that social system. When Postone focuses on the commodity form in the abstract – *as opposed to the commodity labour power* – he not only denudes Lukács' theory of its historical thrust, but in the same moment, he absolves the bureaucracy of its specifically capitalist character. This is the essence of the Weberian vision – it imposes a generic form of rationality and modernization which smothers the social forces and the specific historical conditions of the class conflict which sets the basis for it. Of course it is worth noting just how much Lukács was influenced by Weber, a one-time mentor – for this reason Postone's use of Weber seems almost viable – but what Postone hasn't in the slightest comprehended is that Lukács' theory of reification marks a radical break with Weberianism precisely because it conceives of the rise of capitalism in terms of the class conflict which underpins it.

It should be said, at this point, that Postone – in reading Lukács' theory of reification through Weber and in dissolving its basis in class struggle therein – is actually very positive about the Lukács he has managed to bowdlerize. And there is a reason for this. The Lukácsian theory of reification as reimagined by Postone is actually very close to the political and ontological standpoint of the Frankfurt School, a group Postone was heavily influenced by. Weber deploys a form of idealism to counter class-based historical materialism; he asserts that the idea (Protestantism) simply creates the forms and structures of capitalist modernity – but the idea has no origination in its own right, no necessary genesis in historical development more broadly. Adorno and Horkheimer deploy a similar idealist operation – they argue that, at a certain point in time, something called 'Enlightenment thought' emerges. They stipulate that reason itself – the use of rational thought on the part of human beings is essentially inadequate to the world; that the application of rationality to nature falls short because reason is not capable of divulging all the quality and idiosyncrasy of the natural object, instead reducing it to purely quantitative and rational dimensions which abstract from its richness and particularity.

For Adorno and Horkheimer, Enlightenment thought is wholly 'instrumental'; it is incapable of grasping the natural object in its full and variegated reality but regards it merely as a source to be rationalized, stripped down and converted into an abstract material which humanity uses purely for its own aggrandizement. However, the more human beings regard the world around them from a purely rational and instrumentalist perspective, the more they apply such a vision to other human beings, to society more broadly. As their scientific power and dominion over nature increases, so does the ability to rationalize, quantify and ultimately subject human relations in their entirety: 'Human beings purchase the increase in their power with estrangement from that over which it is exerted. Enlightenment stands in the same relationship to things as the dictator to human beings. He knows them to the extent that he can manipulate them.'[20] In this way, the capitalist social system and the tyranny of exchange value – i.e. the aspect of the commodity form which dissolves the richness and the particularity of the individual labour operation in the quantified and abstract category of labour time – are called into being.

In both Adorno and Horkheimer, and Weber too – the capitalist social system does not evolve out of the development of the living class struggle, out of the mode of exploitation which opens up between bourgeoisie and proletariat at the level of historical existence. Rather capitalism evolves out of an idea – in the case of Weber, it is Protestantism; in the case of Adorno and Horkheimer, it is 'Enlightenment thought'. Because the Frankfurt luminaries conjure up the capitalist system not from the forms of socio-historical existence that it developed out of – but from the pristine abstraction of something called 'Enlightenment thought' – they conceptualize a capitalism which is generic and eternal; it has not been historically created, and for the same reason it cannot be historically superseded. This, ultimately, is the key to the pessimism which is an inevitable part of the Frankfurt School perspective. By seeing Lukács through a Weberian lens, Postone is able to achieve something similar. He is able to remove the aspect of class struggle which is essential to Lukács' theory and remove thereby the one social agency, the proletariat, which has the ability to transform a reified world.

Of course, the Lukács Postone presents us with has little in common with the original. In fact, in order to create an ahistorical Lukács, Postone must first disavow the philosophical and historical roots of Lukács' actual theory of reification. Postone essentially tells us that, in fact, there are two versions of Lukács' theory – there is the one which he, Postone, believes to be the salutary one – i.e. the one which does away with class struggle and the revolutionary succession of the proletariat in favour of creating a 'Marxism' in which capitalism appears in the guise of a Weberian rational bureaucracy underpinned by the transhistorical template of the commodity form (the commodity form abstracted from its manifestation as labour power). And then there is the 'traditional Marxism', that old defunct form of Marxism which still harps on about class struggle and the like, and which sophisticates like Postone have long since moved beyond. He writes:

There is an apparent tension in Lukács's thought. On the one hand, his focus on the commodity form allows for a critique of capitalism that explodes the limits of the traditional Marxist framework. On the other hand, when he addresses the question of the possible overcoming of capitalism, he has recourse to the notion of the proletariat as the revolutionary Subject of history. This idea, however, is bound to a traditional conception of capitalism where labour is considered to be the standpoint of the critique. And it is difficult to see how the notion of the proletariat as the revolutionary Subject points to the possibility of a historical transformation of the quantitative, rationalized and rationalizing character of modern institutions that Lukács critically analyzes as capitalist.[21]

It is difficult to understand why the notion of the 'proletariat as the revolutionary Subject points to the possibility of a historical transformation of the quantitative, rationalized and rationalizing character of modern institutions that Lukács critically analyzes as capitalist' only in as much as Postone has not understood the very basics of it! His essay does not display the slightest awareness of the way in which Hegelian categories inform Lukács' analysis of reification. He, Postone, writes:

> As is well-known, Hegel attempted to overcome the classical theoretical dichotomy of subject and object with his theory that reality, natural as well as social, subjective as well as objective, is constituted by practice – by the objectifying practice of the Geist, the world-historical Subject. The Geist constitutes objective reality by means of a process of externalization, or self-objectification, and, in the process, reflexively constitutes itself.[22]

In fact, this is a surprisingly good summary of Hegel's approach to the historical process *in its generality* – but what Postone doesn't do at any point in the essay is to actually examine how Lukács applies the 'subject object' category to his analysis of capitalism and reification. Actually, that's not quite true; Postone informs us that 'Lukács identifies the proletariat in a "materialized" Hegelian manner as the identical subject-object of the historical process, as the historical Subject, constituting the social world and itself through its labour'[23] but says nothing more. From this brief description, it sounds as though Lukács has imposed a rather mysterious and abstract Hegelian 'teleology' onto the proletariat from the outside – indeed this is how many a criticism of Lukács' 'proletariat as the identical subject-object of the historical process' has been phrased.

But if you actually examine Lukács' argument on this issue – and Postone most certainly does not – you see that not only is Lukács' Hegelian reading of Marxism faithful to Marx's original theory, but that it involves a very specific and highly contextualized historically materialist reading of both the way capitalism develops and the revolutionary possibilities which inhere within it therein. In actual fact, Lukács examines both the proletariat and the bourgeoisie as historical 'subjects'; he looks at the class position of both in their subjective guises *vis-à-vis* their relation to the means of production. And he notes that their 'subjectivity' has different 'objective' limits precisely because of the virtue of such class positions.

For the bourgeoisie as a historical subject, the object of appropriation is capital. Such appropriation is predicated on its encounter with an object which exists forever 'out there', something which is not the manifestation of its own immanent productions, but is instead to be arrogated from an external power (proletariat) which exists in irreconcilable contradiction to itself. Capital is the social relation of exploitation which opens up between bourgeoisie and proletariat; it is the portion of labour power which is generated by the working class and which is then appropriated by the bourgeoisie for the purposes of investment and capital expansion. The object of appropriation which becomes capital is simultaneously the product of another; it is the alienated labour-power of the proletariat brought within the remit of the bourgeoisie *vis-à-vis* production. The dualism of subject and object is thus built into the social existence of the bourgeoisie as something fundamentally irreconcilable.

But with the proletariat, the situation is different. It is true that the proletariat as a class stands in an irrevocable and dualistic opposition to the bourgeoisie every bit as much as the bourgeoisie does to the proletariat. But the difference lies in this. For the proletariat, capital, the object 'out there' is not something which it appropriates; rather it is something which has been appropriated from it; capital is the labour-power of the proletariat which has been alienated by the bourgeoisie. For the proletariat, the object 'out there' is not something which exists in inexorable difference to itself; rather capital is a product of the proletariat's most essential nature albeit one which is then manifested in an alien guise. For the bourgeoisie the subject-object distinction will always remain untraversable, for subject and object are antipodes. For the proletariat, however, the object is, on the most fundamental level, identical with the subject.

In the last analysis, the revolutionary move of the proletariat to take over the means of production, to create workers' councils which regulate the production and distribution of all social goods and services, to submit to itself the totality of the objective forms of organization of the capitalist social system – involves reclaiming the estranged essence of its own subjectivity – its alienated labour in the form of capital. In so doing, the proletariat achieves 'subject-object' identity.

When one understands the Hegelian inflection of Lukács' Marxism as springing from the concrete forms and categories of capitalism at the level of social being – the subject-object identity formulation ceases to appear as some kind of quasi-mystical Hegelian 'teleology' which is imposed on the historical process from without and acts as a *deus ex machina* to resolve any and every contradiction. Rather Lukács' formulation of the 'proletariat as the identical subject-object of the historical process' is really a more explicitly philosophical way of describing what is already Marx's revolutionary position when the latter talks about how the socialization of labour under industrial conditions sets the basis for the abolition of capitalism in and through the 'cooperation and the possession in common of the land and of the means of production'[24] on the part of the direct producers. The achievement of subject-object identity on the part of the proletariat is simply the philosophical expression of the political slogan by which Marx characterizes the culmination of communism more broadly – i.e. '[t]he expropriators are expropriated'.[25] Subject-object identity, then, is simply a euphemism for a successful proletarian revolution.

But what bearing does this have on Lukács' notion of reification? Well, if you consider how reification for Lukács is a consequence of one: the way in which the extraction of surplus labour from the proletariat by the bourgeoisie appears at the level of the appearance of economic relations to manifest as a mere exchange of things: and two, the way in which industrial labour becomes fragmented such that the labour of the individual worker manifests as an abstract force in terms of an unspecialized labour operation – in acknowledging both these criteria you come to realize that, for Lukács, putting an end to the phenomenon of reification must, of necessity, involve ending the appropriation of labour-power by capital at the level of socio-historical existence. Or to say the same, reification is an expression of the dualism of the subject-object expressed by the class exploitation of proletariat by bourgeoisie; for the same reason, the reification of social relationships in the world we live in can only be abolished when such subject-object dualism is overcome, i.e. when the proletariat, the historical subject, is able to realize subject-object identity in practice in and through the revolutionary appropriation of the means of production.

By this point we can recognize how, for Lukács, the theory of reification is inexorably bound up to his philosophical conception of subject-object dualism expressed in the dichotomy which opens up at the level of historical existence between proletariat and bourgeoisie; moreover we can also understand how the subject-object identity achieved by the proletariat in terms of its own historical process culminating in the revolutionary control of the means of production is the only means by which the emanations of the reified reality can be dissipated. With this in mind, we can return to Postone's critique once more. Postone's critique of Lukács is confused, unlettered and utterly contradictory. In one moment he asserts that Lukács' concept of reification is 'transhistorical' and 'commonsensical', in the next he asserts that it is particular to 'fragmented' bourgeois conditions. In another moment he says that Lukács looks at capitalism from the standpoint of labour whereas Marx looks at it from the point of view of capital; but in the next, he says they both look at it from the standpoint of labour.

But when all these rather clumsy errors – inevitably disguised by the pontificating language of a Very Important Intellectual – are set aside, what essentially remains on Postone's part is the attempt to convert a Marxist-Lukácsian description of capitalism as being pregnant with the class contradictions which are centred around the commodity in its form as labour power – to an anti-Marxist description of capitalism as a rational and bureaucratic system centred around the commodity form as a general and generic concept which renders the living class struggle between proletariat and bourgeoisie virtually obsolete.

In order to realize this vision it is necessary for Postone to go to the core, to attack the philosophical roots of Lukács' Marxism in terms of its Hegelian origins – to attack the possibility of the proletariat reclaiming its own alienated labour through subject-object identity as the control of the means of production. To achieve this, Postone opposes to Hegelian historicity – Weberian idealism, and using the template of a Weberian rational bureaucracy – albeit one which is articulated in the Marxist idiom of the commodity form – Postone is able to vanquish the spectre of historical development driven by class contradiction and ultimately, therefore, he is able to do away with the idea of 'socialist revolution as the "self-realization" of the proletariat'.

In conclusion, Postone purports to provide a critical analysis of Lukács' theory of reification, but in providing such analysis, Postone himself presents us with a key instance of reification; that is to say, he transforms Lukács' Marxism from one where the capitalist social system is the expression of social categories of class struggle and class exploitation to one in which capitalism is a generic, 'thing-like' entity indifferent to living social-historical forces and, consequently, impervious to historical change. Postone's analysis becomes the very embodiment of the tendency Lukács so eloquently and so profoundly helped diagnose, the converting of fluid social relationships into the ossified form of the thing – and yet, the irony is that Postone is utterly oblivious to the nature of his own methodological procedure.

Partly this is because, like so many of his brethren, Postone writes in a rather convoluted way – and the sheer rambling portentousness of his world-historic pontifications actually works to disguise the crude and simplistic nature of his errors. He contradicts what he himself says again and again – and yet, despite the fact that the writing is all over the place, there is nevertheless a unity to it, a singleness of purpose, even if this occurs on an unconscious and protean level. Ultimately, everything in Postone's essay works to dissolve the notion of class struggle which is so integral to both Marx, and the Marxism of the Lukács who wrote *History and Class Consciousness*. In dissolving the role of class, quite naturally, Postone is able to annul the possibility of proletarian revolution therein.

Postone's essay on Lukács – and his more general critique of 'traditional Marxism' – doesn't represent an attempt to go back to the fundaments of Marx himself. It doesn't represent a methodological contribution to the ever-evolving tradition of Marxism. It represents nothing more than a form of the most virulent anti-Marxism. But it is being packaged and sold in the language of Marxism itself – and in the figure of a Very Important Intellectual. And having endured decades of neoliberalism and the retreat of class struggle more broadly, it is often quite tempting to find the answers to history not in the force and the energy of the mass movement but in the pristine, untroubled and lofty depths of the mind of the brilliant academic whose radical rhetoric disguises the fact that he is far more at home in the capitalist social world than it might at first seem.

Chapter 8
Revolution and counterrevolution in thought

You might have noticed something in the preceding pages of this book. Some of the writing is less than dispassionate. Sometimes the tone crosses over into the emotive. On occasion, the writer is even insulting to the thinkers under discussion. Now, as someone who has spent a little time in academia as a student, perhaps I should offer up a *mia culpa*. After all, one of the prevailing themes in my own experience of university education was that 'polemic' was considered to be off-limits. If you were rude in your criticisms, if your tone was emotive – the suggestion was that you were losing your sense of objectivity. That heated polemic was anathema to cool, crisp reason. That the delivery of a barbed comment or sarcastic rejoinder was often indicative of an insubstantial or weaker argument. After all, respectability and decorum should be observed at all times in any truly *civilized* debate.

Of course, the rich intellectual tradition which I have the honour of calling my own – that of revolutionary Marxism – involves a long history of polemical exchanges often conducted in a spirit of lacerating irony or white-hot fury. Consider the withering critique which Marx and Engels levelled against Max Stirner in *The German Ideology* rife with insult and mockery, or think about Lenin's furious denunciation of 'the renegade Kautsky' in the aftermath of the First World War, or later still,

Trotsky's sardonic and scornful takedown of James Burnham and the combination of pragmatism and empiricism the latter was peddling in the late 1930s. On a simple emotional level, it can feel refreshing to have the pettiness and folly of others laid bare, crisply dissected in clean withering prose by a penetrating mind, and some of the finest writers often turn their most memorable and iconic phrases in the crucible of bitter and heated dispute. But if this was all there was to recommend polemic, it would remain a merely cosmetic diversion, providing a purely psychological satisfaction on the part of the reader, or the rich stylistic rewards which come from the employment of it by the writer. I think, however, there is something more at stake here, that polemic has a more necessary and historical function.

I remember something more from my time at university too. I advocate what might be called 'classical' Marxism. I continue to believe that the solution to the capitalist riddle of oppression and exploitation in the modern world is to be found in the working class and its ability to take power in and through its control over the factories and the schools, the call centres and the shops, the docks and the offices and the workplaces more generally. I think it is only the vast majority of humanity – humanity in the broadest and most universal sense – who are capable of solving humanity's problems in and through economic and social practice. In a university discussion group, when I would raise these kinds of arguments, people would sometimes shoot glances at each other, raise their eyebrows, smile knowingly, and I often felt this was for my benefit; that they were communicating to me in another way, because etiquette wouldn't allow them to be explicitly rude or dismissive out loud (remember polemic is always a 'no-no'). They were resorting to a different type of language, a mute language in which contempt could be expressed with an ironic cock of the head or a surreptitious gaze. As a Marxist more broadly, I am used to people explaining to me in a considerably more direct fashion just how out-of-date and prehistoric Marxism actually is; how the promise of its quasi-religious utopia has been refuted by reality; how, if Marxist/proletarian movements eventually do come to power they will always degenerate into a form of dictatorship or totalitarianism. It is often frustrating because, the majority of time, the people who say these things with such world-weary wisdom are also the same people who have never actually sat down and read a single word of Marx. Sometimes I will try and unpack the arguments by talking about what Marx 'actually said'; other times I will try and explain something about Stalinism, how it did not emerge as part and parcel of the Russian Revolution but came about in and through processes of counterrevolution and foreign invasion.[1]

My view is in the minority. And, for that reason, I am no longer surprised by the 'refutations' of Marxism which people I am sometimes meeting for the first time feel compelled to treat me to. But I mention the university discussion group for a reason. The attitudes of some of the people there were more surprising to me. Their contempt for the very idea of working-class power was, on the surface, paradoxical. For the group itself – the group I was attending – was a Marxist discussion group. Many of its members stood within that particular tradition. They considered themselves as Marxists. And yet, despite this, most of them felt that the idea of workers actually taking power, taking control of the means of production, control of everything their labour sets the basis for – was a ridiculous delusion to which no sane person would subscribe. My time in that university discussion group taught me definitively that the Marxism which is cultivated in academia often stands in sharp contrast to that advocated by Marx, i.e. a philosophy of practice which traces the process of proletarian self-emancipation and the necessary creation of a society which is not premised on the exploitation of one class by another.

In other words, one of the features of the type of Marxism which held sway in this discussion group is that it allowed theory to be divorced from practice and thus denuded Marxism of its revolutionary implications. It was a Marxism which could quite happily coexist within the foundations and forms of capitalism itself. The lecturers, PHD students and professors who were espousing it were, in the main, from the middle classes and a good few of them were products of the public school[2] system. They were people with many and multifarious radical leanings but at the same time their career trajectories had depended on those they'd met through an elevated professional *milieu* and their membership of a network of class privilege and connection which had given both support and succour to their lives more broadly. The assimilation of your own sense of privilege is often an unconscious one. It doesn't always have a rational or ideological clarity. Rather it expresses itself in a deep-seated anxiety to or hostility towards popular forms or ideas which threaten to radically transfigure the nature of a social system whose 'stability' has previously guaranteed your own position, even your own sense of identity perhaps. On the one hand, many of these extremely bright people were clearly aware of the horrors of capitalism, its day-to-day injustices and so they had automatically a certain left leaning and yet the thought that the system could be practically transformed or superseded in practice through revolutionary means was one which – on some primordial level – managed to disturb and threaten their deeper sense of equilibrium and sense of place in the world more broadly.

Such anxiety is only ever the crystallization on a psychological level of a certain semi-conscious awareness of the deeper historical forces – the tensions and pressure of class conflict – always at work just beneath the surface of human life. One of the palliatives to such an anxiety is to soften and nullify that sense of class struggle at the level of theory in and through the civilized, airy and peaceful environs of the lecture hall or seminar room. There is a strong tendency within the university world to develop a form of Marxism in which the possibilities of class struggle and revolutionary overcoming in practice are abated. And so, Marxism becomes a section of theory, an intellectual tradition separated from its radical practice; a component of philosophy or sociology to be discussed in much the same way one might discuss Durkheim's notion of egoistic suicide or Leucippus' and Democritus' theory of atoms. It wouldn't make much sense to hurl insults at someone who favoured Epicurus' atomic theory over that of his pre-Socratic precursors, however much you were convinced of your view.

But in the case of Lenin arguing against Kautsky, for instance, something else is true. Lenin was so furious with Kautsky not only because he felt that Kautsky had an inadequate grip on Marxist theory at the time, but because he, Lenin, believed that Kautsky's theoretical errors had practical implications; i.e. by inferring that the path to socialism could be won through bourgeois democracy Kautsky was stymieing support for the newly formed workers' councils which underpinned the revolutionary proletarian democracy. Whether one sides with Kautsky or Lenin here is beside the point; the important thing to note is that the polemical tone which Lenin's counterargument had assumed was also an expression of the fact that he thought the theoretical posing of these issues had the most immediate and grievous of practical consequences.

I would argue, therefore, the disdain for polemics which is part and parcel of the academic *milieu* – the attempt to 'sanitize' Marxism by absolving it of any fraught emotional content – is part and parcel of the need to look at it in terms of a purely academic and theoretical pursuit which is abstracted from the practical life of society more broadly; to thus absolve it of its revolutionary connotations. The 'way' it is discussed, the 'tone' with which it is talked about; these things (which seem relatively superficial) are themselves in fact determined by class interests.

Of course this is just one way in which Marxism becomes 'neutered' when it is brought into the academic world. At a more fundamental level, the actual workings of Marxism are tinkered with, its method distorted and its revolutionary conclusions forgone – in order to create a Marxism which resonates more sympathetically with the life of the bourgeois intellectual. As we have seen in some of the previous chapters, much of the power of revolutionary Marxism is described in terms of the notion of 'totality' which takes the form of a socio-historical unfolding. But now consider the following passage where Louis Althusser explains the category of the 'social totality':

If historical time is the existence of the social totality we must be precise about the structure of this existence. The fact that the relation between the social totality and its historical existence is a relation with an immediate existence implies that this relation is itself immediate. In other words: the structure of historical existence is such that all the elements of the whole always co-exist in one and the same time, one and the same present, and are therefore contemporaneous with one another in one and the same present. This means that the structure of the historical existence of the Hegelian social totality allows what I propose to call an 'essential section' (coupe d'essence), i.e., an intellectual operation in which a vertical break is made at any moment in historical time, a break in the present such that all the elements of the whole revealed by this section are in an immediate relationship with one another, a relationship that immediately expresses their internal essence. When I speak of an 'essential section', I shall therefore be referring to the specific structure of the social totality that allows this section, in which all the elements of the whole are given in a co-presence, itself the immediate presence of their essences, which thus become immediately legible in them. It is clear that it is the specific structure of the social totality which allows this essential section: for this section is only possible because of the peculiar nature of the unity of this totality, a 'spiritual' unity, if we can express in this way the type of unity possessed by an expressive totality, i.e., a totality all of whose parts are so many 'total parts', each expressing the others, and each expressing the social totality that contains them, because each in itself contains in the immediate form of its expression the essence of the totality itself.[3]

What can one make of this? Is it even possible to have a 'social totality' which doesn't have a 'historical existence'? And what does it mean to say that a 'social totality' and 'historical existence' are 'immediate'? Such a statement is certainly not untrue, of course. We all experience history as something 'immediate' in as much as we live in the present moment and we encounter society, the social world – 'the social totality' – directly so to say. Saying that 'historical existence' is 'immediate' is really a very wordy way of saying something as simple as 'we live in the present'. And that, of course, is difficult to deny. But in the same moment our lives are formed by the past. And we look to the future with the expectation of change. 'Historical existence', therefore, is something we encounter in an immediate fashion, but it is also something we encounter in a mediated and indirect way. All Althusser has managed to do is utter a very simple, one-sided generality in a very complicated and torturous form of prose. It all sounds very portentous and it all sounds very significant, but once you strip away the veneer and the pretence, you realize that he has said almost nothing of meaning whatsoever.

The same procedure is repeated further down the paragraph. We are informed in a lofty fashion: 'the structure of historical existence is such that all the elements of the whole always co-exist in one and the same time'. In the very next sentence he adds that it is for this reason that they are 'contemporaneous with one another in one and the same present'. This, of course, is just repetition, no new information has been provided, and yet it is presented in the high-faluting and pontificating tone of one who is certain they are making world-historical strides in the history of thought. More importantly, the same question arises: What has Althusser actually said here? We understand that there is a 'social whole' and all its elements exist at 'the same time'. Again, one can hardly disagree, but the information is less that revelatory. A whole exists at the same time as its parts. It is hardly a eureka moment.

But besides providing a rather banal generality, Althusser's description of a 'social totality' fails to reference any living social agency or tendency which constitutes a 'part' of that totality. There is no reference to a class, a state or any other social group; it talks about the 'social totality' and 'historical existence'; but these things are abstracted from the actual socio-historical categories which might give them some meaning. Conceptual categories increasingly take on the semblance and properties of physical structures and objects which are alienated from any social content. Socio-historical entities are depicted as purely structural fetishes. For instance, Althusser analyses the social totality 'in which all the elements of the whole are given in a co-presence, itself the immediate presence of their essences, which thus become immediately legible in them'. Each 'essence' is able to express 'the social totality that contains them' but what is the essence of this 'social totality in the first place'? Are we dealing with a capitalist social world in which the commodity form is the fundamental economic unit? Are we dealing with a social whole in which hunter-gathering is the central mode of production? We do not know. Althusser does not deign to say. But he does tell us that such a 'social totality' can be subject to a sudden interruption in its historical continuity. Does such an interruption come from revolution, from civil war, from global-economic crisis perhaps?

Not at all, rather it is simply described as 'a vertical break'. Again we can see that the socio-historical element is transformed into something which is purely physical and structural: 'a vertical break' – something which has quite literally a geographical position ('vertical') in the context of physical space. Of course there is something of the nonsensical about this once more; the idea of describing any historical event as a 'vertical break' makes about as much sense as describing it as a 'horizontal break' or a 'diagonal break', i.e. none whatsoever – but there is method in this madness; once more, that which is socio-historical in nature has by the tortuous mechanics of Althusser's thought been transformed into a 'thing'.

George Orwell once commented that 'good prose is like a window pane'; that is to say, it should be clear and understandable to all. I don't share Orwell's view on this. It seems to me that as the sciences and social sciences probe ever deeper into our reality, such an increased specialization and depth of knowledge require a more technical and intricate language in order to express it. I wouldn't expect a medical treatise on Lymphedema to be 'like a window pane' in terms of its clarity, and I, for one, would lack the specialist knowledge to understand the terminology and the arguments. For this reason, my criticisms of an Adorno or Althusser do not boil down to the fact that they use a technical language which is often difficult for a non-specialist reader; the works of Aristotle, Hegel and Marx all do that at times, and with good reason. My critique is not motivated by anti-intellectualism. Rather I would suggest that the sheer obscurity in style and language of a writer like Althusser has two main functions. One, it works to foster a pronounced sense of elitism. What you are reading is so profound, so monumental, and so esoteric, that only a few great minds will ever be able to master it. What a thinker like Althusser or Adorno does with their ridiculously complex jargon is to differentiate themselves from the mass of humanity, to better facilitate the image of themselves as a world-historic genius while at the same time disguising the paucity and crudity of the arguments they are actually making. Two, and this is the more important issue: much of the complex and opaque language overlays a process of reification; that is, the thinker in question is able to take what are living and fluid socio-historical entities and contradictions – particularly the contradictions of class – and convert them into things which interrelate in a purely structural and physical manner.

To take an example. In the following, the Trotskyist thinker Ernest Mandel offers up a 'historical reading' of the work of the detective-noir novelist Raymond Chandler. Mandel argues that we should interpret Chandler's work in and through a precise understanding of the specific historical conditions from which it arose. Hence Mandel writes:

> The evolution of the crime story reflects the history of crime itself. With Prohibition in the United States crime came of age … Organized crime came to dominate … [taking] over … bootlegging, prostitution, gambling and the numbers game … With the expansion

of activities more capital was required for investment in trucks, weapons, killers, bribes for police and politicians, exploitation of foreign sources of supply (export of capital) ... The coming of age of organized crime tolled the death knell of the drawing-room detective story. It is impossible to imagine Hercule Poirot, not to mention Lord Peter Wimsey or Father Brown, battling against the Mafia ... It was an abrupt break with the gentility of the classical detective story, especially with crime based on individual psychological motives like greed and revenge. Social corruption, especially among the rich, now moves into the centre of the plots, along with brutality, a reflection of both the change in bourgeois values brought about by the first world war and the impact of organized gangsterism.[4]

Mandel's analysis also reveals why Chandler's protagonist Philip Marlowe needed to be drawn. For those crimes which are more social and endemic in nature, and which presuppose a systematic network of bureaucratic (class) corruption, a detective in the vein of a Miss Marple or a Lord Peter Wimsey is utterly inadequate to the task. One requires a more hardboiled, plebeian character who carries within themselves the tenor and character of vast swathes of people, who is himself a microcosm of the masses, and is able to navigate the underlying and veiled relationships of power and exploitation which open up behind the scenes and impact their lives. While Marlowe has the sense of justice, the moral purpose, of a Miss Marple or Father Brown (albeit cosseted behind a jaded exterior), the key to his literary power lies in the way he is able to speak the language of the streets and thus penetrate their secrets (which is why, incidentally, dialogue is so important and so uniquely emphasized in Chandler). Marlowe is a particle of the very social mystery he inhabits – blemished, tainted, a soul of a soulless world. In other words, Chandler's characterization of Marlowe is a necessary one which evolves out of the broader historical trajectory, and it is this relationship which Mandel is able to elucidate so finely.

As we have already seen in an earlier chapter, the Grand Old Man of Literary Theory, Fredric Jameson, published a small book on Raymond Chandler and there he advocates a different approach to 'reading' Chandler. Let's remind ourselves again of the methodological thrust of his reading:

The tension in Chandler criticism will reproduce the henceforth inevitable one between semiotic analysis and interpretation as such, between the formal exploration of a space that returns again and again and can be apprehended only by way of its identity with itself and a theme or a meaning ('down these mean streets', etc., Chandler's own romantic ideology, the concept of honor, the very mise en abyme of the stained glass window that welcomes Marlowe to the Sternwood mansion).

But 'space' must be read: unless conventional modes of reading are presupposed (conventions being themselves everywhere in crisis in this society), the reader may expect to pass through an initial period of programmation, through some inaugural entry chamber in which the appropriate decoding techniques are taught and learned. Even as far as the category of space itself is concerned, it cannot be assumed to pre-exist the text either, but must be projected by the latter as that 'code' of space which the reader must learn to read. We might therefore have begun by noticing receptacle space in The Big Sleep, halls and interiors too capacious for their furnishings.[5]

What can you say? Just as with Althusser, there is method in this madness. Beyond the ridiculousness of the language, we see the same specific shift; that which was socio-historical in nature in Mandel becomes in Jameson something which is primarily physical – i.e. it becomes a question of 'physical space' which 'the reader must learn to read'. The novel The Big Sleep is to be understood by the fact that there are 'halls and interiors too capacious for their furnishings', again something which detracts from the historical categories and social relationships which underpin the characters and their conflicts – and instead makes a fetish of an abstract sense of physicality ('mapping space'). 'Space' itself assumes an almost mystical meaning, the type of meaning only the most sophisticated of minds can access by first entering into Jameson's magical 'inaugural entry chamber'!!! But although some of this stuff undoubtedly verges on parody, it nevertheless overlays a profound act of reification; that is, it allows for the conversion of socio-historical relationships into things. The clunky and abstruse language is an expression of the absolute dead, 'thing-like' nature of the reified realm Jameson has called into being. Compare this to Mandel's analysis. Look at how deftly and how fluidly Mandel uses a shift in organic historical development as the basis for the creation of new archetype (Marlowe) on Chandler's part and a new way of exhibiting the social and endemic nature of crime in terms of twentieth-century capitalism. Mandel's analysis is utterly superior in every respect; in terms of style, clarity, profundity and innovation, and yet it is Jameson's book which has been received so favourably in many of the largest outlets of the liberal left media, garnering rave reviews in prestigious papers and journals like *The Guardian* or *London Review of Books*. Mandel's very fine book – *Delightful Murder – A Social History of the Crime Story* – languishes virtually forgotten. To turn to another comparison. Here is Georg Lukács writing about the emergence of the historical novel:

> It was the French Revolution, the revolutionary wars, and the rise and fall of Napoleon which for the first time made history a mass experience, and moreover on a European scale ... The wars of absolute states in the pre-Revolutionary period were waged by small professional armies. They were conducted so as to isolate the army as sharply as possible from the civilian population ... This changes at one stroke with the French Revolution. In its defensive struggle against the coalition of absolute monarchies, the French Republic was compelled to create mass armies ... If ... a mass army is to be created, then the content and purpose of the war must be made clear to the masses by means of propaganda ... The inner life of a nation is linked with the modern mass army ... in France the estate barrier between nobleman, officer and common soldier disappears.[6]

Lukács goes on to argue that this shift in the historical weather – i.e. the masses becoming ever more sensitive to historical development as they are pulled into the historical maelstrom in and through the bourgeois revolutions and an emergent sense of national consciousness – that such a shift was inevitably expressed in the literary aesthetic. Specifically, whereas the literature of old was nearly always written from the purview of great aristocratic generals or kings, now was created a form of literature which more and more put the 'ordinary' man or woman at the centre of its story as protagonist. Lukács talks about this in relation to Walter Scott whom he sees as the instigator of the new 'historical novel'. Lukács argues that the hero of a Scott novel is often an 'average' figure from a lower social stratum who possesses 'practical intelligence, a certain moral fortitude and decency which even rises to a capacity for self-sacrifice'.[7] Scott's heroes tend to be more egalitarian in their demographic, because – at the level of historical existence during the epoch of the classical bourgeois revolutions – the masses were evermore entering into the stage of history as protagonists (certainly in comparison to the period of the Middle Ages). Again, like Mandel, Lukács is able to pinpoint a qualitative change in historical development more broadly and show us how such a change helped to reconfigure, on an unconscious and protean level, the way in which writers came to frame their protagonist and the form of the novel *vis-à-vis* the epoch they were living in.

Next to Jameson, the most famous 'Marxist' literary critic writing today is Terry Eagleton. In 2013 Eagleton published a book – *The Event of Literature* – which we already looked at in Chapter 5. But I'd like to return to it again now – because it is worth contrasting Eagleton's approach in that work to that of the historical approach evinced by Lukács. To recap, Eagleton describes the 'literary text' in the following way:

Language works by a kind of double inscription, both clinging to the singular and departing from it. A lyric poem or realist novel presents what is meant to be an irreducibly specific reality; but because the signs it uses are only signs because they are iterable, capable of being deployed in other contexts, any particular literary statement packs a wealth of general connotations into itself. It is thus that the singular comes to behave as a microcosm, condensing whole possible worlds in its slim compass. The more texts are fashioned or framed to display this duality, the more they conventionally approach the condition of literature. Literary texts typically exploit the doubled nature of discourse by portraying irreducibly specific situations which are at the same time, by the very nature of language, of more general import.[8]

Again, the sheer convoluted monotony of the writing impresses itself by way of a grotesque dirge. The attunement to historical development and socio-historical categories which underpins Lukács' analysis is, in Eagleton, annulled in favour of a rambling consideration of 'signs', 'the double nature of discourse' and 'the nature of language' which, despite the highbrow tone, is almost pathologically vacuous managing to tell us next to nothing about literature itself. It does, however, provide yet another demonstration of reification in action.

To take one final comparison. Here is Leon Trotsky talking about swearing.

> Abusive language and swearing are a legacy of slavery, humiliation, and disrespect for human dignity – one's own and that of other people. This is particularly the case with swearing in Russia. I should like to hear from our philologists, our linguists and experts in folklore, whether they know of such loose, sticky, and low terms of abuse in any other language than Russian. As far as I know, there is nothing, or nearly nothing, of the kind outside Russia. Russian swearing in 'the lower depths' was the result of despair, embitterment and, above all, slavery without hope, without escape. The swearing of the upper classes, on the other hand, the swearing that came out of the throats of the gentry, the authorities, was the outcome of class rule, slaveowner's pride, unshakable power.[9]

What is at once noticeable – whether or not you agree with the thrust of the argument – is that Trotsky suggests that there are two main currents of swearing: the current which expresses the despair of the impoverished and downtrodden, and the current which elucidates the vulgarity of the naked power employed by those in the upper classes as they manifest their 'class rule'. Again socio-historical categories and class contradictions become the way in which meaning is shaped; the contradictions of real human life as they are played out in the world receive their expression in the forms of language which take flight from them. Now let's look at the doyen of Literary Theory once more – Professor Fredric Jameson – this time discussing slang:

> The literary problem of slang forms a parallel in the microcosm of style to the problem of the presentation of the serial society itself, never present fully in any of its manifestations, without a privileged center,

offering the impossible alternative between an objective and abstract lexical working of it as a whole and a lived concrete experience of its worthless components.[10]

It is not easy to read this with a straight face, to avoid the sneaking suspicion that Jameson is making a joke at the reader's expense. But thinkers like Jameson tend to lack humour or irony when it comes to their own work; he is, in other words, being painfully sincere. How is it possible that he could write something like this? Again, I am reminded of the Hans Christian Anderson tale, *The Emperor's New Clothes*. Writers like Jameson, Adorno and Žižek often receive a great deal of adulation; world-famous intellectuals who can fill auditoriums almost like popstars, their books are carried by the largest left publishers and they are nearly always greeted with a cacophony of praise. When you understand yourself to be a world-historic thinker, a great mind, I imagine that even the most unformed thought can be considered as precious as a diamond; any vague and rambling stream of consciousness perceived to contain the deep, buried and mysterious answers to the riddle of humanity which require only the proper 'decoding' on the part of the elite middle-class intellectual. Jameson's book on Raymond Chandler is riddled with these type of passages, but nobody in the pre-publication process, none of the readers for the publishers, nor the editors, actually bothered to stop and query it; for none of them had the simple and obvious integrity of the child who might actually say 'But he isn't wearing anything at all!'

At the same time, even though Jameson's analysis of slang is virtually nonsensical, once again we must note how the one thing it does achieve is the abnegation of socio-historical categories in favour of the purely structural, semiotic or physical ones which become the fundamental concepts of Literary Theory. So, for instance, society loses any socio-historical specificity, and becomes a generic 'something'; that is, it is described as a 'serial society'. And what is the main problem about such a society? It lacks a 'privileged center' – that is to say, its main problem is not conceived of in and through the socio-historical categories, the contradictions which open up between different social agencies with their own historical interests; rather the main problem appears as a structural-physical fetish, that of a 'privileged center' which the 'serial society' lacks. The one thing the whole bizarre paragraph manages to achieve, then, is an act of reification; once more, that which is socio-historical in nature is converted into that which is 'thing-like'. The one thing the paragraph doesn't achieve, however, is to tell us anything whatsoever about the nature of 'slang'.

One might object. The authors have written much else, many more books, and not everything they write is as illegible and verbose as the sections I have homed in on. Such objections are justified. Eagleton, for instance, has written some very useful things in a very beautiful way. He wrote an essay for *New Statesman* on the late Christopher Hitchens which is fluid and incisive. He wrote a very good compendium on the young Marx which is clear and persuasive and provides a useful introduction to basic Marxist thought. Even in Jameson's book on Raymond Chandler there are sections where he does make the odd interesting historical observation or says something pertinent about revolutionary politics. I am not saying that Eagleton or Jameson have nothing of interest to say or that they haven't contributed positively to fields and themes in radical scholarship more broadly. What I am saying, however, is that when it comes to developing the fundaments of something called Literary Theory – i.e. a particular trend which focuses on the fundamental issue of what literature is and how it is created – in their answers, these thinkers at the methodological level consistently transform living socio-historical categories and contradictions into 'things' – by way of various semiotic, psychoanalytical and linguistic concepts.

Between Literary Theory and the other tendencies and schools I have briefly addressed in this book, there are the same points of contact. Jameson speaks of a 'serial society' which 'lacks a privileged center'; for Mouffe and Laclau society has a similar problem, it becomes 'decentred' and also tends to lack 'fullness'; in Althusser, the 'social totality' is disrupted by 'a vertical break' and so on. When one does away with living history driven by social and class contradictions, one needs to find another way with which to describe reality; a genuinely social arrangement is replaced by a purely physical one; the work of these thinkers, therefore, consistently tends towards a systematic reification of the philosophical realm in terms of a set of conceptual categories whose 'physicality' reflects this.

The term 'counterrevolution' brings to mind violent reaction – the peasant *vendeé*, royalist militias, the black hundreds, the *freikorps*, spies and informers, military courts, Stalinist prison camps. It usually involves the attack on the forms of political expression of the masses, i.e. the attempt to smash the unions, to infiltrate radical political parties, to assassinate those political figures who have become the representatives of the mass movement, to imprison and repress protestors, to put down strikes and so on. But a counterrevolution can also involve a backlash in thought. It can involve the attempt to break down, delegitimize or neuter the most revolutionary forms of ideology of an epoch, to render them quiescent and compliant, to assimilate them to the interests of the powers-that-be. Much of this book has been the attempt to show that thinkers such as Althusser, Mouffe and Laclau, Žižek, Adorno, Horkheimer, Eagleton and Jameson have struck out at the core of revolutionary Marxism, specifically at the notion of class as the fundamental motor of the historical process, and of the modern working class culminating that process in and through the revolutionary supersession of the capitalist order and the creation of a society whose political and material interests are determined by the vast majority.

I am not saying that these thinkers set out to do this consciously; they all self-describe as Marxists. And yet, they have all, without exception, worked towards the reification of the Marxist method; that is to say, they have transformed social-historical categories – particularly those centred around class conflict – into physical, structural fetishes which are described in terms of the most fashionable concepts doing the rounds in linguistics, psychoanalysis, semiotics, structuralism and so on. Or to say the same thing, they have worked to smuggle in profoundly ahistorical categories into a philosophy whose life's blood is a radical historicism cultivated in and through an ontology of labour. One of the symptoms of this reification is the deployment of a language which is often so thick and so dense that it verges on the nonsensical. And this is in some way inevitable. Once genuine social relations are transfigured into physical or transcendental 'things', then a meaningful language – a language which describes real social agencies and contradictions – is inevitably transformed into a language which describes strange and empty abstractions and physical oddities; the terrain of social struggle is transformed into a terrain which is no longer constituted by real flesh-and-blood people fighting for concrete freedoms but becomes an alien and surreal realm of 'micro-episodic dimensions' across which 'signifiers' tend to 'float' (Jameson). In other words, the ridiculous jargon into which so many of these 'significant' thinkers fall is bound up with the act of reification which is being carried out and which converts genuinely human concerns of social struggle and emancipation into a transcendental realm of mysterious and contorted 'things'.

I have tried to show 'how' the process of reification works at the level of theory by drawing attention to some examples of the work of these thinkers, but I have not devoted so much time as to the 'why'. Why has this kind of thing become so fashionable, grown so ubiquitous in the last half-century or more? In the case of people like Jameson and Eagleton much of the most jargon-heavy and nonsensical stuff they write is twinned with their concerns as literary theorists. Literary Theory in the broadest sense of the word has been around since the ancient Greeks. But in its modern form it emerged from around the 1950s, centred on the universities, part and parcel of the broader impact of structuralism, in this case a structuralism which focused on linguistics. But Literary Theory really achieved its most wide-ranging and international impact from around the late 1960s to the late '80s. In this period its popularity became immense and virtually every university with an English department sought to integrate Literary Theory into its prospectus. It was considered bold, cutting-edge, left-wing, critical and deeply intellectual, and its often impenetrable language and surreal terminology became part and parcel of its avant-garde mystique.

The epoch in which Literary Theory achieved precedence in the academy also coincided with a global economic slump and a period of neoliberalism which saw in many of the developed Western countries industries decimated, the power of the unions curtailed and great political movements sent into a sluggish abeyance. In the United States the Civil Rights struggles went into retreat; an iconic party like the Black Panthers which in the '60s had many thousands of members, by the early '80s was reduced to a husk of a few dozen, having had its leaders incarcerated and assassinated, having been targeted by the infamous Cointelpro programme directed by the FBI and designed to nullify the resistance of the radical parties which emerged out of those same Civil Rights struggles. In England, the last great flame of resistance of the industrial working class was quashed with the crushing of the miners' strike in 1984. Across Europe a process of deindustrialization took place, state industries were dismantled, sold off, put into the service of private and financial capital, which – parasitic and rapacious – expanded exponentially, eating away at the social safety net which was provided by state welfare and public institutions. It was a time of malaise, of disenchantment for radical and revolutionary politics and as the years rolled into decades, the supremacy of the 'yuppie', the high flier, the egoistic individual – rolling the dice of a glitzy, high-octane casino capitalism and reaping massive financial rewards – was more and more enshrined. That sense of defeat, the sense of collective struggle on a class-wide social basis becoming ever thinner, disappearing into the ether was perhaps most evoked in Margaret Thatcher's pithy statement 'there's no such thing as society'.

I think in some way this underpins the very success Literary Theory enjoyed. That mood of defeat, despair, which the decades of neoliberalism had provoked quite naturally permeated the colleges and the universities. Those academics who had been inspired by the Civil Rights movements, the protests against Vietnam, the heyday of the activism of the radical '60s increasingly found themselves marginalized within the university environment, condescended to by their colleagues who experienced in them an antiquated and dogmatic mentality which was a hangover from a vanishing past. In the harsh light of economic crisis and neoliberalism, the belief the more radical faculty could repose in the viability of revolutionary movements was increasingly diminished. A dedicated and honourable few remained welded to the notion of genuine class struggle, but for many, the idea of speaking out at ever more poorly attended union meetings, or partaking in dwindling rainy-day rallies began to feel a little ridiculous and archaic. And yet, if one type of revolution felt increasingly faraway, another type was much closer to hand. If it was impossible to revolutionize the fundamental social structures of the capitalist system, the structures of language could prove more amenable to the revolutionary impulse, for language – even meaning itself – could be reshaped and reformed on a far more radical basis. In this way, a revolution which might spring out of the historical trajectory of capitalist development could now be reimagined, projected onto a fantastical terrain in which the clash of social classes was replaced by the clash of linguistic structures and forms with all their mystical properties and in all their esoteric complexity. The possibility of a revolution in practice fell away, slipping into an inward, reified and imaginary landscape with its own surreal and strange laws, laws which could be deciphered only by the high priests of the temple, those who would reveal the mysteries, letting the rest of humanity in on the secret. This was a movement by which revolutionary despair was translated through a reifying process into a realm in which the sublime ingenuity of the middle-class intellectual and academic becomes the prime mover of human progress. Despite their own class backgrounds, thinkers like Eagleton and Jameson rose to prominence on the back of such a movement; they made their bones in and through it; they absorbed its mantras and methods organically and allowed its prestige and benefits to rub off on them.

And yet, although the kind of reifying processes we have described were intensified in and through the development and consolidation of Literary Theory on the world stage, we must remember that figures like Adorno and Horkheimer, almost a generation before, had performed a similar act of reification, albeit one which transformed the living breathing processes of class conflict into their own set of transcendental categories. And these were overlaid by the same impenetrable and rambling idiom. It is worth noting, of course, that Adorno and Horkheimer were also products of a certain historical despair. Whereas Literary Theory had reached its peak in the great recession of the 1970s and the neoliberal turn, the material for Critical Theory was forged out of bleaker circumstances still. In 1918 and then again in 1923 proletarian revolutions had broken out in Germany and they had been defeated. In the USSR the only ever working-class revolution in history which had succeeded in bringing the proletariat to power had been smashed by a combination of counterrevolution and international invasion, and out of the wreckage of the workers' democracy arose the most grotesque form of dictatorship. In Germany, at around the same time, the Nazis were on the march, consolidating their fascist regime in 1933. An aghast and radical layer of the intelligentsia, which would eventually constitute the earliest iteration of the Frankfurt School, came to understand that a genuine socialist revolution was impossible, and it explained this in and through the fact that the modern-day masses were bovine and suggestible and particularly susceptible to the forces of consumerism and modern entertainment. The sense of despair which the Frankfurt School mobilized in the theoretical realm was a product of a faithlessness in the masses and just as with the thinkers in Literary Theory a generation later, the brilliant mind of the middle-class intellectual and academic – elevated to a pristine realm beyond all the vulgarities of class struggle – would become the transcendental key to deciphering the world.

But the contempt for the masses, which is buried at the heart of such a theoretical perspective, has a longer theoretical lineage. In the latter part of the nineteenth century the masses had vastly increased their numbers in Western Europe and were ever more pressing the forms of their own political representation. The numbers of the cities were swelling and the presence of the masses in the public and cultural sphere was something which was ever more felt. The upper classes did not simply oppose this process with a coherent ideological prospectus – though this, of course, would be realized throughout the century from Malthus to Nietzsche. But more than that, the feeling of being swamped by the masses was something many of the privileged layers felt at an emotional almost visceral level. It was something which provoked a shudder of patrician disgust. The novelist Thomas Hardy, for instance, described the feeling of lying awake in his London apartment one night – unable to fall asleep because of that sense of being so close to the teeming masses of the city's population, 'a monster whose body had four million heads and eight million eyes'.[11]

The Marxist thinker Ishay Landa has chronicled the process by which the 'massification' of society which took place in the nineteenth century was channelled into a mood of disgust and abhorrence on the part of the ruling classes which would eventually be expressed in a theoretical body of work, most infamously, in the philosophy of Nietzsche. Nietzsche, in particular, would help inform the later ideology of the Nazis; the notion of the masses representing a uniform quantity which stifled the quality of the higher human individual is fundamental to fascist ideology. Adorno's methodology would lift such themes almost wholesale from Nietzsche, but rephrasing them in a left-wing idiom. But while Nietzsche's philosophy was essentially proto-fascist and the central figures of the Frankfurt School were all anti-fascist – because the latter shared Nietzsche's methodological premises they came to a particularly paradoxical and anti-Marxist conclusion. From the point of view of the Frankfurt School's leading lights and their Nietzschean trappings, fascism is not the class process which is historically evolved in order to neuter the political power of the proletariat in and through the most lethal means (as a Marxism which draws life from the reality of class conflict would have it); no, rather fascism is the inevitable outcrop of the culture of the masses themselves.

Because (for the Frankfurt School) the masses in the modern epoch are denuded of the ability to think critically, because their behaviour is that of the mindless collective before the altar of mass entertainment – the Nazis through their rallies and propaganda were in the perfect position to pick up on this; to use the means of information and mass entertainment to beam their propaganda into the heart of the mass and co-opt and determine its behaviour therein. The obscenity of such a claim is hard to stomach, especially given the fact that the Nazis enacted a civil war of the most ferocious violence against the German proletariat, not only savaging the organs of their political representation, but also conducting a campaign against popular culture which saw anything deemed subversive or non-conducive to fascist power censored or destroyed. But the conclusion that the vulgarity and bovine nature of the masses set the basis for the fascist triumph flows from the Nietzschean methodical premises of the Frankfurt School. Landa notes that, in July 1942, at the height of the fascist violence compounded by the atomic pressures of the Second World War, notable members of the Frankfurt School including Adorno, Horkheimer, Günter Anders, Herbert Marcuse, Ludwig Marcuse and others met in order to discuss a paper by Ludwig Marcuse. The premise of the paper was 'the idea that the horror of fascism and the war were manifestations of the reign of the Last Humans [masses]'.[12] As Landa went on to note: 'Not one among those eminent social theorists gathering to discuss Marcuse's paper saw fit to question the Last Human's alleged responsibility for the cataclysm.'[13] This in itself is quite remarkable. A form of 'Marxism' which has been so grotesquely infiltrated by the intellectual sensibility which issues from a bourgeois elite that it now works to describe the social agency which holds the key to the emancipation of humanity as that which is implicated in its abasement and destruction through fascist barbarism. What is more remarkable still is just how much respect figures such as Adorno continue to command in explicitly Marxist circles; the theorists and publications prepared to call them out as class enemies, despite their clear and immense disdain for the working class, remain few and far between. The respectable *literati* no doubt feel there would be something philistine, perhaps, about being rude about such a towering figure as an Adorno. Something almost uncouth.

As the masses more and more increased in number and pressed their political and cultural power, the disgust – the almost elemental loathing for them which more and more took shape from the nineteenth century onwards on the part of the ruling class – often had one other key characteristic, according to Landa. He writes:

> While the roots of such conceptions and anxieties are in the 19th century, they bear important cultural consequences mainly in the 20th century. Among them was the demand to develop an alternative to mass culture designed especially for connoisseurs, keeping the masses purposely at arm's length. In order to insulate themselves and their audiences from the masses, many artists chose to write, draw or compose in such a way that the person of average education, now universally available, would not be able to comprehend the work's messages, would not be thrilled by such art and would not, therefore, wish to take part in it. Many advocates of 'high culture' started to espouse works of art that are difficult, complex, abstract, combining elements of special or antiquated education, such as phrases in Latin and ancient Greek in order to exclude the mass. This does not imply that the attempt to innovate in artistic form or subject matter was necessarily elitist; experimentation, personal expression, crossing the boundaries and violation of consecrated codes and norms, are integral to artistic creativity in all fields, and often involves social and political defiance. Yet it is possible that never before the 20th century did the bid to remain incomprehensible form such an integral part of art.[14]

The contention of this chapter, and this book, has been that such a process has not only infected literature and philosophy more generally, but has also penetrated to a great degree Marxism as a subject particularly in academia. Throughout the twentieth century to the current point there have been iterations of this: The Critical Theory of the Frankfurt School, the Literary Theory which reached its zenith in the 1980s and the post-Marxism of figures like Laclau or Žižek which is so popular today. I have tried to show, in outline, how all these intellectual tendencies are part and parcel of the one ongoing trend, i.e. a vast process of reification which takes place at the level of theory and involves the conversion of class process and class conflict – and the social agencies which carry it – into transcendental categories or 'things' which exist in a declassed, dehistoricized realm abstracted inexorably from the life of the historical whole. A consequence of this is the deployment of a language which is both ridiculously dense and ultimately meaningless. Human categories cleaved away from human life in such a way will inevitably ring barren and empty. At the same time the complexity and the impenetrability of the language have another ideological consequence; it serves to create the illusion that the person who has produced it is a 'great' thinker, far above the ordinary, mundane and everyday mental processes of the people he or she is deigning to edify.

One might, of course, point out that Marx himself was a great thinker, and that is certainly true, but such a claim to greatness is undergirded by the fact that Marxism itself was only ever the theoretical expression of the class process of the proletariat; that is to say, it diagnosed the secret of capital in the ability of labour to generate surplus value, and therefore revealed the possibility, with systematic and scientific clarity, of the proletariat reclaiming its own alienated substance in and through revolutionary means. Marxism, as a theoretical prospectus, was crystallized out of the class processes of the proletariat, i.e. the processes of that class struggling for emancipation at the level of practical existence. For this reason, there was built into classical Marxism the unity of theory and practice in and through the most profound democratic impulse, 'the emancipation of the working classes must be conquered by the working classes'. What the thinkers of Critical Theory, Literary Theory and post Marxism do, when they perform the kind of reification that they do – when they transform class agencies into transcendental 'things' – is to sever irrevocably the world of theory from the world of practical existence, radical thought from social revolution; and in so doing all the power and creativity of the broader social struggle devolves onto the mind of the brilliant middle-class academic. Whereas Marxism is democratic precisely because its theoretic power issues from the vast majority of human beings in the process of changing the world, the tendencies and schools we have considered here are elitist in the extreme because their 'power' flows from the 'sublime intellectuality' of the high priests who preach them – the Žižeks, the Eagletons and so on.

And this, I think, is particularly distasteful. Figures like Jameson, Adorno, Žižek and others have had lucrative careers, but these have been premised on their role as academics, and more specifically, their role as teachers. When you read their work, however, you realize how little of it is designed to teach and provide the kind of clarity which can uplift people coming to some of these ideas for the first time. Not only is much of it imbued with the reifying tendency which I have tried to draw attention to, and so actively obscures and undercuts the Marxism it claims to be better developing – but also its ridiculous, impenetrable and often outright nonsensical language works to enforce the vision of a privileged and intellectual elite which is higher, more prescient and more perceptive than the majority of humanity. Again this speaks to what class tendency is really at work here, whether the thinker in question is consciously aware of it or not. These individuals, these ground-breaking geniuses, form in an elite clique; self-regarding and incestuous, they lavish praise upon one another as the world-historic thinkers they know themselves to be. Jameson lauds Adorno as 'the finest stylist ... of them all', someone in whom 'the shifting of the world's gears ... find[s] sudden and dramatic formulation',[15] while Eagleton knows that history will vindicate Jameson as the giant of Literary Theory he is, and when fascism moves towards its fruition once more, when we are again confronted with that existential choice between socialism and barbarism, in terms of 'the averting of fascism or nuclear holocaust' – Jameson will be 'one of the forlornly few names we will stammeringly evoke'.[16] The use of 'stammeringly' is particularly good here; it nicely offsets the grandiosity of the claim Eagleton is making. Eagleton – so humble, so tentative in the face of the great historical mission which has been handed to thinkers like Jameson (and himself), the mission which will no doubts avert the impending fascist apocalypse – 'stammeringly' evokes the name of his cohort, and who could disagree? What chance will the atomic heat and violence of fascist reaction on a global scale have when confronted by sentences like this? 'The constitutive feature of the Balzacian narrative apparatus, however, is something more fundamental than either authorial omniscience or authorial intervention, something that may be designated as libidinal investment or authorial wish-fulfillment, a form of symbolic satisfaction in which the working distinction between biographical subject, Implied Author, reader, and characters is virtually effaced'.[17]

In actual fact, the leading lights of Critical Theory, Literary Theory and post Marxism have done more than anyone else to render the true meaning of Marxism indecipherable and opaque while at the same time blunting its revolutionary edge. Jameson, Eagleton, Žižek and so on are published in the most prestigious journals, receive such extensive coverage and plaudits for their work, not because they are revolutionary thinkers but for the very opposite reason. By reifying categories of class and thereby annulling the revolutionary essence of Marxism, they perform an important task for the bourgeoisie; they shift the focus of progress and truth from the vast majority of people shaping and reshaping the world through their labour activity – to the privileged brain of the elite thinker, surveying all humanity from a lofty perch of the most pristine superiority, expressed in the esoteric and avant-garde language of the great and the good. At the same time, the revolutionary tenor of the form is preserved, allowing the bourgeois reader to imagine that they are being terribly radical, while at the same time confirming in them the nature of their own social superiority and making sure that the fundamental forms and structures of their own class position and power remain absolutely undisturbed.

And that brings us back to the beginning of this particular essay – back to the question of polemic. These people, the majority of the time, speak and write in such a way – verbose, rambling, pompous and abstruse – because they are utterly convinced of the necessity of their own genius; they are confirmed in this prejudice by the fact that their books are gobbled up by prestigious publishers, that they are reviewed in significant publications often by their fawning and uncritical acolytes. But we don't need to confirm this prejudice and bolster their already inflated egos. We have a duty to take these people far less seriously than they take themselves. A student who is coming to Marxism for the first time and is genuinely inspired by radical ideas and the prospect of real change is likely to be daunted and depressed if they encounter someone like Jameson or Žižek in full-on portentous rambling mode.

And we have a duty to help that person understand that, in fact, such figures are not the mystical geniuses they make themselves out to be; that they are rather more suited to the social system they are purporting to 'radically' critique, and that true genius springs not from the isolated head of the superior individual or a select elite but flows from collective humanity and is the common possession of all.

We need to be able to laugh out loud at a figure who is so deluded that he is capable of writing something like this – 'the introverted thought-architect lives behind the moon which extroverted technicians have confiscated' – while simultaneously imagining that in so doing he is helping to solve the grievous and fundamental problems faced by humanity in the modern era. We should not be taking someone like this (in this case Adorno) seriously when it comes to revolutionary politics; rather we should be laughing at him out loud, not because we wish to be unduly cruel or 'polemical' for the sake of it, but because in ridiculing these type of thinkers, we also help undo something of the incredibly powerful hegemony they have established for themselves, not just in the field of cultural radicalism more generally, but specifically in terms of a Marxism that they have helped bastardize so thoroughly. It is far from unreasonable to mock such figures, to show them up for the ridiculous, pretentious, waddling overinflated windbags that they are – and above all, confirm to the next generation of radicals and revolutionaries that these 'emperors' of academia, for all their pretentions and self-importance, remain noticeably bereft of garments.

Notes

Introduction

1 Frederick Engels, 'Preface to the 1883 German Edition', *Manifesto of the Communist Party* (Karl Marx and Frederick Engels) Marxist Internet Archive: https://www.marxists.org/archive/marx/works/download/pdf/Manifesto.pdf

2 Karl Marx and Frederick Engels, *Manifesto of the Communist Party*, Marxist Internet Archive, p.26: https://www.marxists.org/archive/marx/works/download/pdf/Manifesto.pdf

3 Karl Marx. Capital Volume One, 'Chapter Thirty-Two: Historical Tendency of Capitalist Accumulation', Marxist Internet Archive: https://www.marxists.org/archive/marx/works/1867-c1/ch32.htm

4 Marx and Engels, *Manifesto of the Communist Party*.

5 Ibid., p.21.

6 Ibid., p.21.

7 Ibid., p.22.

8 Ibid., p.27.

9 Karl Marx. Capital Volume One, 'Chapter Thirty-Two: Historical Tendency of Capitalist Accumulation', Marx Internet Archive: https://www.marxists.org/archive/marx/works/1867-c1/ch32.htm#1a

10 See Tony McKenna, 'The Political Psyche of Hillary Rodham Clinton', *Angels and Demons – A Radical Anthology of Political Lives* (Winchester: Zero Books, 2018), pp.204–17.

11 Megan Twohey, Jodi Kantor, Susan Dominus, Jim Rutenberg and Steve Eder, 'Weinstein's Complicity Machine', *New York Times*, 5 December 2017: https://www.nytimes.com/interactive/2017/12/05/us/harvey-weinstein-complicity.html

12 DNAinfo Staff, 'How Seeing Rev. King Speak in Chicago Changed Hillary Clinton's Life', *DNA Info,* 28 July 2016: https://www.dnainfo.com/chicago/20160728/downtown/how-seeing-dr-king-speak-chicago-changed-hillary-clintons-life/

13 Hillary Clinton on 'superpredators' (C-SPAN): https://www.youtube.com/watch?v=j0uCrA7ePno

14 A religion which in its early phases the pagan critic Celsus had denigrated as a movement of 'slaves, women and children', but in so doing the same critic gives us a sense of early-Christianity's basis in the broader demographic of the oppressed.

15 Friedrich Engels, 'Engels to J. Bloch In Königsberg', *Marx-Engels Correspondence* 1890, Marx Engels Archive: https://www.marxists.org/archive/marx/works/1890/letters/90_09_21.htm

16 For an account of the way in which Stalinist totalitarianism represented not the continuation of a Marxist revolution but the destruction of it, may I be so immodest as to recommend my own *The Dictator, the Revolution, the Machine: A Political Account of Joseph Stalin* (Brighton, Chicago and Toronto: Sussex Academic Press, 2016).

17 Karl Marx, *Capital* (London: Penguin Classics, 1990), p.165.

18 Lukács would examine in detail the way in which, under advanced capitalism, underlying relationships of economic exploitation were increasingly manifested at the level of the appearance as the exchange of things on the market, and furthermore, the way in which such an underling process of 'reification' helped warp the shape of consciousness and ideology with its gravity; Lukács explored how reification had left its imprint on philosophy, culture, politics, economics and so forth, how reification had a powerful impact in terms of structuring our thought, consciousness and outlook on the world in the capitalist epoch, and finally how it could be overcome by the collective and democratic control of the means of production by the majority.

19 In the context of elucidating the concept of 'reification' many of the chapters in this book also deal with the subject-object contradiction in philosophy and the way in which an authentic and revolutionary Marxism had responded to it. Indeed, I'd go as far as to say that the Lukács' conception of reification doesn't have any coherence or sense without an understanding of the role of subject and object in the philosophy of Marxism more broadly. In this connection, Lukács' notion of the modern proletariat as being the 'identical subject-object of the historical process' is of particular importance, and something I hope to elucidate and elaborate in the chapters which follow.

Chapter 1

1 Walter Benjamin, 'The Work of Art in the Age of Mechanical Reproduction' (1936), Philosophy Archive @ marxists.org: https://www.marxists.org/reference/subject/philosophy/works/ge/benjamin.htm

2 Ibid.

3 Ibid.

4   Walter Benjamin cited in Stuart Jefferies, 'The 10 Lies about Black Friday's Consumerist Circle of Hell', *The Guardian,* 24 November 2016: https://www.theguardian.com/lifeandstyle/2016/nov/24/black-friday-shopping-lies-consumerist-hell

5   Walter Benjamin, 'The Work of Art in the Age of Mechanical Reproduction' (1936), *Philosophy Archive* @ marxists.org: https://www.marxists.org/reference/subject/philosophy/works/ge/benjamin.htm

6   Ibid.

7   Ibid.

8   Ibid.

9   Ibid.

10 Ibid.

11 Ibid.

12 Adorno and many other intellectual figures of the time would relocate to the United States fleeing Nazi persecution.

13 Theodor Adorno and Max Horkheimer, *Dialectic of Enlightenment*, 'The Culture Industry: Enlightenment as Mass Deception' 1944, Marxist Internet Archive: https://www.marxists.org/reference/archive/adorno/1944/culture-industry.htm

14 Ibid.

15 Ibid.

16 Ibid.

17 Ibid.

18 Ibid.

19 Friedrich Nietzsche cited in Ishay Landa, *Fascism and the Masses: The Revolt against the Last Humans, 1848–1945* (New York and London: Routledge, 2018), p.24.

20 Theodore Adorno, *'The Culture Industry – Selected Essays on Mass Culture', The Schema of Mass Culture* (London and New York: Routledge, 1991), p.95.

21 Ibid.

22 Max Horkheimer and Theodore Adorno, *Dialectic of Enlightenment* (California: Stanford University Press, 2002), p.94.

23 For more on this, see Tony McKenna, 'Method in the Madness: Three Moments in Nietzsche's philosophy – An Exposition', Critique, Vol. 41:3, 2013, pp. 391–409, DOI: 10.1080/03017605.2013.851938

24 Friedrich Nietzsche cited in Ishay Landa, *Fascism and the Masses: The Revolt against the Last Humans, 1848–1945* (New York and London: Routledge, 2018), p.92.

25 Andrew Fagan, 'Theodor Adorno (1903 – 1969)', Internet Encyclopaedia of Philosophy: https://www.iep.utm.edu/adorno/#H2

26 Ibid.

27 Of course it does, unbeknownst to itself, express a very clear class interest, i.e. that of the bourgeoisie which is compelled to comprehend the

capitalist social system in terms of what István Mészáros very eloquently described as 'an eternal present'.

28 Georg Lukács, *History and Class Consciousness*, 'Reification and the Class Consciousness of the Proletariat' (London: The Merlin Press, 1983), p.93.
29 Ibid., p.166.
30 Ibid., p.164.
31 Ibid., p.168.
32 Ibid., p.166.
33 Ibid., p.169.
34 Max Horkheimer and Theodore Adorno, *Dialectic of Enlightenment* (California: Stanford University Press, 2002), p.1.
35 Ibid., p.6.
36 Timothy Hall, 'Reification, Materialism, and Praxis: Adorno's Critique of Lukács', *Telos*, Vol. 155 (Summer 2011): 61–8.
37 Max Horkheimer and Theodore Adorno, *Dialectic of Enlightenment* (California: Stanford University Press, 2002), p.6.
38 Hall, 'Reification, Materialism, and Praxis', 61–8.
39 Naturally this has to be qualified by the fact that although equality was a fundamental principle of Enlightenment thought, it often took centuries for that equality in the political realm to be extended to groups such as women, the working class, the indigenous, ethnic minorities and so on, and in many places such a lack of representation is indeed still in effect.
40 *Le Lys Rouge* (The Red Lily, Paris: Calmann-Lévy, 1894, chapter 7).
41 Hall, 'Reification, Materialism, and Praxis', 61–8.
42 It is worth noting how utterly idealistic Adorno's thought is; that is, the relationship between man and nature becomes primarily a question of thought (Enlightenment thought) rather than the social forms of labour activity by which man acts upon the word in practice – i.e. the ontology of labour which is the very foundation of the Marxist theory of history.
43 It's interesting that in arguing this, Adorno seems to be completely unaware of how Hegel's own philosophy of 'identity in difference' was partly shaped in accordance with Hegel's critique of 'identity' thinking as when he memorably criticized Schelling's philosophy as 'a night in which all cows are black'.
44 Theodore Adorno, *Negative Dialectics*, LibCom.org, 2001: https://libcom.org/library/negative-dialectics-theodor-adorno
45 Ibid.
46 Ibid.
47 Ibid.
48 It is true that in *The Logic* Hegel treats the doctrine of the notion in terms of a subjective logic and an objective logic – but the use of 'subjective' and 'objective' here relates to those logical propositions which move from simply being asserted to eventually being deduced as part of an objective rational 'science'. The terms 'subjectivity' and 'objectivity' here obviously

have very different connotations to the way Adorno employs the concepts of 'subject' and 'object' in terms of his theorization of 'Enlightenment thought' and, subsequently, his critique of Hegel's theorization of the state and Lukács' theorization of the proletariat as 'identical subject-object'.

49 If thought is posed in abstraction – cordoned off from its embodiment in the object, in the world, through labour, then thought of necessity does appear as something infinitely and forever removed from the thought object.

50 David Held, 'Overview – Negative Dialectic', Oxford Reference: https://www.oxfordreference.com/view/10.1093/oi/ authority.20110803100227235

51 Adorno, *Negative Dialectics*.

52 Ibid.

53 Ibid.

54 As Engels would later write, it was only 'after Marx has completed his proof on the basis of historical and economic facts does he point out that the anticipated movement has the logical form of "negation of the negation"'. Marx does not impose the template of 'the negation of negation' in order to bend reality to its fit, rather an exhaustive study of the empirical details eventually revealed a more fundamental and underlying tendency which corresponded in its essential and 'ideal' outline to a logical form in which the negative is negated.

55 Karl Marx. Capital Volume One, 'Chapter Thirty-Two: Historical Tendency of Capitalist Accumulation', Marxist Internet Archive: https://www.marxists.org/archive/marx/works/1867-c1/ch32.htm

56 Theodore Adorno, *Negative Dialectics*, 'Preface' (UK: Routledge, 2004), p.xix.

57 Jefferies, 'The 10 Lies about Black Friday's Consumerist Circle of Hell'.

58 Herbert Marcuse cited in ibid.

59 How anyone can see beyond the veil of consumerism based on this kind of model is anyone's guess. Habermas made a similar point when critiquing Adorno; that is, neither Jeffries nor Adorno is able to explain how the critic of the system comes to know anything external to the system.

60 Kaylin Johnson, 'Black Friday Is Consumerism at Its Finest', *The Odyssey* 29 November 2016: https://www.theodysseyonline.com/black-friday-consumerism-finest

61 Andrew Leonard, 'Black Friday: Consumerism Minus Civilization', *Salon,* 25 November 2011: https://www.salon.com/2011/11/25/black_friday_consumerism_minus_civilization/

62 Kashmira Gander, 'Why Black Friday Should Be Buy Nothing Day – How to Escape the "Shopocalypse"', *International Business Times*, 23 November 2017: https://www.ibtimes.co.uk/why-black-friday-should-be-buy-nothing-day-how-escape-shopocalypse–1648451

63 M. Moore cited by Blake Thorne, 'Michael Moore Derides "Hipsters" Who Tease Black Friday Shoppers', *Michigan Live*, 1 December 2014: http://

www.mlive.com/news/flint/index.ssf/2014/12/michael_moore_derides_
hipsters.html

64 R. Williams, *Resources of Hope: Culture, Democracy, Socialism* (London: Verso, 1989), pp.3–14

65 Obviously these do not include the workers the capitalist himself employs, for it is in his interests to pay them as low a wage as possible.

66 Karl Marx cited in Ishay Landa, 'The Left and the Masses: The Question of Consumerism', Marxist Humanist Initiative: https://www.marxisthumanistinitiative.org/the-left-and-the-masses-the-question-of-consumerism

67 Karl Marx cited, ibid.

68 Karl Marx cited, ibid.

69 Karl Marx cited, ibid.

70 Karl Marx cited, ibid.

71 T. Mckenna, 'Harry Potter and the Modern Age', *Critique: Journal of Socialist Theory*, Vol. 39:3, 2011.

72 It is worth noting that, in terms of her politics, J. K. Rowling has become ever more conservative and reactionary, culminating – most recently – in a very public and obscene display of transphobia. Nevertheless, a novelist's conscious political sensibilities are often at odds with the political and aesthetic spirit of the works they create, as both Marx and Engels noted apropos of the works of Balzac.

73 Georg Lukács, 'Preface to The Theory of the Novel', Lukács Archive: https://www.marxists.org/archive/lukacs/works/theory-novel/preface.htm

Chapter 2

1 *Planes, Trains and Automobiles*, 1987 (Director/Screenwriter John Hughes, Hughes Entertainment, Paramount Pictures) Script – 'Dialogue Transcript', Drew's Script-O-Rama: http://www.script-o-rama.com/movie_scripts/p/planes-trains-and-automobiles-script.html

2 Ibid.

3 Ibid.

4 Ibid.

5 Or at least a majority of them. Could well be that the taxi driver owns the cab and in this case would not, of course, be counted as a wage labourer.

6 Ibid.

7 Ibid.

8 By the collective control of the working class of the means of production.

9 Ibid.

10 Ibid.

11 Ibid.

12 Ibid.

13 Ibid.

Chapter 3

1 Peter D. Thomas, *The Gramscian Moment* (Chicago: Haymarket, 2010), p.171.
2 Ibid (Marx cited).
3 Ibid.
4 Ibid.
5 Ibid., p.172.
6 Ibid.
7 I capitalize 'Ideology' here in order to distinguish it from 'particular ideologies' which Althusser discusses in terms of the conventional usage.
8 Louis Althusser, *For Marx* (London: The Penguin Press, 1969), p.231.
9 Chantal Mouffe, 'Hegemony and Ideology in Gramsci', *Gramsci and Marxist Theory* (London, Boston and Henley: Routledge & Kegan Paul, 1979), p.186.
10 Althusser, *For Marx*, p.233.
11 Ibid.
12 Ibid.
13 Louis Althusser, *Lenin and Philosophy and Other Essays*, 'Ideology and the State' (London: NLB, 1977), p.155.
14 Louis Althusser, *Reading Capital* (London: NLB, 1975), p.67.
15 Leszek Kolakowski, 'Althusser's Marx', *Socialist Register*, Vol. 8, 1971, p.114.
16 Mouffe (Antonio Gramsci cited), 'Hegemony and Ideology in Gramsci', p.181–2.
17 Chantal Mouffe, ibid., p.181.
18 Ibid., p.184.
19 Ibid.
20 Ibid.
21 Ibid., p.188.
22 Ibid., p.197.
23 Ibid.
24 Ibid., p.193.
25 Ibid., p.195.
26 Althusser, *Lenin and Philosophy and Other Essays*, p.158
27 Mouffe, 'Hegemony and Ideology in Gramsci', p.192.
28 Ibid.
29 Ernesto Laclau and Chantal Mouffe, 'Post-Marxism without Apologies', *New Left Review* I/166, November/December 1987, p.86.
30 See Tony McKenna, 'Hegelian Dialectics', *Critique*, Vol. 39:1, 2011, pp.155–72, DOI: 10.1080/03017605.2011.537458.
31 It is a credit to Hegel that he was clear-eyed enough to see that no such state in the present had realized this condition – certainly not the Prussian one – though this is a view many commentators still mistakenly attribute to him.

32 Ernesto Laclau and Chantal Mouffe, *Hegemony and Socialist Strategy* (London and New York: Verso,1985), pp.106–7.
33 Ibid., p.109.
34 Ibid., p.125.
35 Jacob Tofing, *New Theories of Discourse* (Malden, MA: Wiley-Blackwell, 1999), p.85.
36 Ibid., p.101.
37 The term 'floating signifier' was originated by Claude Levi Strauss.
38 Laclau and Mouffe, *Hegemony and Socialist Strategy*, p.112.
39 Ibid., p.110.
40 Slavoj Žižek, *Less than Nothing: Hegel and the Shadow of Dialectical Materialism* (London: Verso, 2012), pp.47–8.
41 Hiroshi Uchida, *Marx's Grundrisse and Hegel's Logic (1988)*, philosophy archive – marxist.org: http://www.marxists.org/subject/japan/uchida/ch02.htm
42 Ibid.
43 Ibid.
44 Žižek, *Less than Nothing*, p.250.
45 Slavoj Žižek, *They Know Not What They Do* (London and New York: Verso, 2008), p.214.
46 Žižek, *Less than Nothing*, p.389.
47 Ibid., p.381.
48 Ibid., p.535.
49 G. W. F. Hegel, *Hegel's Science of Logic* (London: George Allen & Unwin Ltd, 1969), p.105.
50 Žižek, *Less than Nothing*, p.48.
51 G. W. F. Hegel, *Lectures in the History of Philosophy Vol III* (London: Routledge and Kegan Paul, 1968), p.479.
52 Žižek, *Less than Nothing*, p.188.
53 Ibid., p.220.
54 I think Lukács was mistaken in this, and his argument here should be understood in the context of a political demoralization on his part which was a consequence of the Stalinification of the Soviet Union – with the important exception of a short burst of activity when he became a minister of the short-lived government which opposed the Soviet Union during the 1956 Hungarian Revolution.
55 Slavoj Žižek, *Living in the End Times* (London and New York: Verso, 2014), p.232.
56 Incidentally, the most effective struggles on the part of slum dwellers like those in El Paz El Alto are often the product of combined communitarian and working-class organization.
57 Slavoj Žižek, 'Where to Look for a Revolutionary Potential?' *Adbusters* March/April 2005.
58 Ibid.
59 Žižek, *Less than Nothing*, p.517.
60 Ibid., p.189.

61 Ibid., p.1006.
62 Ibid., p.1008.

Chapter 4

1   G. Lukács, *History and Class Consciousness* (London: Merlin Press, 1983), p.89.
2   'Amazon: What's It Like Where You Work?' *Organise*: https://static1.squarespace.com/static/5a3af3e22aeba594ad56d8cb/t/5ad098b3562fa7b8c90d5e1b/1523620020369/Amazon+Warehouse+Staff+Survey+Results.pdf
3   Olivia Solon, 'Amazon Patents Wristband That Tracks Warehouse Workers' Movements', *The Guardian*, 1 February 2018: https://www.theguardian.com/technology/2018/jan/31/amazon-warehouse-wristband-tracking
4   Maya Wolfe-Robinson, 'Union Stages Final Protest Over "Horrific" Amazon Work Practices', *The Guardian*, 22 July 2019: https://www.theguardian.com/technology/2019/jul/22/union-stages-final-protest-over-horrific-amazon-work-practices
5   I would, of course, exclude arranged marriage with an eye to develop economic and property connections between families, particularly those on the land in the context of feudal relations.
6   Jason Wilson, 'The "Man-o-sphere" Is Outraged about Mad Max? Hand Me My Popcorn!' *The Guardian*, 15 May 2015: https://www.theguardian.com/commentisfree/2015/may/15/the-man-o-sphere-is-outraged-about-mad-max-hand-me-my-popcorn
7   K. Marx cited in M. Lebowitz, *Following Marx: Method, Critique and Crisis* (Chicago: Haymarket Books, 2009), p.8.
8   Ibid., p.9.
9   B. Foley, *Marxist Literary Criticism Today* (London: Pluto Press, 2019), p.115.
10 Ibid.
11 T. Carlyle, *On Heroes, Hero-Worship and the Heroic in History*. 1841: https://www.gutenberg.org/files/1091/1091-h/1091-h.htm
12 H. Spencer, *The Study of Sociology*, 1873: https://oll.libertyfund.org/titles/spencer-the-study-of-sociology–1873
13 C. Hitchens, 'Against Rationalisation', *The Nation*, 20 September 2001: https://www.thenation.com/article/against-rationalization/
14 Ibid.
15 H. Haq, 'Christopher Hitchens On Osama bin Laden: "A Near-Flawless Personification" of Evil', *The Christian Science Moniter*, 18 May 2011: https://www.csmonitor.com/Books/chapter-and-verse/2011/0518/Christopher-Hitchens-on-Osama-bin-Laden-a-near-flawless-personification-of-evil
16 C. Brotheridge, *Brave New Girl* (UK: Random House, 2019), p.3.

17 Ibid., p.3.

18 Ibid., p.188.

19 Ibid.

20 Ibid., p.226.

21 Ibid., pp.295–6.

22 Ibid., p.296.

23 It is a paper which, when it is not spending its time demonizing immigrants and benefit seekers as the root of all ills, indulges in the grossest fantasies about alternative medicine and the crackpot pseudo-science which underpins it, and the crudest forms of spiritualism welded to commercialism in and through mail order junk.

24 Jane McGonigal, 'An Excerpt from SuperBetter', *Penguin Books*: https://www.penguin.com/ajax/books/excerpt/9780698185500

25 Jane McGonigal cited in A. Swartz, 'Improving Ourselves to Death', *The New Yorker*, 15 January 2018: https://www.newyorker.com/magazine/2018/01/15/improving-ourselves-to-death

26 A. Swartz, 'Improving Ourselves to Death', *The New Yorker*, 15 January 2018: https://www.newyorker.com/magazine/2018/01/15/improving-ourselves-to-death

27 Ibid.

28 A Hochschild cited in Sophie Wilkinson, 'Why Was Everyone Talking about Emotional Labour in 2018?' *BBC 3*, 24 December 2018: https://www.bbc.co.uk/bbcthree/article/5ea9f140-f722-4214-bb57-8b84f9418a7e

29 A Hochschild, *The Managed Heart* (USA: University of California Press, 2012): https://www.ucpress.edu/book/9780520272941/the-managed-heart

Chapter 5

1   Whatever one's criticisms of him, Freud was clearly a great thinker. The same cannot be said of the others mentioned here.

2   S. S. Prawer, *Karl Marx and World Literature* (London and New York: Verso, 2011), p.283.

3   Terry Eagleton, *Literary Theory: An Introduction* (USA: University of Minnesota Press, 1996), p.10.

4   Ibid., p.9.

5   Ibid., p.10.

6   Ibid.

7   Ibid.

8   Ibid.

9   G. W. F. Hegel, *Hegel's Phenomenology of Mind* (London: George Allen & Unwin, 1966), p.68.

10 Terry Eagleton, *Criticism and Ideology – A Study in Marxist Literary Theory* (London: New Left Books, 1976), p.26.

11 Terry Eagleton, 'Self-Realization, Ethics and Socialism', *New Left Review*, I/237 September/October 1999: https://newleftreview.org/issues/I237/articles/terry-eagleton-self-realization-ethics-and-socialism

12 Ibid.

13 Ibid.

14 Ibid.

15 It is interesting to note how close Eagleton's critique edges to people like Popper who also saw in Hegelian historicism and teleology a propensity towards a more totalitarian form of determinism.

16 Ibid.

17 Ibid.

18 Ibid.

19 Georg Lukács, *The Historical Novel* (London: Merlin Press, 1965), p.93.

20 Terry Eagleton, *Marxism and Literary Criticism* (London: Methuen & Co, 1976), p.34.

21 Ibid.

22 Ibid., p.35.

23 Ibid., p.35.

24 Terry Eagleton, *Literary Theory: An Introduction* (USA: University of Minnesota Press, 1996), p.8.

25 Ibid., p.9.

26 Terry Eagleton, *The Event of Literature* (New Haven and London: Yale University Press, 2013), p.71.

27 Terry Eagleton, *Literary Theory: An Introduction* (USA: University of Minnesota Press, 1996), p.94.

28 Eagleton, *Marxism and Literary Criticism*, p.75.

29 Ibid., pp.74–5.

30 Ibid., p.80.

31 Eagleton, *The Event of Literature*, p.83.

32 Ibid., p.105.

33 Ibid., p.140.

34 Ibid., p.22.

35 Ibid., p.149.

36 Eagleton, *Marxism and Literary Criticism*, p.90.

37 Ibid., p.73.

38 Ibid., p.146.

39 Ibid., pp.74–5.

40 Ibid., p.72.

41 Ibid., p.76.

42 Ibid., p.74.

43 Ibid., pp.71–2.

44 Lacan's 'real' is actually a highly dogmatic form of neo-Kantianism which emphasizes wholesale that aspect of irrationalism which was part of the original Kantian system; Lacan simply asserts there is this natural unity which provides the precondition for social development and to which we

in some way yearn to return, and yet at the same time, we never can, for 'the real' is noumenal in its aspect, being both unknown and unknowable. Hegelian historicism was developed, in part, to deal with the rationally unknowable 'thing in itself', so Eagleton's reversion to a crude form of Kantianism – via Lacan – of itself suggests the return to an ahistorical model.

45 Eagleton, *Literary Theory*, p.145

46 Ibid., p.172.

47 Roger Kimball, 'The Contradictions of Terry Eagleton', *The New Criterion*, September 1990: https://newcriterion.com/issues/1990/9/the-contradictions-of-terry-eagleton

48 Roger Kimball, 'Fredric Jameson's Laments', *The New Criterion*, June 1991: https://newcriterion.com/issues/1991/6/fredric-jamesonas-laments

49 Fredric Jameson, *The Political Unconscious* (New York: Cornell University Press, 1981), p.47.

50 Ibid., p.48.

51 A seme is, apparently, the smallest unit of meaning in semiotics though how anyone can differentiate a 'large meaning' from a 'small meaning' is beyond the wits of the current writer.

52 Ibid., p.75.

53 Ibid., p.76.

54 Fredric Jameson, *Marxism and Form* (New Jersey: Princeton University Press, 1974), p.185.

55 Ibid.

56 Ibid.

57 Ibid.

58 Georg Lukács, *History and Class Consciousness*, 'Reification and the Class Consciousness of the Proletariat' (London: The Merlin Press, 1983), p.166.

59 Jameson, *Marxism and Form*, p.185.

60 Ibid., pp.187–8.

61 Lukács, *History and Class Consciousness*, p.166.

62 Ibid., p.169.

63 Karl Marx, Capital Volume One, 'Chapter Thirty-Two: Historical Tendency of Capitalist Accumulation', Marxist Internet Archive: https://www.marxists.org/archive/marx/works/1867-c1/ch32.htm

64 Ibid.

65 Lukács, *History and Class Consciousness*, p.80.

66 Jameson, *Marxism and Form*, p.188.

67 Fredric Jameson, *Raymond Chandler: The Detections of Totality* (London: Verso, 2016), p.51.

68 Ibid., p.40.

69 Ibid.

70 Ibid., p.49.
71 Ibid.
72 Ibid.
73 Ibid., p.51.
74 Ibid., p.31.

Chapter 6

1 Stephen King, *IT* (UK: Hodder and Stoughton, 1987), p.31.
2 Ibid., p.39.
3 Ibid., p. 455.
4 Ibid., p.457.
5 Ibid., p.459.
6 Ibid., pp.459–60.
7 Ibid., p.463.
8 Ibid., p.999.
9 Stephen King, *Danse Macabre* (UK: Time Warner, 2002), pp.132–3.
10 Georg Lukács, *History and Class Consciousness*, 'Reification and the Consciousness of the Proletariat' (London: Merlin Press, 1983), p.116.
11 Ibid., p.128.
12 Ibid., p.164.
13 'Outside' in this context is problematic; it denotes a spatial position which is the purview of phenomenal reality and for this reason I put it in quote marks.
14 It is true that Lukács himself doesn't put this view forward in *History and Class Consciousness* – but I am designating it as Lukácsian because, in my view, it follows from his analysis of the proletariat as identical subject-object of history in that great work.
15 Lukács, *History and Class Consciousness*, p.168.
16 I'd like to add a final note about the subject-object analysis more generally which was brought to the fore by Lukács as very much part and parcel of the Hegelian Marxism the current writer ascribes to. In his preface to the 1967 version of *History and Class Consciousness* Lukács rejected the 'identical subject-object of the historical process' thesis as 'idealistic'. I think he was wrong in this though naturally there is not space to go into details here. I wish to confine myself to one remark; that is, Lukács' rejection of the subject-object description of the proletariat also coincides with the disappearance of the workers' councils or 'soviets' from his theoretical corpus more broadly. In *History and Class Consciousness* the workers' councils are the very lynchpin of the analysis. When he pens a defence of *History and Class Consciousness* only a couple of years after its publication (*Tailism and the Dialectic*), the 'soviets' are notably absent

from his theoretical considerations. Despite his support for, and active role in, the Hungarian Revolution of 1956, Lukács' theoretical defence of Marxism in his later life very much resembled the idea of a bureaucratic caste or vanguard which was able to direct the state in the workers' best interests rather than a radical democracy from below which fused society's economic and political spheres.

Chapter 7

1   Moishe Postone, 'Lukács and the Dialectical Critique of Capitalism': https://platypus1917.org/wp-content/uploads/readings/postone_ lukacsdialecticalcritique2003.pdf?fbclid=IwAR2Soa2da1P–NJ2Nylk_ f6fcUt72hr4-ReLOORkz89Wh0WQ-oPnnGjWD_
2   This is the popular view advocated by people like Žižek, Hardt and Negri, among others.
3   Moishe Postone, 'Lukács and the Dialectical Critique of Capitalism': https://platypus1917.org/wp-content/uploads/readings/postone_ lukacsdialecticalcritique2003.pdf?fbclid=IwAR2Soa2da1P–NJ2Nylk_ f6fcUt72hr4-ReLOORkz89Wh0WQ-oPnnGjWD_
4   Ibid.
5   K. Marx, 'Marx to Kugelmann in Hanover', Marx-Engels Correspondence 1868, Marx Internet Archive: https://www.marxists.org/archive/marx/ works/1868/letters/68_07_11-abs.htm
6   Ibid.
7   Ibid.
8   Ibid.
9   Ibid.
10 Chris Arther, 'Marx, Hegel and the Value-Form', *Marx's Capital and Hegel's Logic – A Reexamination* (Ed. Fred Moseley and Tony Smith) (Lieden and Boston: Brill, 2014), p.270.
11 Ibid., p.269.
12 Moishe Postone, 'Lukács and the Dialectical Critique of Capitalism': https://platypus1917.org/wp-content/uploads/readings/postone_ lukacsdialecticalcritique2003.pdf?fbclid=IwAR2Soa2da1P–NJ2Nylk_ f6fcUt72hr4-ReLOORkz89Wh0WQ-oPnnGjWD_
13 Ibid.
14 Ibid.
15 Ibid.
16 I don't mean this in the sense of the typical Marxist understanding of abstract labour – i.e. a quantum of labour time – though this applies also.
17 Ibid.
18 Ibid.
19 Ibid.

20 Max Horkheimer and Theodore Adorno, *Dialectic of Enlightenment* (California: Stanford University Press, 2002), p.6.
21 Moishe Postone, 'Lukács and the Dialectical Critique of Capitalism': https://platypus1917.org/wp-content/uploads/readings/postone_ lukacsdialecticalcritique2003.pdf?fbclid=IwAR2Soa2da1P–NJ2Nylk_ f6fcUt72hr4-ReL0ORkz89Wh0WQ-oPnnGjWD_
22 Ibid.
23 Ibid.
24 Karl Marx. Capital Volume One, 'Chapter Thirty-Two: Historical Tendency of Capitalist Accumulation', Marxist Internet Archive: https://www. marxists.org/archive/marx/works/1867-c1/ch32.htm
25 Ibid.

Chapter 8

1 I would (again) point the reader to my own book on the subject, *The Dictator, the Revolution, the Machine: A Political Account of Joseph Stalin* (Brighton, Chicago and Toronto: Sussex Academic Press, 2016) which traces the genesis and development of Stalinism as it consumed the revolution from the inside out much like a malignant parasite.
2 In the UK, paradoxically, when we refer to public school we mean private school.
3 Louis Althusser, 'Louis Althusser on Hegel's Expressive Totality', Autodidactic Project: http://www.autodidactproject.org/quote/althusser_ expressive.html
4 Ernest Mandel, *Delightful Murder: A Social History of the Crime Story* (London: Pluto Press, 1984), pp.31–5.
5 Fredric Jameson, *Raymond Chandler – The Detections of Totality* (New York: Verso, 2016), p.31.
6 Georg Lukács, *The Historical Novel* (London: Merlin Press, 1965), pp.23–4.
7 Lukács, *The Historical Novel*.
8 Terry Eagleton, *The Event of Literature* (Connecticut: Yale University Press, 2013), p.146.
9 Leon Trotsky, 'The Struggle for Cultured Speech', Pravda, May 1923: https://www.marxists.org/archive/trotsky/women/life/23_05_16.htm:
10 Jameson, *Raymond Chandler – The Detections of Totality*, p.14.
11 Thomas Hardy cited in Ishay Landa, *Fascism and the Masses – The Revolt against the Last Humans, 1848–1945* (Oxon: Routledge, 2018), p.126.
12 Landa, *Fascism and the Masses – The Revolt against the Last Humans, 1848–1945*, p.416.
13 Ibid., p.416.
14 Ibid., p.126.

15 Fredric Jameson cited in Roger Kimball, 'Fredric Jameson's Lament', *The New Criterion*, June 1991: https://newcriterion.com/issues/1991/6/fredric-jamesonas-laments
16 Terry Eagleton cited in Kimball, 'Fredric Jameson's Lament'.
17 Fredric Jameson, *The Political Unconscious* (London and New York: Routledge, 2002), p.141.

Index